THE *Other* TROJAN WAR

The Chronicles of Dictys of Crete

and

Dares the Phrygian

The *Other* TROJAN WAR

The Chronicles of Dictys of Crete

and

Dares the Phrygian

A parallel text edition with the Latin texts of
Werner Eisenhut and Ferdinandus Meister opposed
by the English translation of R. M. Frazer, Jr.
Introduction, and notes by Fraser.

Edited by Giles Laurén

SOPHRON IMPRIMIT 2012

The illustration on the back cover:
'Hercules slaying Troilus',
from an Etruscan fresco,
Tomb of the Bulls, Tarquina. c.535.

Design by Sophron

CONTENTS

Prologue

Dictys and Dares have been out of print for a number years in both Latin and English editions and obtaining copies has become expensive. For this reason it is hoped that the present combined edition at a reasonable price will fill a need of both scholars and the general reader.

R. M. Fraser's introduction, notes and bibliography have been preserved and will more that serve the needs of all but a few very specialised readers. Here and there the translation has been amended in the interests of clarity.

Both writers have enjoyed periods of credibility and periods of doubt; are they forgeries or not? Are they derivatives of the Homeric cycle? Are they fragments unknown to the sixth century editors? If they are forgeries, to what end?

Quintus of Smyrna, who postdated Dictys and Dares by at least a century was surely familiar with their writing, he makes no mention of Briseida/Cressida and limits Troilus to the following account of the games at Achilles' funeral:

> Then Teucer, with spirit most intent, shot his arrow. The sharp
> missile quickly cut away the horsehair crest. The people, when
> they saw it, gave a loud shout and praised him greatly, because
> the hurt his swift foot had received in the race still pained
> him, but it did him no harm as he directed the swift missile.
> Pelus' wife gave him the beautiful armour of godlike Troilus.
> He was the finest by far of Hecabe's unmarried sons in holy
> Troy, but she got no good from so splendid a son, because
> fearless Achilles' spear and strength together robbed him of
> his life. Just as when in a dewy, flourishing field that grows
> luxuriantly, close to an irrigation ditch, someone with a freshly
> sharpened scythe cuts off a stalk of grain or a poppy before it
> ripens and does not allow it to reach its sweet goal and come
> to another sowing, but reaps it when it is empty and has no
> seed for men yet to come, when it might have grown in the
> dewy spring; so Peleusson killed Priam's son who looked like

the gods, still beardless, still with no knowledge of a bride, still youthful as a child. Fate brought him to destructive war when his joyous youth was just beginning, the time when men are bold, and their courage is full-grown.* (**Quintus of Smyrna**. *The War at Troy*. I. 412-430. Combellack trans. & note.)

Any suggestions, corrections or additions will be grateful received by the editor at: [liberdux@gmail.com].

*The care that Quintus devotes to Troilus anticipates the day when Troilus (only a name in Homer) will become a leading figure in the mediaeval Troy story. There was a tradition in antiquity that after killing Troilus Achilles cut his head off. Some have found an allusion to this in Quintus' simile of the grain or poppy cut with the scythe.

INTRODUCTION

The Medieval Troy Story

The works of Dictys and Dares are short prose narratives about the Trojan War. Though they were probably composed, in their original Greek forms during the first century A.D., they claim to antedate Homer. Their authors are supposed to have fought at Troy and to have made first-hand reports of the War. The longer and fuller work is that of Dictys which alone of the two describes how the Greeks returned to their homelands.

Several writers of the Byzantine period based their accounts of the Trojan War on the original Dictys, but there is little traceable influence of Dares on later Greek literature. This is because Dictys is written from the Greek point of view, Dares from that of the Trojans.[1]

The Greek texts of both authors, with the exception of a small fragment of Dictys, have not survived. They were, however, during the early middle ages, translated, more or less completely, into Latin; and this is how we know them.

The Latin Dictys and Dares exercised a major influence on the medieval Troy story. At that time Dares was more popular than Dictys, for the Latin-speaking West had inherited a pro-Trojan bias from the Romans, who claimed descent from the Trojans. About 1160 A.D. Benoit de Sainte-Maure based his *Le Roman de Troie* upon our authors. His main source was Dares, but he also used Dictys, especially toward the end of his work where the former authority failed him.

---

1 The following Byzantine writers based their stories of the Trojan War on the Greek Dictys: Joannes Malalas (6th c.), Joannes Antiochenos (7th c.), and Georgias Kedrenos (11th c.). See Nathaniel Edward Griffin, *Dares and Dictys, An Introduction to the Study of Medieval Versions of the Story of Troy*, (Baltimore, 1907), pp. 34-108. On the influence of the original Dares on Malalas, see Introduction below.

The most famous story contained in the *Roman* is that of Troilus and Briseida, which Benoit himself presumably created on the basis of a few disconnected passages in Dares. Dares' contributions to the Troilus romance can be summarised as follows:[2] First, he describes the appearance of the main characters: Troilus, Briseida, and Diomedes.[3] Secondly, he relates that Troilus, in one of his fights, wounds Diomedes.[4] And finally, he reports that Calchas, the Trojan priest, meets Achilles at Delphi and joins the Greeks at the command of the oracle.[5]

Benoit's poem found many translators and imitators, and thus was largely responsible for spreading the accounts of Dictys and Dares throughout Western Europe. The most influential of Benoit's adapters was the thirteenth-century Sicilian judge Guido delle Colonne, who wrote his *Historia Destructionis Troiae* in Latin prose.[6] Guido cites Dictys and Dares as his sources and never so much as mentions Benoit. Nevertheless, the *Historia* has been proved to be, for the most part, an abridging paraphrase of the *Roman*.[7] It offers a shortened and somewhat altered Troilus and Briseida story.[8]

In the *Roman* (and therefore in the *Historia*) the Troilus story must be pieced together from several different passages. A unified version was first created by Boccaccio in his *Il Filostrato* ('The One Prostrated by Love'). Boccaccio's main source was

---

2 This summary is given by Karl Young, The Origin and Development of the Story of Troilus and Criseyde, Chaucer Soc., 2nd Ser., No. 40 (London, 1908 [for 1904]), p. 2. Young, p. 2, n. 2, contrasts Dictys' account as follows: Hippodamia, and not Briseida, is the daughter of Brises; there are no equivalents for Dares' portraits; Troilus, who is mentioned only in a passage recording his death, is never connected with the often mentioned Diomedes; Calchas is a Greek priest.

3 These portraits are given in Dares 12 (Troilus) and 13 (Briseida and Diomedes).

4 Dares 31.

5 Dares 15.

6 Guido's work was widely adapted, as, for instance, by John Lydgate in his *Troy-book*. See Wilhelm Greif, *Die Mittelalterlichen Bearbeitungen der Trojanersage* (Marburg, 1886), pp. 64-70.

7 Guido shows some direct knowledge of Dares too. See Greif, pp. 57-64.

8 See R. M. Lumiansky, 'The Story of Troilus and Briseida according to Benoit and Guido', Speculum, XXIX, 4 (October 1954), 727-733.

Benoit; he is probably indebted to Guido for only a few incidental touches.[9] The *Filostrato* expands the original version by describing how Troilo becomes enamoured of Criseida (for thus the heroine is renamed)[10] and how he wins her love; it also adds the character Pandaro.[11]

The description of Troilo's falling in love and the addition of the pander were undoubtedly influenced by another story in the *Roman*, which told how Achilles fell under the spell of Polyxena. Some of the striking similarities between this Troilo episode as told by Boccaccio and that of Achilles as told by Benoit are as follows:[12] (1) Both men are stricken with love while in a temple at a annual ritual. (2) Both are at first aloof toward the women they see at the temple. (3) Both, on returning to their homes, suffer the pangs of love and finally summon faithful friends to act as intermediaries. Although Benoit claims to be following only Dares here, he seems to have used Dictys too.[13]

Boccaccio, supplemented by Benoit and probably by Guido, was the main source of Chaucer's *Troilus and Criseyde*.[14] About a third of the lines in Chaucer's poem are adaptations from the *Filostrato*.[15] Nevertheless, the English work is much longer and much more complex than its Italian model. Chaucer has transformed Boccaccio's characters into fuller, richer beings and

---

9 Young, p. 12.

10 The renaming of Briseida is perhaps due to a confusion of her father, the seer Calchas, with the priest of Apollo, Chryses, the father of Chryseis (in the Iliad). Boccaccio may have been influenced to make this change of name by Armannino's Florita, which uses 'Criseida' instead of 'Briseida', and which was composed slightly earlier than the *Filostrato*. See Griffin's Introduction, *The Filostrato of Giovanni Boccaccio*, trans. Nathaniel Edward Griffin and Arthur Beckwith Myrick (Philadelphia, 1929), p. 26, n. 1.

11 Pandaro seems to have no other connection than his name with the Pandarus of Lycia mentioned in Dictys and Dares and in the Iliad. Griffin, Introduction, pp. 41-42, thinks that Boccaccio used this particular name only because of its fancied etymology: Pandaro is the one who 'gives all' to Troilo.

12 Young, pp. 36-55, lists these similarities along with many others.

13 Compare Dictys 3.2-3 and Dares 27.

14 Young, p. 139.

15 Young, p. 105.

has touched the prevailing sadness of the story with his gentle humour.

Two other important English works which stand in the tradition of the medieval Troy story are Robert Henryson's *Testament of Cresseid* and Shakespeare's *Troilus and Cressida*. Henryson's poem is a sequel to Chaucer's; it tells how Cresseid goes from bad to worse and ends her life as a beggar and leper. Shakespeare's play shows the influence of both Chaucer and Henryson; but it was based primarily on William Caxton's *Recuyell of the Historyes of Troye*, an English translation of a French translation of Guido.[16]

The Anti-Homeric Tradition

Dictys and Dares are frequently at odds with Homer in spite of the fact that he was the likely source of much of what they report and they promise to give more accurate accounts than his.

Both writers actually claim, as we know, to have lived at the time of the Trojan War, whereas Homer lived much later. The one, designating himself Dictys (otherwise unknown), states that he is a follower of Idomeneus, the leader of the Cretans; the other calls himself Dares the Phrygian (perhaps to be identified with the priest of Vulcan first mentioned in *Iliad* 5.9), a follower of the Trojan Antenor. Thus, if we can believe our authors (who often disagree with each other), they are primary sources for the events they describe, and Homer, wherever he fails to agree with them, is wrong. The pro-Trojan Dares tends to be more anti-Homeric than Dictys, perhaps because of the belief (false) that Homer had favoured the Greeks.

Dictys and Dares were influenced by two criticisms which had been brought against Homer from very early times. First, Homer was criticised for picturing the gods as thieves and adulterers and for showing them doing battle with mortals. Our authors, on the

---

16 The French translator of Guido was Raoul le Fevre. See Alice Walker, ed., *Troilus and Cressida by Shakespeare* (Cambridge, 1957), xxxviii-xlvi.

other hand, present the gods as without human foibles and wholly worthy of worship. Furthermore, they use none of the divine machinery typical of epic poetry, and they tend to describe supernatural occurrences in rational language. Sometimes Dictys openly flouts the traditional account by offering the reader a choice between rational and supernatural explanations.[17]

Secondly, Homer was accused of favouring certain heroes. Why, for instance, does he completely ignore Palamedes and mention Troilus only once? Our anti-Homeric authors emphasise these and other characters slighted by Homer. Dares does this especially, for in his account Palamedes and Troilus play more prominent roles than in Dictys' version. Polyxena is another character never mentioned by Homer: Achilles does not fall in love with her in the *Iliad* as he does in Dictys and Dares.

Homer's Achilles embodies the Greek heroic ideal by which the virtues of manly courage and personal honour are placed above long life and ease. The antithesis of this ideal is represented by the barbarian Paris who, enamoured of Helen, places his pleasure above the good of his country. Some time after Homer the heroic ideal began to be debased; and finally, as in the works of our authors, it disappeared altogether and the formerly great Achilles becomes no better than Paris. In the traditional account an heroic Achilles meets his end while fiercely attacking the city of Troy.[18] In Dictys and Dares an enamoured Achilles is ambushed and killed in the temple of the Thymbraean Apollo, a place of sanctuary, where he has come to bargain with the enemy for Polyxena's hand in marriage.[19]

The Christian middle ages were even more anti-Homeric than later antiquity. In Western Europe, the knowledge of Greek, and

---

17 See Dictys 1.19 and 6.10.

18 Aethiopis, frag. 1 in *Hesiod, the Homeric Hymns, and Homerica,* ed. by Hugh G. Evelyn-White in the Loeb series, 1936, pp. 507-509.

19 Dictys 4.10-11 and Dares 34.

therefore of Homer, died out. Medieval writers, as we have seen, based their accounts on Dictys and Dares; furthering the anti-Homeric tendencies they found in these sources, they created the romance of Troilus and Cressida.[20]

Belief in the truth of Dictys and Dares survived the Revival of Learning and it was not until the beginning of the eighteenth century that Jacob Perizonius demonstrated that our present authors were forgers.[21]

Dictys

All of our surviving manuscripts of Dictys are written in medieval Latin. They can be divided into two groups, each of which has a separate introduction. The manuscripts of one group are introduced by a Preface, those of the other group are introduced by a Letter.[22]

The author of the Letter makes three claims: (1) He is the Latin translator of an original Greek Dictys; (2) he has made a free, not a literal, translation; and (3) while reproducing the first five books of the original complete, he has condensed the last books into one.[23]

For a long time many scholars were unable to believe that a Greek Dictys had ever existed. Finally, however, in the winter of 1899-1900 a Greek papyrus fragment closely corresponding to a portion of our Latin text was found on the back of tax records for the year 206 A.D.[24] Thus our Latin Dictys, which we know was

---

20 See N. E. Griffin, 'Un-Homeric Elements in the Story of Troy', The Journal of English and Germanic Philology, VII (1907-1908), 32-52.

21 Griffin, 'Un-Homeric Elements', p. 37.

22 Werner Eisenhut, ed. *Dictyis Cretensis Ephemeridos Belli Troiani Libri* (Teubner, Leipzig, 1958), p. xii (praefatio).

23 These claims are discussed by Nathaniel E. Griffin, 'The Greek Dictys', American Journal of Philology, XXIX (1908), 331.

24 *The Tebtunis Papyri*, ed. Grenfell-Hunt-Goodspeed, Part II (London, 1907), pp. 9 ff. The Dictys fragment is also edited by Eisenhut, pp. 134-139. The fragment covers Dictys 4.8 (end)-4.15 (middle).

composed much later than the Greek of the papyrus fragment, was proved to be a translation of a Greek original. Furthermore, the papyrus fragment helps us to prove that this is a free translation, and that its last book is an abridgement.

The following comparison of the same passage (Dictys 4.9) in the Greek papyrus fragment and in the Latin translation clearly illustrates the greater fullness of the latter.

πενθος δε ου μικρον τοις εν Ιλιω εγενετο
Τρωιλου απολομενου. ν γαρ ετι νεος και
γενναιος και [ωραιος]. [25]

Troiani tollunt gemitus et clamore lugubri Troili casum miserandum in modum deflent recordati aetatem eius admodum immaturam qui in primis pueritiae annis cum verecundia ac probitate, tum praecipue forma corporis amabilis atque acceptus popularibus adolescebat. [26]

Moreover, even before the discovery of the papyrus fragment, it was quite certain that the Latin Dictys could not be a literal translation of a Greek original since its style is heavily indebted to earlier Latin literature. The translator has imitated Plautus, Terence, Cicero, Livy, Caesar, Cornelius Nepos, Vergil, and especially Sallust.[27] The influence of Sallust has been detected in more than 350 places.[28] For instance, in the passage quoted above, *acceptus popularibus*, for which there is no equivalent in the Greek, is probably derived from the Sallustian *tam acceptum popularibus*.[29]

In spite of the fact that the Latin Dictys is a free translation, it seems for the most part to represent faithfully the essential matter of the original. The freedom of the translator consisted in

---

25 Which may be translated: 'No small grief came upon the Trojans when Troilus died, for he was still young and noble and handsome'.

26 See our text (the last sentence of Dictys 4.9) for a translation.

27 Hermann Dunger, 'Dictys-Septimius: Ober die unsprungliche Abfassung und die Quellen der Ephemeris Belli Troiani', Programm des Vitzhumschens Gymnasiums (Dresden, 1878), p. 7.

28 Henrich Pratje, *Quaestiones Sallustianae ad Lucium Septimium et Sulpicium Severum Gai Sallusti Crispi imitatores spectantes* (Gottingen, 1874).

29 Griffin, AJP, 331, who cites Pratje, p. 10. The reference to Sallust is Bellum Jugurthinum 7.1.

amplifying on the bare bones of the Greek, often by drawing appropriate phrases from earlier Latin authors. Even so, his own work is exceptionally dry and straightforward.

The fullness of the translation in the above passage from Book 4 of the Latin Dictys also tends to confirm the claim of the author of the Letter to have translated the first five books without abridgement, for the rest of the Latin text in Books 1 through 5 seems to be as full as this passage.

On the other hand, in comparison with Books 1 through 5, Book 6, with which the Latin Dictys ends, seems very compressed; it attempts to summarise the whole story of the return of the Greeks after the Trojan War. Furthermore, the Byzantine writer Malalas, whose work was derived from the Greek Dictys, gives a much longer and more detailed account of the returns than that of the Latin Dictys. [30]

We also know, from two other Byzantine sources, that the Greek Dictys contained nine books. [31] Thus we can conclude that the first five books of our Latin text are a fairly faithful reproduction of the first five books of the original Greek, but that Book 6 of our text is a condensation of the last four books of the Greek.

Since the author of the Letter has correctly described the composition of our Latin Dictys, we have every reason to believe that he was the one who composed it. The heading of the Letter gives his name as Lucius Septimius; unfortunately, this is all we know about him.

We can date the composition of the Letter and the Latin Dictys to the fourth century A.D. First, considerations of language and style point to this time. Secondly, the word *consularis* which is used in the Letter, with reference to Rutilius Rufus, to mean 'governor of a

---

30 Malalas Chronographia 5. See Griffin, AJP, 334-335.

31 These sources are Eudokia and Suidas. See note 7 to the Letter and note 3 to the Preface.

province' did not acquire this sense until the reign of Constantine (323-337 A.D.).[32]

The Quintus Aradius Rufinus to whom the Letter is addressed is probably to be identified with an Aradius Rufinus who was a commander of the east in 363 A.D. There is, however, another possible identification, for we also know of a Quintus Aradius Rufinus who was a prefect of Rome in the fourth century A.D., in the early years before Constantine's reign.[33]

Both the Letter and the Preface (which introduces the other group of Latin manuscripts) describe how the Greek Dictys was originally composed and how it was eventually discovered. They do not, however, give quite the same account. For instance, in the Preface an earthquake lays open Dictys' tomb, and shepherds take the manuscript to Eupraxides; whereas in the Letter the tomb collapses from the passage of time, and the shepherds take the manuscript to Praxis.[34]

N. E. Griffin has given the following explanation for these two introductions: Our Latin Preface represents the original Greek Preface written by the author of the Greek Dictys; its genuineness is indicated by the fact that it gives 'more specific and circumstantial' readings, such as the name Eupraxides instead of Praxis. The author of the Letter is, as he says, the Latin translator of the Greek Dictys; the Greek Preface, which he must have read somewhere, was missing from the Greek manuscript he used to make his Latin translation, and this is why he thought it necessary to reproduce the information of the Preface in his Letter, and why his Letter disagrees with the Preface to such an extent.[35]

---

32 Leopold Constans, ed. *Le Roman de Troie* par Benoit de Sainte-Maure, Vol. VI, Societe des Anciens Textes Francais (Paris, 1912),pp. 196-197.

33 Constans, pp. 196-197.

34 Other discrepancies are pointed out in the notes to the Dictys Letter.

35 Nathaniel E. Griffin, *Dares and Dictys* (Baltimore, 1907), pp. 118-120.

Accordingly, probably after our Latin Dictys, along with its introductory Letter, had been composed, another translator must have turned the Greek Preface into Latin. Perhaps he had read the Letter but preferred the Preface as the original and therefore truer introduction.

If, as seems likely, the author of the original Dictys wrote the Preface as an introduction to his work (thus filling the roles of two men who lived a thousand years apart), we can date the original to after 66 A.D., 'the thirteenth year of Nero's reign', when the Preface claims that it was discovered. Furthermore, we know, on the basis of palaeographical evidence, that the Greek papyrus fragment was written before 250 A.D.[36] Thus the original Greek Dictys must have been composed between 66 A.D. and 250 A.D. Griffin argues for a date soon after Nero's reign; he points out that 'occasional variations in the fragment from what we must suppose to have been the original Dictys' memoirs' (that is, where the fragment omits details contained in both the Latin Dictys and Malalas) tend to support this view.[37]

The name 'Dictys' is probably derived from "Dicte," the name of the famous mountain on Crete; 'Dictaean' is a synonym for 'Cretan'. Our author throughout his work shows a bias toward the Cretans: for instance, Idomeneus, the leader of the Cretans, is the one to whom Ulysses tells his adventures. Accordingly, we can surmise that our author may well have been a Cretan. To judge from his work, he seems to have had the character of the Cretan described in the New Testament text of the first century: 'One of themselves, even a prophet of their own, said, The Cretians are always liars, evil beasts, slow bellies. This witness is true'.[38]

The title of our author's work, in Latin, is *Ephemeris Belli Troiani (A Journal of the Trojan War)*. The word *ephemeris* is borrowed from

---

36 Papyri, p. 10.

37 Griffin, AJP, 335.

38 Titus 1.12-13 (King James Version).

the Greek, and must have stood in the Greek original. It means 'diary' or 'journal' and is often used in the sense of a military record. Thus the Greek writer Plutarch refers to Caesar's *Commentarii* as *Ephemerides*.[39] Caesar's *Gallic War* is a military record written in a simple prose style by a man who took part in the events which he describes; and this is exactly what Dictys' *Trojan War* purports to be.

Dares

Dares is known to us only in a medieval Latin version. This Latin Dares is introduced by a Letter whose author claims that he is the Latin translator of an original Greek Dares and that he has made a word-for-word translation. Since no papyrus fragment of a Greek original has as yet been found, we must test these claims in other ways.

Schissel von Fleschenberg has given two main reasons for believing that a Greek text of Dares once existed.[40] First, our Latin text, for the description of heroes and heroines in Sections 12 and 13, depends on the same source as the Byzantine writer Malalas, who knew no Latin. Secondly, the influence of a Greek original can be detected in the wording of the Latin translation. There are, moreover, references to Dares which go as far back as Ptolemy Chennos in the first century A.D., probably soon after the Greek text of Dares was composed.[41]

Thus we are able to grant that the author of the Letter is, as he says, the translator of an original Greek work. His other claim, however, to have made a simple word-for-word translation, cannot be entirely true. Schissel von Fleschenberg has described our Latin Dares as a compilation consisting of the following parts:[42]

---

39 Plutarch Caesar 22. See Eisenhut, p. vi (praefatio).

40 Otmar Schissel von Fleschenberg, *Dares Studien* (Halle an-der-Salle, 1908), pp. 84-85.

41 The reference of Ptolemy Chennos is found in Photius Bibliotheca, cod. 190, p. 147 (Bekker).

42 Schissel von Fleschenberg, pp. 84-157.

(1) a history of events before the Trojan War (Sections 1-10) which the translator-compiler has taken from Latin sources and prefixed to his work; (2) the remains, in Latin translation, of an original Greek Preface to be found in the Letter and in Sections 12 (beginning) and 44; and (3) the translation of the Greek Dares (Sections 11-43).

Sections 1 through 10 describe events which happened before the Trojan War, such as the adventure of the Argonauts. This in itself is enough to make us suspect that they never belonged to the original Dares. The case against them is conclusively proved by the fact that they are derived from Latin, and not from Greek, sources. They betray their Latin origin in mistakes no Greek would make: for instance, Pelias is called the king of the Peloponnese! Sections 5 through 10 are based on the work of the Latin author Dracontius.[43]

These additions by the Latin translator-compiler enable us to date the composition of the Latin Dares to the early sixth century A.D. Dracontius, at the beginning of that century, supplies the *terminus post quem*. The *terminus ante quem* is set by a Latin work, composed about fifty years after Dracontius, which is based on Sections 1 through 3 of our text.[44]

The heading of the Letter, 'Cornelius Nepos sends greetings to Sallustius Crispus', may have been added in later medieval times. If not, the translator-compiler is pretending to have done his work in the late first century B.C., when Nepos and Sallust lived. It seems not improbable that he adopted this idea from an original Greek Preface, which told how the Roman scholar Nepos had discovered Dares' work in Athens. Thus we have a Letter and a Preface for Dares whose relationship is very similar to that of the Letter and the Preface which introduce Dictys.

---

43 Dracontius Romulea 8. See Schissel von Fleschenberg, p. 169.

44 Mythographus Vaticanus Primus 24. See Schissel von Fleschenberg, p. 169.

The Dares Letter is, in fact, more like a preface than a letter.[45] It seems to be addressed to the public in general and not to any particular person, for the author speaks of his 'readers', whom he exhorts to judge the worth of Dares' work. Nor does he end, as is customary in letters, with any *vale;* instead, we are simply told to start reading Dares.

The Letter shows signs that it is dependent on an original Greek Preface by the similarity of its contents to that of two other places in our text which speak of Dares in the third person and give information of a prefatory character. (An eyewitness reporter, like Dictys when referring to himself, speaks in the first person.) These places are Sections 12 (beginning) and 44, and form, respectively, an introduction and a conclusion to the main work in Sections 12 through 43. The first place tells how Dares the Phrygian, who wrote this history, had been a soldier until the capture of Troy, and how he saw the major personages during times of truce or when fighting. The second tells how Dares the Phrygian stayed on at Troy as a faithful follower of Antenor, and how the *Acta Diurna* that Dares wrote gives the number of casualties on both sides.

The connection with Antenor, which is comparable to Dictys' connection with Idomeneus, explains how Dares was able to survive the War and so to write his history. Antenor had helped the Greeks to bring the War to an end, and they, being grateful, had left him and his party unharmed.

The Latin words *acta diurna* are the translation of the Greek *ephemeris,* and thus *Ephemeris (Journal)* must have stood in Dares' original title, just as in Dictys'. The Letter lends force to this conclusion with its assertion that 'the history was written, as the title indicates, in Dares' own hand', for the word *ephemeris,* like our word 'diary', connotes the penman.[46]

---

45 Schissel von Fleschenberg, pp. 84-96.
46 Schissel von Fleschenberg, pp. 89-90.

The present title, in Latin, is *De Excidio Troiae Historia (The Fall of Troy; A History)*. It was probably added later by someone who was influenced by the first sentence of the Letter which speaks of 'the history which Dares the Phrygian wrote about the Greeks and the Trojans'.[47]

Dares' work, as contained in Sections 11 through 43, is much shorter than that of Dictys, Books 1 through 5, which cover much the same matter. The question, therefore, arises whether our Latin translation has abridged the original Greek. The answer to this question, in the absence of any papyrus fragment, cannot be given with certainty. Schissel von Fleschenberg argues, on the basis of the artistic unity of the Latin translation, that our text offers, with some exceptions,[48] a reliable reproduction of the original. He divides Dares' work into an introduction (Sections 11-18) and the ephemeris proper (Sections 19-43). The introduction, he feels, with its character sketches of the chief personages involved, its foretelling of the War's result by means of an oracle, and its description of the short war with Teuthras as a prelude to the main events, shows parallels with the Greek romances, such as the *Ephesian Tale* by Xenophon of Ephesus; and the *ephemeris* proper reveals its orderly composition in the chronological references which begin almost all of its sections.

We know no more about Dares' original author than we do about Dictys'. He was, however, to judge from the remarks about Athens and the Athenians in the Letter and from the pro-Athenian bias to be found in his work, probably an Athenian.[49] He makes the Athenian leaders play greater parts than they do in Homer; and his Palamedes, who never appears in Homer and whom the Athenians favoured above Ulysses, replaces the seldom mentioned Ulysses

---

47 Schissel von Fleschenberg, pp. 89-90.

48 Schissel von Fleschenberg, pp. 160-169. For the exceptions, see notes 9, 10, 11, 12, 13, 17, and 31 to Dares.

49 Schissel von Fleschenberg, p. 91.

and, for a while, replaces Agamemnon as chief commander of the Greeks.

The Translation

Dictys' Latin prose is simple and fairly good. Dares', on the other hand, is very bad; it is, as Gilbert Highet says, 'of extreme simplicity, verging on stupidity'.[50] My English translations are simple, too, but not so simple, I hope, as to verge on stupidity. I have tried to translate accurately, but not word for word, or even sentence for sentence. Sentences in my translation do not always correspond exactly, in structure or extent, with those of the Latin text. Sometimes I have used a proper name instead of a pronoun, or even instead of an alternate proper name, such as 'Neoptolemus' for 'Pyrrhus'. Thus I have striven for clarity and readability as well as for accuracy.

The Latin texts which I have used for my translations are Werner Eisenhut's 1958 edition of Dictys[51] and Ferdinand [Otto] Meister's 1873 edition of Dares.[52]

There is, to my knowledge, no previous complete translation of Dictys in English. There is, however, a translation of the first three books in an unpublished thesis by William Huie Hess.[53]

The only previous English translations of Dares which I have been able to find are both based on inferior Latin texts. The first of these was made by Thomas Paynell in 1553.[54] The second was

---

50 Gilbert Highet, *The Classical Tradition: Greek and Roman Influences on Western Literature*, third printing with corrections (Oxford, 1953), p. 51.

51 Ephemeridos Belli Troiani Libri.

52 *Daretis Phrygii De Excidio Troiae Historia*, ed. Ferdinand Meister (Teubner, Leipzig, 1873).

53 Unpubl. thesis (Univ. of Texas, 1959) by William Huie Hess, 'Dictys the Cretan, Journal of the Trojan War, A Translation'.

54 *Dares Phrygius, The faythfull and true storye of the Destruction of Troy*, trans. Thomas Paynell (London, 1553). This translation has not been seen; according to Clarissa P. Farrar and Austin P. Evans, Bibliography of English Translations from Medieval Sources (Columbia Univ. Press, 1946), p. 148, it 'appears to exist only in a unique copy in the Bodleian Library'.

made by Margaret Schlauch in 1928, who used as her text the Delphin edition of 1825.[55]

---

55 *Dares Phrygius, The History of the Fall of Troy*, trans. Margaret Schlauch, in Medieval Narrative, A Book of Translations (New York, 1928, pp. 247-279. The Delphin edition is *Dictys Cretensis et Dares Phrygius De Bello Trojano* ex editione Samuelis Artopoei, pub. with notes of previous scholars by A. J. Valpy (London, 1825). This edition, as its title page indicates, is based on that of Samuel Artopoeus (Strasbourg, 1691).

A JOURNAL
OF THE
TROJAN WAR
by Dictys of Crete

TRANSLATED FROM GREEK INTO LATIN

BY

LUCIUS SEPTIMIUS

EPISTVLA

(L.) SEPTIMIUS Q. ARADIO RUFINO SALVTEM.

Ephemeridem belli Troiani Dictys Cretensis, qui in ea militia cum Idomeneo meruit, primo conscripsit litteris Punicis, quae tum Cadmo et Agenore auctoribus per Graeciam frequentabantur. Deinde post multa saecula collapso per vetustatem apud Gnosum, olim Cretensis regis sedem, sepulchro eius, pastores cum eo devenissent, forte inter ceteram ruinam loculum stagno affabre clausum offendere ac thesaurum rati mox dissolvunt, non aurum neque aliud quicquam praedae, sed libros ex philyra in lucem ‡ prodierunt ‡. At ubi spes frustrata est, ad Praxim dominum loci eos deferunt, qui commutatos litteris Atticis, nam oratio Graeca fuerat, Neroni Romano Caesari obtulit, pro quo plurimis ab eo donatus est. Nobis cum in manus forte libelli venissent, avidos verae historiae cupido incessit ea, uti erant, Latine disserere, non magis confisi ingenio, quam ut otiosi animi desidiam discuteremus. Itaque priorum quinque voluminum, quae bello contracta gestaque sunt, eundem numerum servavimus, residua de reditu Graecorum quidem in unum redegimus atque ita ad te misimus. Tu, Rufine mi, ut par est, fave coeptis atque in legendo Dictym ...

Letter[1]

Lucius Septimius sends greetings to Quintus Aradius Rufinus.

Dictys of Crete originally wrote his *Journal of the Trojan War* in the Phoenician alphabet, which Cadmus and Agenor[2] had spread throughout Greece. Dictys had served in the War with Idomeneus.

After many centuries the tomb of Dictys at Cnossos (formerly the seat of the Cretan king) collapsed with age.[3] Then shepherds, wandering near the ruins, happened upon a little box skilfully enclosed in tin. Thinking it was treasure, they soon broke it open, but brought to light, instead of gold or some other kind of wealth, books written on linden tablets. Their hopes thus frustrated, they took their find to Praxis,[4] the owner of that place. Praxis had the books transliterated into the Attic alphabet (the language was Greek)[5] and presented them to the Roman Emperor Nero.[6] Nero rewarded him richly.

When these little books had by chance come into my hands, I, as a student of true history, was seized with the desire of making a free translation into Latin; I felt I had no special talent but wanted only to occupy my leisure time. I have preserved without abridgement the first five volumes which deal with the happenings of the War, but have reduced into one volume the others[7] which are concerned with the Return of the Greeks. Thus, my Rufinus, I have sent them to you. Favour my work as it deserves, and in reading Dictys. . .

---

1 For a discussion of problems concerning the Letter and the Preface, see Introduction.

2 The Preface names only Cadmus. Dictys 5.17 names Cadmus and Danaus; here we must suppose that the author of the Letter has forgotten his own translation.

3 In the Preface an earthquake lays open the tomb.

4 Praxis is the Eupraxides of the Preface.

5 In the Preface the language is Phoenician instead of Greek.

6 In the Preface Eupraxides gives the books to Rutilius Rufus, the governor of Crete, and Rufus sees that they get to Nero.

7 The manuscripts, all of which give the number of abridged books as five, have been corrected to agree with the reports of Eudokia and Suidas that the total number of books was nine. See Preface, note 3.

PROLOGVS

Dictys, Cretensis genere, Gnoso civitate, isdem temporibus, quibus et Atridae, fuit, peritus vocis ac litterarum Phoenicum, quae a Cadmo in Achaiam fuerant delatae. Hic fuit socius Idomenei, Deucalionis filii, et Merionis ex Molo, qui duces cum exercitu contra Ilium venerant, a quibus ordinatus est, ut annales belli Troiani conscriberet. Igitur de toto bello novem volumina in tilias digessit Phoeniceis litteris. Quae iam reversus senior in Cretam praecepit moriens, ut secum sepelirentur. itaque, ut ille iusserat, memoratas tilias in stagnea arcula repositas eius tumulo condiderunt. Verum secutis temporibus, tertio decimo anno Neronis imperii, in Gnoso civitate terrae motus facti cum multa, tum etiam sepulchrum Dictys ita patefecerunt, ut a transeuntibus arcula viseretur. pastores itaque praetereuntes cum hanc vidissent, thesaurum rati sepulchro abstulerunt. Et aperta ea invenerunt tilias incognitis sibi litteris conscriptas continuoque ad suum dominum. Eupraxidem quendam nomine, pertulerunt. Qui agnitas, quaenam essent, litteras Rutilio Rufo, illius insulae tunc consulari, obtulit. ille cum ipso Eupraxide ad Neronem oblata sibi transmisit existimans quaedam in his secretiora contineri. Haec igitur cum Nero accepisset advertissetque Punicas esse litteras, harum peritos ad se evocavit. qui cum venissent, interpretati sunt omnia, cumque Nero cognosset antiqui viri, qui apud Ilium fuerat, haec esse monumenta, iussit in Graecum sermonem ista transferri, e quibus Troiani belli verior textus cunctis innotuit. Tunc Eupraxidem muneribus et Romana civitate donatum ad propria remisit. annales vero nomine Dictys inscriptos in Graecam bibliothecam recepit, quorum seriem, qui sequitur, textus ostendit.

DICTYS I.

Preface

Dictys, a native of Crete from the city of Cnossos and a contemporary of the Atridae,[8] knew the Phoenician language and alphabet, which Cadmus brought to Achaea.[9] He accompanied the leaders Idomeneus and Meriones with the army that went against Troy. (Idomeneus and Meriones were the sons of Deucalion and Molus respectively.) They chose him to write down a history of this campaign. Accordingly, writing on linden tablets and using the Phoenician alphabet, he composed nine volumes[10] about the whole war.

When he returned to Crete, he was an old man. On his deathbed he gave instructions that his books be buried with him. In accordance with his wishes they put the linden tablets in a little tin box and hid it in his tomb.

Time passed. In the thirteenth year of Nero's[11] reign an earthquake struck at Cnossos and, in the course of its devastation, laid open the tomb of Dictys in such a way that people, as they passed, could see the little box. And so shepherds who had seen it as they passed stole it from the tomb, thinking it was treasure. But when they opened it and found the linden tablets inscribed with characters unknown to them, they took this find to their master. Their master, whose name was Eupraxides, recognized the characters, and presented the books to Rutilius Rufus, who was at that time governor of the island. Since Rufus, when the books had been presented to him, thought they contained certain mysteries, he, along with Eupraxides himself, carried them to Nero.[12]

Nero, having received the tablets and having noticed that they were written in the Phoenician alphabet, ordered his Phoenician philologists to come and decipher whatever was written. When this had been done, since he realized that these were the records of an ancient man who had been at Troy, he had them translated into Greek; thus a more accurate text of the Trojan War was made known to all. Then he bestowed gifts and Roman citizenship upon Eupraxides, and sent him home.

The Greek Library, according to Nero's command, acquired this history that Dictys had written, the contents of which the following text sets forth in order.

---

8 The Atridae are Agamemnon and Menelaus, who, however, in Dictys, are not the real sons of Atreus, but of Plisthenes. See Dictys 1.1.

9 Achaea is the Roman province of Greece

10 The manuscripts, all of which give the total number of books as six, have been corrected to agree with the reports of Eudokia and Suidas. See Letter, note 7.

11 i.e. 67 A.D.

12 This sentence might also be translated: 'Rufus . . . sent them to Nero along with Eupraxides himself'.

5

LIBER PRIMVS

I.1. Cuncti reges, qui Minois Iove geniti pronepotes Graeciae imperitabant, ad dividendas inter se Atrei opes Cretam convenere. Atreus namque ex Minoe postrema sua ordinans, quicquid auri atque argenti, pecorum etiam fuit, nepotibus, quos filiae genuerant, ex aequo dividendum reliquerat, excepto civitatum terrarumque imperio; haec quippe Idomeneus cum Merione, Deucalionis Idomeneus, alter Moli, iussu eius seorsum habuere. Convenere autem Clymenae et Naupli Palamedes et Oeax. item Menelaus, Aeropa et Plisthene genitus, a qua Anaxibia soror, quae eo tempore Nestori denupta erat, et Agamemnon maior frater, ut vice sua in divisione uteretur, petiverant. sed hi non Plisthenis, ut erat, magis quam Atrei dicebantur, ob eam causam, quod, cum Plisthenes admodum parvis ipse agens in primis annis vita functus, nihil dignum ad memoriam nominis reliquisset, Atreus miseratione aetatis secum eos habuerat neque minus quam regios educaverat. In qua divisione singuli pro nominis celebritate inter se quisque magnifice transiere.

Book One

I. 1.   All the kings who were greatgrandsons of Minos, the son of Jupiter, and who ruled over Greece, came to Crete to divide the wealth of Atreus. Atreus, the son of Minos,[13] when making his last will and testament, had left all his gold and silver, and even his herds, to them; for they were his grandsons, the sons of his daughters. Everything was to be equally divided among them, excepting only the rule of his cities and lands. This he bequeathed to Idomeneus, the son of Deucalion, and Meriones, the son of Molus.

Among those who came to Crete were Palamedes and Oeax, the sons of Clymene and Nauplius.

Also Menelaus and his older brother Agamemnon, the sons of Aerope and Plisthenes,[14] came to get their share. (They had a sister, Anaxibia, who at that time was married to Nestor.) People often thought that their father was Atreus, because when their real father, Plisthenes, died young without having made a name for himself, Atreus, pitying their plight, had taken them in and brought them up like princes.

In the division of Atreus' property everyone, as befitted his rank, acquired a handsome inheritance.

---

13 Atreus is apparently identified with Catreus, the son of Minos (Apollodorus 3.1.2).

14 Agamemnon and Menelaus are the sons of Plisthenes in Hesiod The Catalogues of Women (frag. 69, p. 203, ed. Evelyn-White) .

I. 2.   Ad eos re cognita omnes ex origine Europae, quae in ea
insula summa religione colitur, confluunt benigneque salutatos in templum
deducunt. Ibi multarum hostiarum immolatione more patrio celebrata
exhibitisque epulis largiter magnificeque eos habuere itemque insecutis
diebus. Reges Graeciae etsi ea, quae exhibebantur, cum laetitia accipiebant,
tamen multo magis templi eius magnifica pulchritudine pretiosaque
exstructione operum afficiebantur, inspicientes repetentesque memoria
singula, quae ex Sidona a Phoenice, patre eius, atque nobilibus matronis
transmissa magnotum decori erant.

I. 3.   Per idem tempus Alexander Phrygius, Priami filius, Aenea
aliisque ex consanguinitate comitibus, Spartae in domum Menelai hospitio
receptus, indignissimum facinus perpetraverat. is namque, ubi animadvertit
regem abesse, quod erat Helena praeter ceteras Graeciae feminas miranda
specie, amore eius captus ipsamque et multas opes domo eius aufert,
Aethram etiam et Clymenam, Menelai adfines, quae ob necessitudinem
cum Helena agebant. Postquam Cretam nuntius venit et cuncta, quae ab
Alexandro adversum domum Menelai commissa erant, aperuit, per omnem
insulam, sicut in tali re fieri amat, fama in maius divulgatur expugnatam
quippe domum regis eversumque regnum et alia in talem modum singuli
disserebant.

I. 2.   All the descendants of Europa (she was worshiped on Crete with the most elaborate ritual), on learning that the heirs of Atreus had landed, hastened to give them a friendly welcome. Escorting them to the temple, they entertained them lavishly with elegant banquets, offering, in accordance with their ancient customs, many sacrificial victims. Thus, day after day, the kings of Greece delighted in this entertainment. They were, however, even more impressed by the temple of Europa itself, so magnificent was the beauty of this structure, so rich its embellishments. Examining all its marvellous features, they called to mind how Europa's father, Phoenix, and the noble matrons, had brought across from Sidon this thing and that.

I. 3.   During the same time the home of Menelaus at Sparta welcomed Alexander the Phrygian,[15] the son of Priam, who had come with Aeneas and other of his relatives. Alexander, taking advantage of Menelaus' absence, committed a very foul crime. Falling desperately in love with Helen, the most beautiful woman in Greece, he carried her off, along with much wealth, and also Aethra and Clymene, who, being Menelaus' relatives, attended on Helen.

A report of this crime came to Crete;[16] but rumour, as commonly happens, spread over the island, making what Alexander had done seem worse than it was. People were even saying that King Menelaus' home had been taken by storm and that his kingdom was conquered.

---

15 Dictys always uses 'Alexander', not 'Paris'. 'Phrygian' is a synonym for 'Trojan'.
16 In the Cypria (frag. 1, p. 491, ed. Evelyn-White), Iris brings this news.

I. 4.   Quis cognitis Menelaus, etsi abstractio coniugis animum permoverat, multo amplius tamen ob iniuriam adfinium, quas supra memoravimus, consternabatur. at ubi animadvertit Palamedes regem ira atque indignatione stupefactum consilio excidisse, ipse naves parat atque omni instrumento conpositas terrae adplicat. Dein pro tempore regem breviter consolatus, positis etiam ex divisione quae in tali negotio tempus patiebatur, navem ascendere facit atque ita ventis ex sententia flantibus paucis diebus Spartam pervenere. eo iam Agamemnon et Nestor omnesque, qui ex origine Pelopis in Graecia regnabant, cognitis rebus confluxerant. Igitur postquam Menelaum advenisse sciunt, omnes in unum coeunt. Et quamquam atrocitas facti ad indignationem ultumque iniurias rapiebat, tamen ex consilii sententia legantur prius ad Troiam Palamedes, Ulixes et Menelaus hisque mandatur, uti conquesti iniurias Helenam et quae cum ea abrepta erant repeterent.

I. 4.   On learning this news, Menelaus was deeply upset by the abduction of his wife, but he was even more disturbed by the fact that the relatives we mentioned above had wronged him.[17]

Palamedes noticed that the king, being distraught with wrath and righteous indignation, had lost all power of reason. Accordingly, he rigged the ships and brought them to shore equipped with all their gear. Loading as much of Menelaus' inheritance as time under the circumstances allowed, and briefly but appropriately offering his sympathy, he made the king go aboard; and thus, the winds blowing as they desired, they came to Sparta within a few days.

Agamemnon, Nestor, and all the rulers of Greece who were descendants of Pelops,[18] having heard the news, had already gathered together at Sparta. On learning of Menelaus' arrival, they all assembled together. First, though the barbarity of the deed demanded immediate vengeance, they decided to send envoys to Troy. Palamedes, Ulysses, and Menelaus were chosen to go, and instructed to complain of the crime and demand the return of Helen and the things that had been carried off.[19]

---

17 According to Malalas (*Chronographia* 5.118-119), Aethra persuaded Helen to yield to Alexander. In the *Cypria* (frag. 1, p. 491), Venus brings Helen and Alexander together.

18 Pelops (sc. Peloponnese) was the great hero of the past from whom aristocratic families liked to claim descent, and often did so falsely.

19 This embassy appears before the Trojan council in Dictys 1.6 and before the Trojan assembly in Dictys 1.10 (middle)-11. It should be compared with the later, similar embassy in Dictys 2.20-26.

I. 5.   Legati paucis diebus ad Troiam veniunt. neque tamen Alexandrum in loco offendere; eum namque properatione navigii inconsulte usum venti ad Cyprum appulere, unde sumptis aliquot navibus Phoenicem delapsus Sidoniorum regem, qui eum amice susceperat, noctu insidiis necat, eademque, qua apud Lacedaemonam, cupiditate universam domum eius in scelus proprium convertit. Ita omnia, quae ad ostentationem regiae magnificentiae fuere, indigne rapta ad naves deferri iubet. sed ubi ex lamentatione eorum, qui casum domini deflentes reliqui praedae aufugerant, tumultus ortus est, populus omnis ad regiam concurrit. Inde, quod iam Alexander abreptis, quae cupiebat, ascensionem properabat, pro tempore armati ad naves veniunt ortoque inter eos acri proelio cadunt utrimque plurimi, cum obstinate hi regis necem defenderent, hi, ne amitterent partam praedam, summis opibus adniterentur. Incensis deinde duabus navibus Troiani reliquas strenue defensas liberant. atque ita fatigatis iam proelio hostibus evadunt.

I. 5.   These, on coming to Troy within a few days, did not find Alexander at home; for when he had sailed from Sparta, hastily and taking no thought of the weather, the winds had forced him to Cyprus. After obtaining some ships, he had then gone on to Phoenicia, where the king of the Sidonians received him kindly. There he treacherously slaughtered the king at night and, venting again that injurious nature he had shown at Sparta, pillaged the palace. He shamelessly ordered his men to seize everything the purpose of which was to show the royal magnificence, and carry it off to the ships. The Sidonians, however, who escaped the general destruction, raised a huge tumult, bewailing the fate of their ruler. All of their people rushed to the palace, and then, arming themselves as best they were able, rushed to the ships; for Alexander had already seized whatever he wanted and now was hastening to sail. A raging battle arose, and many men fell on both sides. While the Sidonians fought fiercely in the cause of their murdered king, the Trojans strove with all their might to keep the booty they had gained. Two of their ships were fired; but finally, after a terrible struggle, they freed the others and thus, having broken the strength of their foe, they escaped.

I. 6.   Interim apud Troiam legatorum Palamedes, cuius maxime ea tempestate domi belloque consilium valuit, ad Priamum adit conductoque consilio primum de Alexandri iniuria conqueritur, exponens communis hospitii eversionem, dein monet, quantas ea res inter duo regna simultates concitatura esset, interiaciens memoriam discordiarum Ili et Pelopis aliorumque, qui ex causis similibus ad internecionem gentium usque pervenissent. Ad postremum belli difficultates contraque pacis commoda adstruens non se ignorare, ait, quantis mortalibus tam atrox facinus indignationem incuteret; ex quo auctores iniuriae ab omnibus derelictos impietatis supplicia subituros. et cum plura dicere cuperet, Priamus medium eius interrumpens sermonem: parcius quaeso Palamede, inquit. Iniquum etenim videtur insimulari eum qui absit, maxime cum fieri possit, uti, quae criminose obiecta sunt, praesenti refutatione diluantur. Haec atque alia huiusmodi inserens differri querelas ad adventum Alexandri iubet. Videbat enim, ut singuli, qui in eo consilio aderant, Palamedis oratione moverentur, ut taciti, vultu tamen admissum facinus condemnarent, cum singula miro genere orationis exponerentur atque in sermone Graeci regis inesset quaedam permixta miserationi vis. Atque ita eo die consilium dimittitur. Sed legatos Antenor, vir hospitalis ct praeter ceteros boni honestique sectator, domum ad se volentes deducit.

I. 6.   Meanwhile, at Troy, one of the envoys, Palamedes (he was known as a skilful adviser and diplomat), prevailed upon Priam to let him speak at a meeting of the council. First, he made his complaint, describing the injurious way Alexander had broken the ties of mutual hostpitality. Next, he warned of the horrible conflict that Greece and Troy might have because of this act, citing, among other examples, the feud between Ilus and Pelops,[20] who for similar reasons had come to the point of committing their countries to war. Then, comparing the hazards of war with the blessings of peace, he said that he knew that most of the Trojans hated this barbarous injury; all would abandon those who were guilty, and the guilty would have to pay for their impious acts.

Palamedes wanted to finish his speech, but Priam interrupted and said: 'I beseech you, Palamedes, to go more slowly. It seems unfair to attack a man who is absent, who, if he were present, might refute the charges you are bringing against him'. Thus Priam ordered Palamedes to defer his complaint until Alexander returned. He had noticed that everyone who was present in the council was being moved by Palamedes' speech; though they were silent, nevertheless they showed by their faces that they were condemning the things Alexander had done. Palamedes was making his points with marvellous eloquence, and there was a certain indescribable force in the moving tone of his speech.

Then the council broke up for that day. The envoys went home with Antenor, pleased to be his guests. He was a gracious host and a man who, more than anyone else, loved the good and the true.

---

20 Ilus had led an army against Pelops and chased him out of Lydia. See Pausanias *Description of Greece* 2.2.24.

I. 7.   Interim paucis post diebus Alexander cum supra dictis comitibus venit Helenam secum habens. cuius adventu, tota civitas cum partim exemplum facinoris exsecrarentur, alii iniurias in Menelaum admissas dolerent, nullo omnium adprobante, postremo cunctis indignantibus tumultus ortus est. Quis rebus anxius Priamus filios convocat eosque, quid super tali agendum negotio vidcrotur, consulit. qui una voce minime reddendam Helenam respondent. Videbant quippe, quantae opes cum ea advectae essent; quae universa, si Helena traderetur, necessario amitterent. Praeter ea permoti forma mulierum, quae cum Helena venerant, nuptias sibi singularum iam animo destinaverant, quippe qui lingua moribusque barbari nihil pensi aut consulti patientes praeda atque libidine transversi agebantur.

I. 8.   Igitur Priamus relictis his senes conducit, sententiam filiorum aperit, dein cunctos, quid agendum esset, consulit. sed priusquam ex more sententiae dicerentur, reguli repente consilium inrumpunt atque inconditis moribus malum singulis minitantur, ei aliter, quam ipsis videretur, decernerent. interim omnis populus indigne admissam iniuriam atque in hunc modum multa alia cum exsecratione reclamabant. Ob quae Alexander cupidine animi praeceps veritus, ne quid adversum se a popularibus oriretur, stipatus armatis fratribus impetum in multitudinem facit, multos obtruncat. Reliqui interventu procerum, qui in consilio fuerant, duce liberantur Antenore. Ita infectis rebus populus contemptui habitus non sine pernicie sua domum discedit.

I. 7.　　　Several days having passed, Alexander came with the companions we mentioned above, and also with Helen. Upon his arrival, all of the people showed their disgust at what he had done: some cursed the evil precedent he had set; others bewailed the injustice Menelaus had suffered, and finally, disgusted and angry, they raised a revolt.

Priam, alarmed by this turn of events, called together his sons and asked what course they advised. They answered unanimously that, no matter what happened, Helen should not be returned. They saw, no doubt, that if this were done, they would lose all the great wealth with which she had come. Furthermore, they had fallen in love with the beautiful women who had come with Helen and had already set their hearts on marrying this or that one. Being barbarians in language and morals, and impatient of weighing their actions or asking advice, they were driven astray by greed for booty and lust.

I. 8.　　　Leaving his sons, Priam called together the elders. After reporting what his sons had decided, he asked each member to give his advice. This was the custom. But before anyone could state his opinion, the princes suddenly broke into the council and, never before had this happened, threatened all of the members that they had better not find anyone opposing their will.

Meanwhile all of the people were cursing and crying out against the injuries Alexander had committed and against many other similar acts. This caused Alexander, who was reckless because of his lust, to surround himself with his brothers in arms and make an attack on the crowd; for he feared that something might happen to him at the hands of the people. Many were killed, but finally the slaughter was stopped by those who had been in the council and the nobles led by Antenor. Thus the people returned to their homes, their numbers not undiminished, frustrated as to their purpose and held in contempt.

I. 9.　　　　Dein secuta die rex hortatu Hecubae ad Helenam adit eamque benigne salutans bonum animum uti gereret hortatur. Quae cuiusque esset, requirit. tum illa Alexandri se adfinem respondit, magisque ad Priamum et Hecubam, quam ad Plisthenis filios genere pertinere, repetens ordinem omnem maiorum. Danaum enim atque Agenorem et sui et Priami generis auctores esse, namque ex Plesiona, Danai filia, et Atlante Electram natam, quam ex Iove gravidam Dardanum genuisse. Ex quo Tros et deinceps insecuti reges Ilii. Agenoris porro Taygetam. Eam ex Iove habuisse Lacedaemona. Ex quo Amyclam natum et ex eo Argalum, patrem Oebali, quem Tyndari, ex quo ipsa genita videretur, patrem constaret. Repetebat etiam cum Hecuba materni generis adfinitatem. Agenoris quippe filium Phoenicem et Dymae, patris Hecubae, et Ledae consanguinitatis originem divisisse. Postquam memoriter cuncta retexuit, ad postremum flens orare, ne, quae semel in fidem eorum recepta esset, prodendam putarent. ea secum domo Menelai adportata, quae propria fuissent, nihil praeter ea ablatum. Sed utrum inmodico amore Alexandri, an poenarum metu, quas ob desertam domum a coniuge metuebat, ita sibi consulere maluerit, parum constabat.

I. 9. On the following day King Priam, at the insistence of Hecuba, went to Helen. Greeting her kindly, he urged her to feel well disposed and asked who she was and what was her family.

She answered that she was Alexander's relative and more closely akin to Priam and Hecuba than to the sons of Plisthenes. She went through the whole list of her ancestors. Danaus and Agenor were the progenitors, respectively, of Priam's line and of hers.[21] The daughter of Danaus was Hesione,[22] who had given birth to Electra by Atlas; Electra had given birth to Dardanus by Jupiter; and from Dardanus were descended Tros and, in order of succession, the other kings of Troy. As for Agenor, he had begotten Taygete; and she had given birth to Lacedaemon by Jupiter; Lacedaemon had begotten Amyclas, and he had begotten Argalus, the father of Oebalus. It was well known that Oebalus was the father of Tyndareus, and he, it seemed, was her father. She also recited the relation of her mother's family with Hecuba, for the son of Agenor, Phoenix, was the ancestor both of Leda and of Hecuba's father, Dymas.

After revealing her whole genealogy, she burst into tears and begged him not to return her. Now that the Trojans had made her welcome, and she had put her trust in them, they must not prove faithless. Everything Alexander had taken from Menelaus' home belonged to her; nothing else had been taken.

It was by no means clear why she preferred to look after her interests in this way. Was it because of her immodest love for Alexander, or because of her fear of the punishment her husband would exact for desertion?

---

21 Danaus and Agenor were related as follows: Neptune was the father of Belus and Agenor by Libya, and Belus was the father of Danaus. See Apollod. 2.1.4.

22 The text, which reads 'Plesione' here, has been corrected to 'Hesione', to agree with Dictys 4.22, where the same genealogy is given.

I. 10.   Igitur Hecuba cognita voluntate, simul ob generis coniunctionem conplexa Helenam, ne proderetur, summis opibus adnitebatur, cum iam Priamus et reliqui reguli non amplius differendos legatos dicerent neque resistendum popularium voluntati, solo omnium Deiphobo Hecubae adsenso, quem non aliter atque Alexandrum Helenae desiderium a recto consilio praepediebat. Itaque cum obstinate Hecuba nunc Priamum, modo filios deprecaretur, modo conplexu eius nulla ratione divelli posset, omnes qui aderant in voluntatem suam transduxit. Ita ad postremum bonum publicum materna gratia corruptum est. Deinde postero die Menelaus cum suis in contionem venit, coniugem et quae cum ea abrepta essent repetens. Tunc Priamus inter regulos medius adstans facto silentio optionem Helenae, quae ob id in conspectum popularium venerat, offert, si ei videretur domum ad suos regredi. Quam ferunt dixisse neque se invitam navigasse, neque sibi cum Menelai matrimonio convenire. Ita reguli habentes Helenam non sine exsultatione ex contione discedunt.

I. 10.   When Hecuba was informed of Helen's attitude and of the relation between their families, she embraced her and did everything she could to prevent her being returned. By this time Priam and most of the princes were saying that they could no longer put off the envoys or resist the will of the people. (Deiphobus was the only one who sided with Hecuba, for his judgment, like Alexander's, had been corrupted by his desire for Helen). Hecuba, however, persisted to intercede in Helen's behalf and accosted Priam and all of her sons who were present. They found it impossible to pull her from Helen's embrace and, therefore, finally decided to do as she wished. Thus by her influence as mother and wife she compromised the good of her country.

On the next day Menelaus, accompanied by the other envoys, came into the assembly. He demanded the return of his wife and the things Alexander had taken.

Then Priam, standing in the midst of the princes and calling for silence, said that Helen (who had come into public view for this purpose) should have the right to decide. When he asked her, 'Do you want to go home'? her answer, so they reported, was 'No'. She had not sailed, she said, unwillingly, for her marriage to Menelaus did not suit her. And so the princes left the assembly, exulting, with Helen.

I. 11. His actis Ulixes contestandi magis gratia quam aliquid ex oratione profuturus cuncta, quae ab Alexandro contra Graeciam indigne commissa essent, retexuit; ob quae ultionem brevi testatus est. dein Menelaus ira percitus atroci vultu exitium minatus consilium dimittit. Quae ubi ad Priamidas perlata sunt, confirmant inter se clam, uti per dolum legatos circumveniant. Credebant quippe, quod non frustra eos habuit, si legati inperfecto negotio revertissent, fore, uti adversum se grande proelium concitaretur. Igitur Antenor, cuius de sanctitate morum supra memoravimus, Priamum convenit coniurationemque factam conqueritur: filios quippe eius non legatis, sed adversus se insidias parare, neque id se passurum. Dein non multo post legatis rem aperit. Ita exploratis omnibus adhibito praesidio, cum primum opportunum visum est, inviolatos eos dimittit.

I. 11. When they had gone, Ulysses, though he knew that nothing he said would make any difference, argued for argument's sake. He reviewed everything Alexander had done and swore that the Greeks would soon be avenging these crimes. Next, Menelaus, full of wrath and scowling blackly, broke up the meeting with threats of destruction.

When Priam's sons were told what had happened, they secretly swore to kidnap the envoys. They believed, quite rightly, that the envoys, having failed to accomplish their mission, would return to Greece and demand war against Troy. Antenor, however, whose pious character we mentioned above, thwarted this plot. Going to Priam, he complained about the conspiracy: Priam's sons were not plotting against the envoys but against himself, and this he would not endure. Soon afterwards he informed the envoys. Thus every precaution was taken; he gave them a guard and at the first opportunity sent them home unharmed.

I. 12.   Dum haec apud Troiam aguntur, disseminata iam per universam Graeciam fama omnes Pelopidae in unum conveniunt atque interposita iuris iurandi religione, ni Helena cum abreptis redderetur, bellum se Priamo inlaturos confirmant. Legati Lacedaemonam redeunt, de Helena eiusque voluntate narrant, dein Priami filiorumque eius adversum se dicta gestaque, grande praeconium fidei erga legatos Antenoris praeferentes. Quae ubi accepere, decernitur, uti singuli in suis locis atque imperiis opes belli parent. Igitur ex consilii sententia opportunus locus ad conveniendum et in quo de apparatu belli ageretur, Argi, Diomedis regnum, deligitur.

I. 13.   Ita ubi tempus visum est, primus omnium ingenti nomine virtutis atque corporis Aiax Telamonius advenit, cum eo Teucer frater. Dein haud multo post Idomeneus et Meriones, summa inter se iuncti concordia. is eorum ego secutus comitatum ea quidem, quae antea apud Troiam gesta sunt, ab Ulixe cognita quam diligentissime rettuli et reliqua, quae deinceps insecuta sunt, quoniam ipse interfui, quam verissime potero exponam. Igitur post eos, quos supra memoravimus, Nestor cum Antilocho et Thrasymede, quos Anaxibia susceperat, supervenit. eos Peneleus insecutus cum Glonio et Arcesilao consanguineis, dein Prothoenor et Leitus Boeotiae principes, itemque Schedius et Epistrophus Phocenses, Ascalaphus et Ialmenus Orchomenii, tum Diores et Meges Phyleo genitus, Thoas ex Andraemone, Eurypylus Euaemonis Ormenius et Leonteus.

I. 12.   While this was happening at Troy, news of the abduction spread throughout Greece. All the descendants of Pelops foregathered and bound themselves with mutual oaths. If Helen was not returned along with the things Alexander had taken, they swore to make war against Priam.

The envoys, having returned to Sparta, reported Helen's decision and described the hostile words and deeds of Priam and his sons against them. Yet they praised Antenor in the highest terms for the good faith he had shown. The members of the Greek council, having heard this report, decided to make preparations for war in their different regions and kingdoms. They chose Argos, which was the realm of Diomedes, as a good place to meet and make plans for the war.

I. 13.   When the time seemed best, Ajax the son of Telamon, who was known for his bravery no less than his hugeness, was the first to arrive, accompanied by Teucer, his brother. Soon afterwards Idomeneus and Meriones came, who were the closest of friends.

(I followed along with these. As to what happened earlier at Troy, I have tried to make my report as accurate as possible, Ulysses being my source. The account that follows, based as it is on my own observations, will satisfy, I hope, the highest critical judgement).

Nestor also came to Argos, accompanied by Antilochus and Thrasymedes, his sons by Anaxibia. Then Peneleus came with his cousins Clonius and Arcesilaus; and these were followed by two other leaders of the Boeotians, Prothoenor and Leitus. Schedius and Epistrophus came from Phocis; Ascalaphus and Ialmenus, from Orchomenus. Then Diores and Meges, the sons of Phyleus, came; then Thoas, the son of Andraemon; Eurypylus, the son of Euaemon, from Ormenion; and then Leonteus.

I. 14.　　　　Post quos Achilles Pelei et Thetidis, quae ex Chirone dicebatur, hic in primis adulescentiae annis, procerus, decora facie, studio rerum bellicarum omnes iam tum virtute atque gloria superabat, neque tamen aberat ab eo vis quaedam inconsulta et effera morum impatientia. cum eo Patroclus et Phoenix, alter propter coniunctionem amicitiae, alter custos atque rector eius. Tlepolemus dein Herculis, eum insecuti sunt Phidippus et Antiphus, insignes armorum specie, avo Hercule; post eos Protesilaus Iphicli cum Podarce fratre. Adfuit et Eumelus Pheraeus, cuius pater Admetus quondam vicaria morte coniugis fata propria protulerat, Podalirius et Machaon Triccenses, Aesculapio geniti, adsciti ad id bellum ob sollertiam medicinae artis. Dein Poeantis Philocteta, qui comes Herculis post discessum eius ad deos sagittas divinas industriae praemium consecutus est, Nireus pulcher, ex Athenis Menestheus et Aiax Oilei ex Locride, Argis Amphilochus et Sthenelus, Amphiarai Amphilochus, Capanei alter, cum his Euryalus Mecistei. dein ex Aetolia Thessandrus Polynicis; postremi omnium Demophoon atque Acamas. Fuere cuncti ex origine Pelopis. Sed eos, quos memoravimus, plures alii ex suis quisque regionibus, partim ex regum comitibus, alii ipsius regni participes insecuti sunt, quorum nomina singillatim exponere haud necessarium visum est.

DICTYS I.

I. 14.   Next Achilles arrived, the son of Peleus and Thetis. (Thetis, so they say, was the daughter of Chiron.) Achilles was in the first years of his manhood, a noble youth and handsome. So great was his zeal for war that he was already known as the bravest champion alive. Nevertheless, it must be admitted, his character showed a certain ill-advised forcefulness, a certain savage impatience. He was accompanied by Patroclus, his close friend, and Phoenix, his guardian and teacher.

Then there was Tlepolemus, the son of Hercules; and after him, Phidippus and Antiphus, the grandsons of Hercules, wearing beautiful armour. After them came Protesilaus, the son of Iphiclus, with his brother Podarces. And Eumelus of Pherae was there. (Eumelus' father, Admetus, had once prolonged his life by having his wife die for him).[23] Podalirius and Machaon came from Tricca; they, being sons of Aesculapius, had been summoned to serve as physicians. Then Philoctetes came, the son of Poeas, carrying the marvellous bow and arrows of Hercules, whom he had formerly served. (As reward for his service, Hercules, when departing to be with the gods, had given these weapons to him).[24] Then the handsome Nireus came. Menestheus came from Athens; Ajax the son of Oileus, from Locris; Amphilochus, the son of Amphiaraus, and Sthenelus, the son of Capaneus, from Argos, and with them was Euryalus, the son of Mecisteus; Thersander, the son of Polynices, came from Aetolia; and, last of all, Demophoon and Acamas. These were all the descendants of Pelops. They were followed by a great number of others, coming from various regions, some being retainers of kings, and others rulers themselves. It seems quite useless, however, to give a list of their names.

---

23 Admetus' wife was Alcestis. See Euripides *Alcestis*.
24 See Sophocles *Trachiniae*.

27

I. 15.   Igitur ubi omnes Argos convenere, Diomedes hospitio cunctos recipit, necessariaque praebet. Dein Agamemnon grande auri pondus Mycenis adportatum per singulos dispertiens promptiores animos omnium ad bellum, quod parabatur, facit. Tum communi consilio super condicione proelii ius iurandum interponi hoc modo placuit. Calchas, Thestoris filius, praescius futurorum, porcum marem in forum medium adferri iubet, quem in duas partes exsectum orienti occidentique dividit, atque ita singulos nudatis gladiis per medium transire iubet. dein mucronibus sanguine eius oblitis, adhibitis etiam aliis ad eam rem necessariis, inimicitias sibi cum Priamo per religionem confirmant: neque prius se bellum deserturos, quam Ilium atque omne regnum eruissent. Quis perfectis pure lauti Martem atque Concordiam multis immolationibus sibi adhospitavere.

I. 15.   When all had assembled at Argos, Diomedes supplied their needs and made them at home. Agamemnon distributed a great amount of gold he had brought from Mycenae, and thus increased their yearning for war. Then they decided unanimously to seal their alliance as follows:

Calchas the prophet, the son of Thestor, having ordered a hog brought into their midst, cut it in half and set the parts towards east and west. Then he commanded them all to draw their swords and pass them through the victim. Thus, smearing their blades with the blood of the hog, and completing the other rites as required, they bound themselves to war against Priam. They swore to fight on until Troy and Priam's whole kingdom was utterly destroyed. After taking this oath and purifying themselves with ablutions, they sacrificed many victims to Mars and Concord, seeking the aid of these gods.

I. 16.   Dein in templo Iunonis Argivae rectorem omnium declarari placuit. igitur singuli in tabellis, quas ad deligendum belli principem quem cuique videretur acceperant, Punicis litteris Agamemnonis nomen designant. Ita consensu omnium secundo rumore summam belli atque exercitus in se suscipit, quod ei et propter germanum, cuius gratia bellum id parabatur, et propter magnam opum vim, quibus praeter ceteros Graeciae reges magnus atque clarus habebatur, merito acciderat. dein duces praefectosque navium Achillem, Aiacem et Phoenicem destinant. praeponuntur etiam campestri exercitui Palamedes cum Diomede et Ulixe, ita ut inter se diurnas vigiliarumque vices dispertiant. His peractis ad parandas opes atque instrumenta militiae singuli sua in regna discedunt. Interim belli studio ardebat omnis Graecia: arma, tela, equi, naves atque haec omnia toto biennio praeparantur, cum iuventus partim sua sponte, alii aequalium ad gloriam aemulatione munia militiae festinarent. Sed inter haec summa cura vis magna navium praecipue fabricatur, scilicet ne multa milia exercituum, undique versum in unum collecta, incuria navigandi tardarentur.

DICTYS I.

I. 16.   Then they decided to appoint a principal leader. Accordingly, in the temple of the Argive Juno, everyone, having received a ballot, wrote (in Phoenician letters) the name of the man he thought would make the best leader. Agamemnon was chosen and thus, with the hearty approval of each and every one, he took upon himself the command of the forces. He deserved this position for two reasons: first, he was the brother of the man for whose sake they were fighting; and second, he was considered the wealthiest and most powerful king in Greece. Then they appointed Achilles, Ajax, and Phoenix to be the leaders in charge of the fleet; and gave Palamedes, Diomedes, and Ulysses joint command of the army-in-camp, that is, the routine duties of the day and the watches of the night. Having made these arrangements, the Greeks departed to their different kingdoms to get ready their forces and equipment for war.

Zeal for war inflamed all Greece during the following period. Within two years everything was ready; weapons for defence and offence, and horses and ships. The men had accelerated their work, some acting with natural zest, others to rival the glory their comrades were gaining. They felt, understandably enough, that their most important task was the construction of a great naval force; the many thousands of soldiers, when once they had been gathered from everywhere, must not be delayed for want of a fleet.

I. 17.   Igitur peracto biennio ad Aulidam Boeotiae, nam is locus delectus fuerat, singuli reges pro facultate opum regnique instructas classes praemittunt: ex quis primus Agamemnon ex Mycenis naves C, aliisque LX, quas ex diversis civitatibus, quae sub eo erant, contraxerat, Agapenorem praeficit, Nestor XC navium instructam classem, Menelaus ex omni Lacedaemona naves LX, Menestheus Athenis L, XL Elephenor ex Euboea, Aiax Telamonius Salamina XII, Diomedes Argis LXXX navium classem, Ascalaphus et Ialmenus Orchomenii naves XXX, Oileus Aiax XL, item ex omni Boeotia Arcesilaus, Prothoenor, Peneleus, Leitus, Clonius naves L, XL ex Phocide Schedius et Epistrophus, dein Thalpius et Diores cum Amphimacho et Polyxeno Elide aliisque civitatibus regionis eius naves XL,Thoas ex Aetolia XL, Meges ex Dulichio et ex insulis Echinadibus XL, Idomeneus cum Merione ex omni Creta classem navium LXXX, ex Ithaca Ulixes XII, XL Prothous Magnes, Tlepolemus Rhodo aliisque circa eam insulis IX, XI Eumelus Pheraeus, Achilles ex Argo Pelasgico L, III Nireus ex Syme, Podarces et Protesilaus ex Phylaca aliisque, quibus praeerant, locis naves XL, XXX Podalirius et Machaon, Philocteta Methona aliisque civitatibus naves VII, Eurypylus Ormenius XL, duas et XX Guneus Perrhaebis, Leonteus et Polypoetes ex suis regionibus XL, XXX ex insulis Co Crapathoque cum Antipho Phidippus, Thessandrus, quem Polynicis supra memoravimus, Thebis naves L, Calehas ex Acarnania XX, Mopsus Colophona XX, Epios ex insulis Cycladibus is XXX. easque magna vi frumenti aliorumque necessariorum cibi replent. quippe ita ab Agamemnone mandatum acceperant, scilicet ne tanta vis militum necessariorum penuria fatigaretur.

DICTYS I.

I. 17.   Thus at the end of two years all the kings had equipped ships varying in number with the wealth and power of their kingdoms,[25] and had sent them on to Aulis in Boeotia; this was the place they had chosen. Agamemnon assembled a fleet of 100 ships from Mycenae, in addition to 60 others from the various cities under his power; he put Agapenor in charge. Nestor equipped a fleet of 90 ships. Menelaus had 60 ships from all Lacedaemon; Menestheus 50 from Athens; Elephenor 40 from Euboea; Ajax, the son of Telamon, 12 from Salamis; Diomedes 80 from Argos; Ascalaphus and Ialmenus 30 from Orchomenus; Ajax, the son of Oileus, 40; Arcesilaus, Prothoenor, Peneleus, Leitus, and Clonius 50 from all of Boeotia; Schedius and Epistrophus 40 from Phocis; Thalpius and Diores, along with Amphimachus and Polyxenus, 40 from Elis and the other cities of this region; Thoas 40 from Aetolia; Meges 40 from Dulichium and the islands of the Echinades; Idomeneus and Meriones 80 from all Crete; Ulysses 12 from Ithaca; Prothous 40 from Magnesia; Tlepolemus 9 from Rhodes and the other islands about; Eumelus 11 from Pherae; Achilles 50 from Pelasgian Argos; Nireus 3 from Syme; Podarces and Protestilaus 40 from Phylaca and the other, places they controlled; Podalirius and Machaon 30; Philoctetes 7 from Methona and other cities; Eurypylus 40 from Ormenion; Guneus 22 from Perrhaebia; Leonteus and Polypoetes 40 from their regions; Phidippus and Antiphus 30 from the islands of Cos and Crapathus; Thersander (the son of Polynices, as we mentioned above) 50 from Thebes; Calchas 20 from Acarnania; Mopsus 20 from Colophon; and Epeus 30 from the islands of the Cyclades.

They filled their ships with large amounts of grain and other necessary goods. Agamemnon had of course ordered them to do this, that so huge a military force might not be stymied with lack of supplies.

---

25 Section 17, with a few exceptions, is based on Homer's catalogue of ships in *Iliad* 2.494-795.

I. 18.   Igitur inter tantum classium apparatum equi atque currus bellici ob locorum condicionem multi, sed pedestres milites pars maxima, ob eam causam, quia per omnem Graeciam multo maiore egestate pabuli, equitatus usus prohibetur. Praeterea fuere multi, qui ob artis peritiam necessarii nautico apparatui credebantur. Per idem tempus Lycius Sarpedon neque pretio neque gratia ‡ Phalidis ‡, Sidoniorum regis, ‡ inlectus, qui virtutis ‡ societatem militae nostrae adversum Troianos sequeretur, quippe quem iam Priamus donis amplioribus eisque postea duplicatis fidissimum sibi retinuerat. Omnium autem classium numerus, quem ex diversis Graeciae regnis contractum supra exposuimus, toto quinquennio praeparatus instructusque est. Ita cum nulla iam res profectionem, nisi absentia militis retardaret, cuncti duces veluti signo dato una atque eodem tempore Aulidam confluunt.

Dictys I.

I. 18. In addition to this huge armada, there were many horses and war chariots, their number being large, considering the lack of good pasture in Greece. The infantry, however, far outnumbered the cavalry. Also there were the many nautical experts who were necessary to maintain and operate the ships.

During this time we were unable, either by bribery or by the influence of Phalis,[26] the king of the Sidonians, to entice the Lycian Sarpedon to follow our alliance. Priam, by offering larger gifts (which afterwards were doubled), had already won his support for the Trojans.

It took five years for all the ships (which, as we have described above, were brought together from the various regions of Greece) to be equipped and readied. When, however, nothing except the soldiers' absence prevented us from sailing, all of our leaders, at the same time, as if at a given signal, came together at Aulis.

---

26 The text is corrupt here. This Phalis is probably to be equated with the Phalas of Dictys 4.4.

I. 19. Interim in ipsa navigandi festinatione Agamemnon, quem a cunctis regem omnium declaratum supra docuimus, longius paulo ab exercitu progressus forte conspicit circa lucum Dianae pascentem capream imprudensque religionis, quae in eo loco erat, iaculo transfigit. Neque multo post irane caelesti an ob mutationem aeris corporibus pertemptatis lues invadit. atque interim in dies magis magisque saeviens multa milia fatigare et promiscue per pecora atque exercitum grassari. Prorsus nullus funeri modus neque requies; uti quidque malo obvium fuerat, vastabatur. quis rebus sollicitis ducibus mulier quaedam deo plena Dianae iram fatur: eam namque ob necem capreae, qua maxime laetabatur, sacrilegii poenam ab exercitu expetere, nec leniri, priusquam auctor tanti sceleris filiam natu maximam vicariam victimam immolavisset. Quae vox ut ad exercitum venit, omnes duces Agamemnonem adeunt eumque primo orare recusantemque ad postremum cogere, uti malo obviam properaret. Sed ubi obstinate renuere vident nec ulla vi queunt flectere, plurimis conviciis insecuti, ad postremum regio honore spoliavere. ac ne tanta vis exercitus sine rectore effusius ac sine modo militiae vagaretur, praeficiunt ante omnes Palamedem, dein Diomedem et Aiacem Telamonium, quartum Idomenea. Ita per aequationem numeri atque partium quadripertitur exercitus.

36

Dictys I.

I. 19.   While we were hastening to sail, Agamemnon (who, as we have said above, had been unanimously chosen commander-in-chief), having gone some way from the camp, noticed a she-goat grazing near a grove of Diana and, feeling no awe because of the place, struck it through with his spear. Soon afterwards, either because of heavenly wrath or atmospheric contamination, a plague began to attack us. Day after day it raged with greater and greater violence, destroying many thousands as it passed indiscriminately through herds and army, laying waste everything that stood in its way, there being no abatement, no end to death.

While our leaders were seeking some remedy, a certain woman,[27] divinely inspired, revealed the reason for our affliction: the wrath of Diana; the goddess was exacting punishment from the army for the sacrilege of slaying the she-goat in which she especially delighted, nor would she relent until the perpetrator of this awful injury had made full atonement by sacrificing his oldest daughter. When this solution was brought to the army, all of our leaders approached Agamemnon. Begging and then threatening, they tried to make him offer the remedy quickly, but he obstinately and absolutely refused and so they reviled him and finally stripped him of his command.

But in order that their huge army, being leaderless, might not become an undisciplined mob, they chose four men to share the command: Palamedes, Diomedes, Ajax the son of Telamon, and Idomeneus. And they divided their forces, according to the number of leaders, into four equal parts.

---

27 Perhaps Agamemnon had consulted the oracle of Apollo, while this woman was Apollo's priestess, the Pythia.

I. 20. Neque interim ullus finis vastitatis, cum Ulixes simulata ex pertinacia Agamemnonis iracundia et ob id domuitionem confirmans magnum atque insperabile cunctis remedium excogitavit. Profectus namque Mycenas nullo consilii participe falsas litteras tamquam ab Agamemnone ad Clytemestram perfert, quarum sententia haec erat: Iphigeniam, nam ea maior natu erat, desponsam Achilli, eumque non prius ad Troiam profecturum, quam promissi fides impleretur; ob quae festinaret eamque et quae nuptiis usui essent, mature mittere. Praeterea multa pro negotio locutus ementito argumento fidem fecerat. Quae ubi accepit Clytemestra cum propter gratiam Helenae, tum maxime, quod tam celeberrimi nominis viro filia traderetur, laeta Iphigeniam Ulixi committit. isque confecto negotio paucis diebus ad exercitum revenit, atque ex inproviso in luco Dianae cum virgine conspicitur. quis cognitis Agamemnon affectione paternae pietatis motus an ne tam inlicito immolationis sceleri interesset, fugam parat. Eumque re cognita Nestor, longam exorsus orationem, ad postremum persuadendi genere, in quo praeter ceteros Graeciae viros iucundus acceptusque erat, a proposito prohibuit.

DICTYS I.

I. 20. Meanwhile the plague continued to rage until Ulysses unexpectedly provided the necessary remedy. No one knew of his plan. He pretended to return to his kingdom because of his anger at Agamemnon's refusal, but went instead to Mycenae and took Clytemnestra a letter he had forged in the name of her husband. The gist of this letter was as follows: Achilles refused to sail for Troy until he had married their oldest daughter, Iphigenia, whom they had promised to him; therefore, she should send Iphigenia to Aulis, along with the dowry, as quickly as possible. In addition to bringing this letter, Ulysses said many things to strengthen Clytemnestra's belief in its contents. Thus she, desiring both to recover her sister Helen and, even more, to marry her daughter to so renowned a man, gladly entrusted Iphigenia to Ulysses. Within a few days he returned to the camp and appeared unexpectedly with the girl in the grove of Diana.

When Agamemnon knew what had happened, he wanted to flee, either because of his love for his daughter or because he wanted no part in so vile a sacrifice. Nestor, however, learned of his plans and, in a long speech, by means of that art of persuasion in which he was more pleasing and effective than anyone else in Greece, prevailed upon him to stay.

I. 21.   Interim virginem Ulixes et Menelaus cum Calchante, quibus id negotium datum erat, remotis procul omnibus sacrificio adornant, cum ecce dies foedari et caelum nubilo tegi coepit, dein repente tonitrua, corusca fulmina et praeterea terrae marisque ingens motus atque ad postremum confusione aeris ereptum lumen. Neque multo post imbrium atque grandinis vis magna praecipitata. inter quae tam taetra nulla requie tempestatis Menelaus cum his, qui sacrificium curabant, metu atque haesitatione diversus agebatur, terreri quippe primo subita caeli permutatione idque signum divinum credere, dein, ne inceptum omitteret, detrimento militum commoveri. Igitur inter tantam animi dubitationem vox quaedam luco emissa: aspernari numen sacrificii genus et ob id abstinendum corpore virginis, misereri namque eius deam; ceteru pro tanto facinore satis poenarum Agamemnoni ab coniuge eius post Troianam victoriam conparatum. Itaque curarent id, quod in vicem virginis oblatum animadverterent, immolare. Dein coepere venti atque fulmina aliaque, quae in magno caeli motu oriri solent, consenescere.

I. 21.   Ulysses, Menelaus, and Calchas were put in charge of the sacrifice; everyone else was kept at a distance. When they had begun to adorn the girl, suddenly, lo and behold, the day began to darken. Thunder roared and lightning flashed, earth and sea were shaken. Finally a whirlwind of dust made the darkness complete. Soon afterwards rain and hail poured down. This ghastly disturbance which showed no signs of abatement threw Menelaus and the other officiants into confusion; they were caught between their fear and perplexity. At first they were frightened by the sudden change in the weather and believed that this was the sign of some god, but then they were worried that the army might suffer some harm if they discontinued the sacrifice. While they were trying to solve their dilemma, they heard a voice from the grove saying that divinity spurned such an offering; the goddess had mercy upon the girl, and they must not touch her; as for Agamemnon, after his victory at Troy, his wife would see to his adequate punishment; they must sacrifice what they would see had been sent in the place of the girl. Then the winds and the lightning and all the storm's fierceness began to diminish.

I. 22.   Sed cum haec in luco aguntur, Achilles litteras seorsum missas sibi a Clytemestra cum auri magno pondere accepit, in quis ei filiam atque omnem domum suam commendaverat. Quae postquam et Ulixis consilium patefactum est, omissis omnibus propere ad lucum pergit, magna voce Menelaum et qui cum eo erant, inclamans, ab inquietudine Iphigeniae cohiberent sese, comminatus perniciem, ni paruissent. mox attonitis his atque obstupefactis ipse supervenit reformatoque iam die virginem abstrahit. Interim deliberantibus cunctis, quidnam vel ubi esset, quod immolari iuberetur, cerva forma corporis admiranda ante ipsam aram intrepida consistit. Eam praedictam hostiam rati oblatamque divinitus conprehendere moxque immolant. Quis peractis sedata lues instarque aestivi temporis reseratum est caelum. Ceterum virginem Achilles atque hi, qui sacrificio praefuere, clam omnes regi Scytharum, qui eo tempore aderat, commendavere.

I. 22.   While these things were happening, Achilles received a personal letter from Clytemnestra, and also a great deal of gold; she commended her daughter and all of her house to him. When he had read the letter, he realized the scheme of Ulysses and, dropping all other concerns, rushed to the grove, shouting for Menelaus and the other officiants to keep their hands off Iphigenia, or else he would kill them. He found them still in a state of disaray; and when the weather had cleared, he freed the girl. But what was the thing, where was the thing that they had been ordered to sacrifice? This was perplexing them all when a marvellously beautiful deer appeared un-trembling before the very altar. Accepting this deer as the victim which had been predicted and which was now divinely offered, they seized upon it and soon slew it. With the performance of this sacrifice, the force of the plague subsided, and the sky became bright as in summer. Then Achilles and the three officiants, acting in complete secrecy, entrusted the girl to the king of the Scythians, who was there at this time.[28]

---

28 In the *Cypria* (frag. 1, p. 495), Diana snatches Iphigenia away and carries her off to the land of the Taurians.

I. 23.   At ubi duces sedatam vim mali animadvertunt ventorumque flatus navigandi prosperos atque aestivam maris faciem, omnes laeti Agamemnonem adeunt, eumque interitu filiae permaestum consolati honorem regni rursus concelebrant. Quae res pergrata atque accepta per exercitum fuit, eum quippe optimum consultorem sui non secus, quam parentem miles omnis percolebat. Sed Agamemnon sive eorum, quae praecesserant, satis prudens, seu humanarum rerum necessitatem animo reputans et ob id adversus infortunia firmissimus, dissimulato quod ei acciderat, honorem suscipit atque eo die duces omnes ad se in convivium deducit. Dein haud multis post diebus exercitus ordinatus per duces, cum opportunum iam tempus navigandi ingrueret, ascendit naves repletas multis rebus pretiosissimis, quae ab incolis regionis eius offerebantur. Ceterum frumenta, vinum aliaque cibi necessaria Anius et eius filiae praebuere, quae oenotropae ac divinae religionis antistites memorabantur. Hoc modo ex Aulide navigatum est.

I. 23.   Our leaders were all delighted, for they saw that the force of the plague had abated and that the winds were good for sailing, the sea being calm as in summer. Going to Agamemnon and consoling him over his daughter's death, they made him principal leader again. This greatly pleased the whole army, for all the soldiers loved Agamemnon, thinking that he would look after their interests no less than a father. Agamemnon showed no signs of knowing what had really happened to Iphigenia. Perhaps he knew. Or had he, having pondered the turns of human fortune, steeled himself to adversity? In either case, resuming his office, he invited the leaders to dinner that day.

Several days later, the weather being good for sailing, our leaders set the army in order; and thus we boarded the ships. We had stowed all sorts of costly supplies which the people who lived near Aulis had given us. Grain, wine, and other necessary foods were furnished by Anius and his daughters; the latter were known as Oenotropae (winegrowers) and priestesses of a holy religion.[29] Thus we sailed from Aulis.

---

29 Anius was a king of Delos. For him and his daughters, see Ovid *Metamorphoses* 13.631-673.

LIBER SECUNDVS

II. 1.   Postquam ad Mysorum regionem universas classes venti appulere, propere omnes signo dato naves litori admovent. Dein egredi cupientibus a custodibus loci eius obviam itum est. eos namque Telephus, qui tum Mysiae imperator erat, quo omnis regio ab incursione maritimorum hostium defensaretur, litori praefecerat. igitur ubi descendere prohibentur neque prius permittitur terram contingere, quam regi quinam essent nuntiaretur, nostri primo quae dicebantur neglegere et singuli navibus egredi; dein postquam a custodibus nihil remittebatur et summa vi resisti et prohiberi coeptum, duces omnes iniuriam manu vindicandam rati arreptis armis evolant navibus incensique ira custodes caedere neque versis his atque in fuga parcere, sed uti quisque fugientem conprehenderat, obtruncare.

DICTYS II.

Book Two

II. 1.   The winds drove our whole fleet toward Mysia, and at a given signal we quickly guided all of the ships to shore, where, however, there were guards who opposed our men and prevented them from debarking. These guards had been stationed there by Telephus, who was at that time the ruler of Mysia, to protect his country from sea invasion. They forbade us to come ashore, or even touch land, until they had told their king who we were. When our men paid no heed to these orders and began, one by one, to debark, the guards relented not in the least but used full force to resist and obstruct us. Thereupon all of our leaders agreed that force must be met with force and, snatching up arms and rushing from the ships, angrily slew some of the guards; and put the others to flight, slaughtering any they happened to catch.

II. 2.   Interim ad Telephum, qui primi fuga Graecos evaserant, veniunt: inruisse multa milia hostium eosque caesis custodibus litora occupasse et multa praeterea singuli pro metu suo adicientes nuntiant. Dein re cognita Telephus cum his, quos circum se habebat, aliisque, qui in ea festinatione in unum conduci potuere, propere Graecis obviam venit ac statim condensatis utrimque frontibus vi magna concurritur. Dein uti quisque in manus venerat, interficitur, cum interim his aut illis ex casu suorum perculsis vehementius invicem instaretur. Sed in ea pugna Thessandrus, quem Polynicis supra memoravimus, congressus cum Telepho ictusque ab eo cadit multis tamen hostium ante interfectis, in quis Telephi comitem, quem rex ob industriam virium atque ingenii inter duces habebat, strenue dimicantem obtruncaverat; atque ita paulatim elatus secundo belli eventu et ob id maiora viribus adgressus interficitur. Atque eius cruentum corpus Diomedes, quod ei iam tum a parentibus coeptum cum eo societatis ius perseverabat, umeris extulit. Idque igni crematum, quod superfuerat, patrio more sepeliit.

II. 2.   The guards who were first to escape the Greeks went and told Telephus about the hostile horde which had attacked their country and which, having slain some of their number, now was holding the shore. And each of the guards, in proportion to his fear, embellished the story with some additional incident.

On learning this news, Telephus, taking the men he had with him and those who were able to be gathered in the emergency, hastened to encounter the Greeks. When the two sides had drawn up their forces, a great battle ensued. They slaughtered each other at close quarters, the deaths of their comrades spurring them on to fight the more fiercely. It was in this battle that Thersander (the son of Polynices, as we mentioned above) attacked Telephus, and fell at his hands. Thersander had killed many of the Mysians, among whom was a doughty fighter, a favourite of Telephus, chosen by him as one of his generals because of his bravery, strength, and natural ability; these successes had gradually caused Thersander to become elated at the prospects of ultimate victory; and thus, daring to do greater deeds, he was killed. Thereupon Diomedes, remembering the friendship their fathers had started,[1] shouldered Thersander's bloody body and carried it off to be cremated and buried according to custom.

---

1 Diomedes' father, Tydeus, had helped Polynices gather an army for the attack against Thebes. See *Iliad* 4.376-379.

II. 3.   At ubi animadvertere Achilles et Aiax Telamonius magno suorum detrimento eventum belli trahi, exercitum in duas partes dispertiunt. Ac pro tempore cohortati suos tamquam restauratis viribus acrius hostes incurrunt, ipsi duces principes certaminis, cum modo insequerentur fugientes, modo ingruentibus semet instar muri opponerent. Atque ita omni modo primi aut inter primos bellantes praeclaram iam tum virtutis suae famam apud hostes atque inter suos effecere. Interim Teuthranius, Teuthrante et Auge genitus, frater Telephi uterinus, ubi animadvertit Aiacem tanta adversum suos gloria dimicantem, propere ad eum convertit ibique pugnando ictus telo eius occubuit. Eius casu Telephus non mediocriter perculsus ultionemque fraternae mortis expetens infestus aciem invadit atque ibi, fugatis quos adversum ierat, cum obstinate Ulixem inter vineas, quae ei loco adiunctae erant, insequeretur, praepeditus trunco vitis ruit. Id ubi Achilles procul animadvertit, telum iaculatus femur sinistrum regi transfigit. At Telephus inpigre resurgens ferrum ex corpore extrahit et protectus concursu suorum ab instanti pernicie liberatus est.

II. 3   Achilles and Ajax the son of Telamon, seeing that the war was resulting in heavy casualties for our side, divided the army between them and, exhorting their troops as the occasion demanded, attacked the enemy more fiercely, their strength apparently renewed. They themselves were in the front of the fighting, now pursuing those who were fleeing, now opposing, like a wall, those who attacked. Thus even then, by being the first or among the first to fight in every encounter, they had won for themselves, both with our men and with the enemy, an illustrious reputation for bravery.

Meanwhile Teuthranius, having noticed that Ajax was winning great glory in battle, hastened to meet him, and there died fighting, felled by Ajax' spear. Teuthranius was the son of Teuthras and Auge; and the half-brother of Telephus, for they had the same mother.[2]

Telephus, being deeply upset by the death of his brother and seeking for vengeance, attacked the enemy line. Having put to flight those who opposed him, he was doggedly pursuing Ulysses in a vineyard nearby when a vine tripped him up. Thereupon Achilles who, from some distance, had seen what had happened, hurled his spear and pierced the king's left thigh. But Telephus rose quickly and, having drawn out the spear, escaped immediate destruction shielded by a group of his men who had come to the rescue.

---

2 Telephus, whose real father was Hercules, was, according to *Apollod.* 3.9.1, Teuthras' adopted son. Compare Dares 16.

II. 4.   Iamque diei plerumque processerat, cum utraque acie intenta proelium sine ulla requie iugi certamine ac strenue adversum se ducibus fatigaretur. Namque nostros multorum dierum navigio in aliquantum exhaustos maxime praesentia Telephi debilitaverat. Is namque Hercule genitus procerus corpore ac pollens viribus, divinis patriis virtutibus propriam gloriam aequiperaverat. Igitur adventante nocte cunctis cupientibus requies belli facta. Ac Mysi ad se domum, nostri ad naves digrediuntur. Ceterum in ea pugna utriusque exercitus interfecti multi mortales, sed et vulnerati pars maxima, prorsus nullo aut perpaucis clade belli eius expertibus. Dein secuta die legati invicem de sepeliendis, qui in bello ceciderant, mittuntur. Atque ita indutiis interpositis collecta corpora atque igni cremata sepeliuntur.

II. 4.   At the close of this day, both sides were exhausted, for the battle had raged without break, the leaders joined in fierce combat. The presence of Telephus had especially dampened our spirits, tired as we already were from sailing so far; for Telephus was a tall and powerful man whose deeds of valour rivalled those of his divine father, Hercules. Thus with the coming of night, all were glad to stop fighting. The Mysians returned to their homes, our men to the ships. Great was the number of those who were slain in this battle, but greater still was the number of those who were wounded: no one, or at least very few, escaped without injury.

On the next day both sides sent envoys to make a truce for burying the dead. Thus the bodies were collected, cremated, and buried.

II. 5.   Interim Tlepolemus et cum fratre Antipho Phidippus, quos Thessalo genitos nepotes Herculis supra memoravimus, cognito Telephum in his locis imperitare, fiducia cognationis ad eum veniunt eique, quinam essent et quibuscum navigassent, aperuere. Dein multa invicem consumpta oratione ad postremum nostri acrius incusare, quod tam hostiliter adversum suos versaretur. Agamemnonem namque et Menelaum Pelopidas, non alienos generis sui, eum exercitum contraxisse. Dein quae circa domum Menelai ab Alexandro commissa essent raptumque Helenae docent. Atque decere eum cum propter consanguinitatem tum praecipue ob scelus violati communis hospitii Graecis ultro ferre auxilium, in quorum gratia ipsius etiam Herculis plurima laborum monumenta per totam Graeciam existere. Ad ea Telephus, etsi dolore vulneris inmodice adflictabatur, benigne tamen respondens ipsorum potius ait culpa factum, quod amicissimos et iunctos sibi generis adfinitate regno suo adpulsos ignoraverit; praemittendos etenim fuisse, per quos cognito eorum adventu obviam ire gratulantem oportuerit atque amice hospitio receptos donatosque muneribus, cum commodum ipsis videretur, remittere. Ceterum militiam adversum Priamum recusare; Astyochen enim Priami iunctam sibi matrimonio, ex qua Eurypylus genitus artissimum adfinitatis pignus intercederet. Dein propere popularibus, uti ab incepto desisterent, nuntiari iubet. atque ita nostris liberam egrediendi navibus potestatem permittit. Tlepolemus et qui cum eo venerant Eurypylo traduntur hique perfectis quae cupierant ad naves pergunt nuntiantes Agamemnoni ac reliquis regibus pacem concordiamque cum Telepho.

DICTYS II.

II. 5. Meanwhile Tlepolemus and the brothers Antiphus and Phidippus (who were sons of Thessalus and grandsons of Hercules, as we mentioned above) learned that Telephus was the ruler of Mysia. Relying for protection on the fact of this kinship, they went and told him who they were, and with whom they had sailed. Finally, after a long conversation, they bitterly accused him of the hostile way he had opposed his own people, pointing out that Agamemnon and Menelaus, who had brought together their army, were descendants of Pelops and therefore not unrelated to him.[3] Then they told him about Alexander's injuries against Menelaus' home and about the abduction of Helen. Telephus therefore, they concluded, should want to aid the Greeks because of his relationship with them, and especially in view of Alexander's violation of the customs of guest-friendship; moreover, Telephus' father, Hercules, had also aided the Greeks by those numerous labours the monuments of which existed throughout Greece.

Telephus, though terribly pained by his wound, answered their charges politely. What had happened, he said, was not his fault, but theirs. He had not known that they who had come were closest friends and cherished relatives. They should have sent ahead messengers to announce their arrival, and he would have gone and met them, bidden them welcome, and made them at home; they would have been his guests, and he would have sent them off with gifts when they thought they must go. As for the expedition against Priam, he refused to take part; he was prevented by the closest bonds of kinship, for his wife Astyoche, the mother of his son Eurypylus, was one of Priam's daughters.

Then he quickly commanded that his people be told to stop preparing for war and freely granted our men the right to debark. Tlepolemus and the other envoys were put in the care of Eurypylus; and thus, their mission accomplished, they returned to the ships to tell Agamemnon and the other nobles about the peace and concord with Telephus.

---

3 According to Euripides (*Heraclidae* 210-211), Hercules' mother Alcmene, was the daughter of Pelops.

II. 6. Quae ubi accepere, apparatum belli laeti omittunt. dein ex consilii sententia Achilles cum Aiace ad Telephum pervenere, eumque iactatum magnis doloribus consolati, ut viriliter incommodum ferret deprecabantur. At Telephus, ubi aliquantum requies doloris intercesserat, Graecos incusare, quod ne nuntium quidem adventus sui praemisissent. Dein percontatur, quinam et quanti Pelopidae in ea militia essent doctusque multis precibus orat, ut ad se omnes veniant. tunc nostri facturos se quae vellet polliciti desiderium regis reliquis nuntiavere. Igitur omnes Pelopidae praeter Agamemnonem et Menelaum in unum congregati ad Telephum veniunt multumque gratulationis atque laetitiae praesentia sua regi obtulere. Ac deinde muneribus largiter donati hospitio recipiuntur. neque tamen miles reliquus, qui apud naves erat, munificentiae regis expers fuit, namque ex numero navium frumentum aliaque necessaria adfatim portabantur. Ceterum rex ubi Agamemnonem fratremque eius abesse animadvertit, multis precibus Ulixem deprecatur, uti ad eos acciendos pergeret. Hi itaque ad Telephum veniunt is ae more regio invicem acceptis datisque donis Machaonem et Podalirium, Aesculapii filios, venire ac vulneri mederi iubent; qui inspecta cura propere apta dolori medicamina inponunt.

II. 6.   On learning this news, we gladly stopped preparing for war; and, in accordance with the will of the council, Achilles and Ajax went to Telephus. Seeing he was suffering great pain, they tried to console him and urged him to bear up bravely. Telephus, when his pain allowed him to speak, accused the Greeks of not even sending a messenger ahead to announce their arrival. Then he asked how many of our men were descendants of Pelops, and who these descendants were. Having been told, he insisted that these relatives should come and see him. Thereupon our men, having promised to do as he wished, returned and told the others what he desired.

Accordingly, all of the descendants of Pelops, with the exception of Agamemnon and Menelaus, came together and went to Telephus. He was very grateful and very delighted to see them and received them hospitably with many gifts. Moreover, he showed his kindness by sending grain and ample supplies to all our men who were left at the ships. Noticing, however, that Agamemnon and Menelaus were absent, he begged Ulysses to go and summon them. Upon their arrival, he and they exchanged gifts, as royal custom demanded; and they ordered Podalirius and Machaon, the sons of Aesculapius, to come and treat him. These latter hastened to discover a cure and to offer a suitable treatment for the wound.

II. 7.   Sed ubi tritis aliquot diebus tempus navigandi remorari ac ventis adversantibus mare in dies magis magisque saevire occepit, Telephum adeunt eumque de opportunitate temporis consulunt. Atque ab eo docti initio veris ex his locis ad Troiam navigandi tempus esse, reliqua adversa, cunctis volentibus Boeotiam revertuntur ibique subductis navibus singuli in regna sua hiematum discedunt. Interim in eo otio regi Agamemnoni cum Menelao fratre exercere discordias vacuum fuit ob proditam Iphigeniam. Is namque auctor et veluti causa luctus eius credebatur.

II. 8.   Per idem tempus, ubi de coniuratione universae Graeciae apud Troiam conpertum est, auctoribus nuntii eius Scythis barbaris, qui mercandi gratia per omnem Hellespontum commutare res cum accolis sueti ultro citroque vagabantur, metus atque maeror universos invasere, cum singuli, quibus ab initio Alexandri facinus displicuerat, male actum adversum Graeciam et ob id paucorum pravitate in communem perniciem praecipitatum iri testarentur. inter quae tam sollicita magna cura plurimi ex omni ordine electi ad contrahenda ex finitimis regionibus auxilia ab Alexandro aliisque pessimis consultoribus dimittuntur hisque mandatur, uti quam primum expedito negotio remearent. Quod ea gratia maxime a Priamidis festinabatur, uti propere instructo exercitu tempus profectionis antecaperent atque omne quod parabatur bellum in regiones Graeciae transportaretur.

II. 7.   When we had been delayed from embarking for several days, and the sea, because of the adverse winds, was becoming increasingly rough, we went to Telephus and asked what was the best time for sailing to Troy from Mysia. The beginning of spring, he said; no other time was good. Thereupon, by unanimous agreement, we returned to Boeotia and, having hauled up our ships, dispersed to spend the winter in our different kingdoms.

During this time of leisure, Agamemnon felt free to blame Menelaus for having betrayed Iphigenia,[4] for he believed that he had advised this and was, so to speak, the cause of his grief.

I. 8.   During this time the Trojans learned of our hostile alliance from the barbarous Scythians, who bartered their goods with the people who lived up and down both sides of the Hellespont. Fear and sorrow prevailed throughout Troy. Everyone who had from the beginning disapproved of Alexander's evil acts swore that Greece had been wronged and that all of the Trojans, because of the sins of a few, were going straight to destruction. To meet this threat to their country, Alexander and his wicked advisers sent men, carefully chosen from every group, to levy forces in the neighbouring regions, and commanded them to return as quickly as possible with their mission accomplished. Thus the sons of Priam sped up preparations in order that, when the army was ready, they might set sail first and carry the entire war to Greece.

---

4 According to Euripides (*Iphigenia in Aulis* 94-414), Menelaus persuaded Agamemnon to sacrifice Iphigenia, and prevented him from countermanding the letter by which she had been summoned to Aulis.

II. 9.   Dum haec apud Troiam geruntur, Diomedes incepti eorum certior factus magna celeritate per omnem Graeciam pervagatus universos duces convenit hisque consilium Troianorum aperiens monet atque hortatur, uti quam primum instructi rebus bello necessariis ad navigandum festinarent. Neque multo post re cognita Argos ab omnibus convenitur. Ibi Achilles regi indignatus, quod propter filiam renueret profectionem, ab Ulixe in gratiam reductus est. Is namque diu maesto ac luctu obsito Agamemnoni insinuans, quae circa filiam eius evenissent, animum atque ornatum regis reformavit. igitur cunctis praesentibus quamquam a nullo officia militiae neglegebantur, praecipue tamen Aiax Telamonius et Achilles cum Diomede curam maximam studiumque inportandi belli susceperant; hisque placet, uti praeter contractam classem naves, quibus loca hostilia incursarent, praeparentur. Ita diebus paucis quinquaginta navium classem instructam omni genere conpingunt. Ceterum ab incepto militiae eius octavo iam anno ad hoc usque tempus consumpto initium noni occeperat.

II. 9.   Meanwhile Diomedes, having learned what was happening at Troy, quickly went throughout Greece; he met with all of our leaders and told them the plan of the Trojans. We must, he urged, gather supplies and equipment and sail as soon as we could.

Thus we assembled at Argos; but there Agamemnon aroused the wrath of Achilles by refusing to sail. He was still crushed with grief because of the loss of his daughter. Finally, however, Ulysses revived his spirits and sense of purpose by letting him know what had really happened to Iphigenia.

Everyone was present at Argos, and no one neglected his military duty. But Ajax the son of Telamon, along with Achilles and Diomedes, had shown the greatest concern and zeal in preparing for war; and now these saw to the construction of extra ships with which to make beachheads on Trojan territory, building within a few days fifty such vessels complete in all points.

Eight years had passed from the time we first began preparing for war, and now the ninth had begun.

II. 10.   At ubi instructae omni modo classes et mare navigii patiens neque ulla res impedimento erat, Scythas, qui forte mercandi gratia eo adpulerant, conductos mercede duces profectionis eius delegere. Per idem tempus Telephus dolore vulneris eius, quod in proelio adversum Graecos acceperat, diu adflictatus, cum nullo remedio mederi posset, ad postremum Apollinis oraculo monitus, uti Achillem atque Aesculapii filios adhiberet, propere Argos navigat. Dein cunctis ducibus causam adventus eius admirantibus oraculum refert atque ita orat, ne sibi praedictum remedium ab amicis negaretur. Quae ubi accepere Achilles cum Machaone et Podalirio adhibentes curam vulneri brevi fidem oraculi firmavere. Ceterum Graeci multis immolationibus deos adiutores incepto invocantes Aulidam cum praedictis navibus veniunt atque inde propere navigare incipientibus dux Telephus ob acceptam gratiam factus. Ita ascensis navibus ventos nacti paucis diebus ad Troiam pervenere.

Dictys II.

II. 10.   When nothing prevented our sailing, the ships being ready and the sea being calm, we hired Scythians to act as our guides.[5] They had landed at Argos to barter their goods.

At the same time Telephus hastened to sail to Argos to find relief for the wound he had received while fighting our men. Having suffered a long time and found no remedy, he had gone to the oracle of Apollo, and there been told to consult Achilles and the sons of Aesculapius. He reported the oracle to all of our leaders, who were wondering why he had come, and begged them, they were his friends, not to deny the predicted remedy. On hearing his plea, Achilles, Machaon, and Podalirius treated his wound, and thus soon proved the oracle true.

After we had made many sacrifices and besought the gods to aid our endeavours, we went to Aulis, taking the ships mentioned above.

And from there we hastened to sail. Telephus, being grateful because of his cure, offered himself as a guide. Thus we boarded the ships and, finding favourable winds, came to Troy several days later.

---

5 This section provides two different guides for the Greeks: the Scythians and Telephus. Furthermore, the part about Telephus seems inconsistent with earlier sections. Previously Telephus had refused to help the Greeks because of his relationship with Priam (Dictys 2.5); and Machaon and Podalirius had already bound his wound (Dictys 2.6).

II. 11.   Per idem tempus Sarpedon Lycius Xanthi et Laodamiae frequentibus nuntiis a Priamo accitus cum magna armatorum manu adventabat. Is ubi animadvertit procul magnam vim classium admotam litori, ratus ut negotium erat, propere suos instruit Graecosque degredi incipientes invadit. Neque multo post re cognita Priamidae arreptis armis accurunt, cum interim Graeci infensis hostibus et omni modo instantibus neque degredi sine pernicie neque arma capere turbatis omnibus et ob id cuncta impedientibus possent. Ad postremum tamen hi, quibus in ea festinatione armandi semet potestas fuit, confirmati inter se invicem acriter hostes incurrunt. Sed in ea pugna Protesilaus, cuius navis prima omnium terrae admota erat, inter primos bellando ad postremum telo Aeneae ictus ruit. Occidere etiam duo Priami filii neque reliqua multitudo utraque ex parte cladis eius expers fuit.

DICTYS II.

II. 11.   Meanwhile the Lycian Sarpedon, the son of
Xanthus and Laodamia, in answer to the summons which
frequent messengers had made for Priam, had led a huge army to
Troy. Having noticed from afar that our great armada was landing,
he realized the situation and, alerting his forces, rushed to prevent
our debarking. Soon afterwards the sons of Priam learned what
was happening and, taking up arms, ran to the aid of Sarpedon.
Thus we were fiercely attacked in every way. At first we could
neither debark without being killed nor arm ourselves, the general
confusion causing our every action to flounder. Finally, however,
some, in spite of the terrible pressure, were able to arm and,
banding together, fiercely counterattacked. In this battle
Protesilaus, whose ship had been first to land, fell among those
who were fighting up front, struck by Aeneas' weapon. Also two
sons of Priam were killed. In fact, no one on either side
completely escaped without injury.

II 12.   Ceterum Achilles et Aiax Telamonius, quorum virtute Graeci sustentabantur, magna gloria dimicantes metum hostibus et fiduciam suis effecere. Neque amplius resisti iam apud eos poterat, quin paulatim decedentibus his, quos adversum ierant, ad postremum cuncti fugarentur. Ita libero ab hostibus tempore Graeci subductas naves atque in ordinem compositas tuto conlocant. Dein ex omnibus Achillem et Aiacem Telamonium, quorum virtute maxime fidebant, custodes deligunt hisque tutelam classium atque exercitus per latera atque cornua distribuentes tradunt. Igitur ordinatis dispositisque omnibus Telephus, cuius ductu ad Troiam navigatum est, magna sui apud exercitum gratia domum discedit. Neque multo post circa Protesilai sepulturam nostris occupatis nihilque tali tempore hostile metuentibus Cycnus, cuius haud procul a Troia regnum, cognito adventu nostro, clam atque insidiis Graecos invadit eosque ancipiti malo territos sine ullo ordine ac disciplina militari fugere coegit. Dein propere reliqui, quibus non ea humatio demandata erat, re cognita armati eunt contra; in quis Achilles congressus cum rege eumque et magnam vim hostium interfecit, conversis in fuga hoc modo liberatis.

II. 12. Achilles and Ajax the son of Telamon fought with great glory, their courage sustaining and increasing the confidence of our men. They struck fear into the enemy, some of whom, having dared to oppose them, soon were retreating, and all of whom finally were taking to flight. Thus we, being free for a time from enemy attack, were able to draw up our ships and set them safely in order.

Then we chose Achilles and Ajax the son of Telamon, since they were the bravest, to guard the ships and the army, stationing them at the ends of our camp to cover our flanks. When everyone was settled in place, Telephus departed for home. Our army was very grateful to him for having led us to Troy.

Soon afterwards Cycnus surprised us with a treacherous attack. He had heard of our coming, for his kingdom was not far off from Troy. His attack was made against those of our men who were preoccupied with the burial of Protesilaus. These, expecting no trouble, were caught unawares and forced to flee in utter disorder. But soon the rest of our men, those not entrusted with the burial, learned what was happening and came to the rescue. Among these was Achilles who encountered and slew Cycnus along with countless numbers of others; thus those who had fled were relieved.

II. 13.   Ceterum sollicitis ducibus et multorum clade ob is crebras hostium incursiones anxiis decernitur, uti primum finitimas Troiae civitates cum parte exercitus adeant easque omni modo incursent. Ita omnium primam Cycni regionem invadunt vastantque circum omnia. Sed ubi Neandriensium civitatem, quae regni caput filiorum Cycni nutrix memorabatur, nullo resistente invasere atque ignem subicere coepere, cives eius multis precibus lacrimisque orare, uti ab incepto desisterent, per omnia humana atque divina nixis genibus deprecantes, ne delicta pessimi ducis civitatem innoxiam et paulo post fidam sibi luere paterentur. Hoc modo per miserationem servata civitas. Ceterum regios pueros Cobin et Corianum eorumque sororem Glaucen expetentibus Graecis tradidere, quam nostri Aiaci ob fortia facta eius exceptam reliquae praedae habendam concedunt. Neque multo post Neandrienses supplices et cum pace ad Graecos conveniunt amicitiam et omnia, quae imperavissent, facturos polliciti. Quis perfectis Graeci Cillam adgressi expugnavere. Neque tamen Carenen, quae haud procul aberat, contingunt in gratiam Neandriorum, qui domini civitatis eius fideles atque amicissimi nobis ad hoc tempus permanserant.

II. 13.   But frequent raids by the enemy caused heavy casualties to our side and deeply disturbed our leaders. Therefore, the first thing we decided to do was to attack the cities in the region near Troy with a part of our army and wreak general destruction. We began with the kingdom of Cycnus and plundered the country around it. When, however, we invaded and began to fire the capital, where it was said the sons of Cycnus were being reared, the people, that is, the Neandrienses, offered no resistance and begged us to forbear. Weeping, they prayed on bended knee, by all things human and divine, that their city be spared. They were not, they said, to be blamed for the wicked acts of their evil king; they had been innocent and, after his death, had sided with us. Thus they stirred us to pity and saved their city. We required, however, that they hand over the sons of the king, Cobis and Corianus, along with their sister Glauce. Then we gave the girl to Ajax, in addition to his regular share of the booty, a due reward for his valourous deeds. Soon afterwards the Neandrienses came to the camp and sued for peace; they promised to be our allies and to do whatever we ordered.

When this campaign had been finished, we stormed Cilla but refrained from touching Carene, though it was near. Thus we showed our gratitude for the faithful friendship of the Neandrienses, for they were lords in Carene.

II. 14.   Eadem tempestate oraculum Pythii Graecis perfertur: concedendum ab omnibus, uti per Palamedem Apollini Zminthio sacrificium exhiberetur. Quae res multis grata ob industriam et amorem viri, quem circa omnem exercitum exhibebat, nonnullis ducum dolori fuerat. Ceterum immolatio centum victimarum, sicuti praedictum erat, pro cuncto exercitu exhibebatur praeeunte Chryse, loci eius sacerdote. Interim re cognita Alexander congregata armatorum manu ad prohibendum venit. Eum duo Aiaces, priusquam ad templum adpropinquaret, interfectis plurimis fugavere. Sed Chryses, quem sacerdotem Zminthii Apollinis supra diximus, utriusque exercitus offensam metuens, quisque partium ad eum venerat, cum his se adiunctum esse simulabat. interim in eo sacrificio Philocteta haud procul ab ara templi eius adstans morsu serpentis forte contingitur. dein ab omnibus, qui animadverterant, clamore sublato Ulixes adcurrens serpentem interficit. Neque multo post Philocteta cum paucis, uti curaretur, Lemnum insulam mittitur, namque in ea sacra Vulcano antistites dei inhabitare ab accolis dicebatur solitos mederi adversus venena huiusmodi.

DICTYS II.

II. 14. At the same time an oracle of the Pythian god was reported to us. We must, it said, choose Palamedes to offer a sacrifice to the Sminthian Apollo; we must all grant Palamedes this honour. Many of us were happy to obey this oracle, remembering the zeal and love Palamedes had shown throughout the army; but some of the leaders disliked him. Nevertheless, whatever our feelings, we did what was ordered and had Palamedes offer a hundred victims in behalf of all the army. Chryses, Apollo's priest in this region, presided over the offering.

Meanwhile Alexander, having learned what was happening, gathered a force of armed men and came to prevent the sacrifice. But before he could reach the temple, the two Ajaxes killed a great number of his men and put him to flight.

Chryses (who, as we have said above, was the priest of the Sminthian Apollo) feared harm from both armies and pretended to favour those from each side who approached him.

During the sacrifice, Philoctetes, who was standing in the temple near the altar, was suddenly bitten by a serpent. Everyone who saw what had happened raised a shout, and Ulysses rushed forward and slew the serpent. Soon afterwards we sent Philoctetes, with a few other men, to be cured of his poison on Lemnos, for the inhabitants of this island, which was sacred to Vulcan, claimed that their priests were wont to cure cases like his.

II. 15.   Per idem tempus Diomedes et Ulixes consilium de interficiendo Palamede ineunt, more ingenii humani, quod inbecillum adversum dolores animi et invidiae plenum anteiri se a meliore haud facile patitur. igitur simulato quod thesaurum repertum in puteo cum eo partiri vellent, remotis procul omnibus persuadent, uti ipse potius descenderet eumque nihil insidiosum metuentem adminiculo funis usum deponunt ac propere arreptis saxis, quae circum erant, desuper obruunt. Ita vir optimus acceptusque in exercitu, cuius is neque consilium umquam neque virtus frustra fuit, circumventus a quibus minime decuerat indigno modo interiit. Sed fuere, qui eius consilii haud expertem Agamemnonem dicerent ob amorem ducis in exercitum et quia pars maxima regi ab eo cupiens tradendum ei imperium palam loquebantur. Igitur a cunctis Graecis veluti publicum funus eius crematum igni, aureo vasculo sepultum est.

II. 15.   During the same time Diomedes and Ulysses devised a plot to kill Palamedes.[6] (It is characteristic of human nature to yield to resentments and envy; one does not easily allow oneself to be surpassed by a better). Accordingly, these two, pretending to have found gold in a well, persuaded Palamedes, they wanted, they said, to share the treasure with him, to be the one to descend. He suspected nothing; and so, when no one else was nearby, they let him down by means of a rope, and then, picking up stones which were lying around, they quickly stoned him to death. Thus Palamedes, the best of men and the army's favourite, one whose counsel and courage had never failed, died in a way he ill deserved, treacherously slain by the most unworthy men. There were those who suspected Agamemnon of having shared in this plot, for Palamedes was very popular with the soldiers, most of whom wanted him as their king and openly said that he should be made commander-in-chief. After burning the body, a ceremony which was attended, like a public funeral, by all the Greeks, the ashes were placed in a golden urn.

---

6 Dictys differs from all other accounts of how Palamedes was slain. For instance, in the *Cypria* (frag. 19, p. 505), Palamedes is drowned by Diomedes and Ulysses when he went out fishing.

II. 16.   Interim Achilles ministras et veluti officinam belli proximas Troiae civitates ratus sumptis aliquot navibus Lesbum adgreditur ac sine ulla difficultate eam capit et Phorbanta, loci eius regem, multa adversum Graecos hostiliter molitum interficit atque inde Diomedeam, filiam regis, cum magna praeda abducit. Dein Scyrum et Hierapolim, urbes refertas divitiis, cunctis suorum poscentibus vi magna adgressus paucis diebus sine ulla difficultate excindit. Ceterum, qua pergebat, agri referti iugi pace depraedati omnibusque vexati neque quicquam, quod amicum Troianis videretur, non eversum aut vastatum relinqui. Quis cognitis finitimi populi ultro ad eum cum pace adcurrere ac, ne vastarentur agri, dimidio fructuum pacti dant fidem pacis atque ab eo accipiunt. His actis Achilles ad exercitum regreditur magnam vim gloriae atque praedae adportans. Eodem tempore rex Scytharum cognito adventu nostrorum cum multis donis adventabat.

II. 16.   Meanwhile Achilles suspected that the states bordering on Troy were Trojan allies and, so to speak, a Trojan arsenal. Accordingly, taking some ships, he attacked Lesbos and easily took it by storm. Having slain Phorbas, the king of this island, who had committed many acts of hostility against us, he carried off Diomedea, Phorbas' daughter, along with much booty. Then, as all of his soldiers demanded it, he attacked the wealthy cities of Scyros and Hierapolis with all of his forces; and these he utterly destroyed without any trouble within a few days. Wherever he went, the country was completely pacified and plundered, and everything was thrown into turmoil; anything that might be helpful to Troy was either overturned or destroyed. The other neighbouring peoples, having learned what was happening, flocked to him in peace and promised him half of their crops if he, in return, would leave their fields unharmed. Thus he made treaties with these and exchanged pledges of peace.

After completing this campaign, Achilles returned to camp, a glorious victor bringing much booty. At the same time the king of the Scythians, having learned that our men had arrived, came and brought many gifts.

II. 17. Ceterum Achilles haud contentus eorum, quae gesserat, Cilicas adgreditur, ibique Lyrnesum paucis diebus pugnando cepit. Interfecto deinde Eetione, qui his locis imperitabat, magnis opibus naves replet, abducens Astynomen, Chrysi filiam, quae eo tempore regi denupta erat. Propere inde Pedasum expugnare occepit, Lelegum urbem, sed eorum rex Brises ubi animadvertit in obsidendo saevire nostros, ratus nulla vi prohiberi hostes aut suos satis defendi posse, desperatione effugii salutisque attentis ceteris adversum hostes domum regressus laqueo interiit. Neque multo post eapta civitas atque interfecti multi mortales et abducta filia regis Hippodamia.

II. 18. Per idem tempus Aiax Telamonius Thracum Cherronesum omni modo infestabat. Sed ubi rex eorum Polymestor virtutem atque gloriam viri cognovit, diffidens rebus suis deditionem occepit. Tuncque Polydorus, Priami filius, quem rex recens natum clam omnes alendum ei transmiserat, merces pacis ab eo traditur. Aurum etiam aliaque dona huiuscemodi ad conciliandum hostium animos adfatim praebebantur. Dehinc frumentum per omnem exercitum totius anni pollicitus naves onerarias, quas ob id Aiax secum habuerat, replet. multis execrationibus amicitiam Priami adversum Graecos renuens in pacis fidem receptus est. His actis Aiax iter ad Phrygas convertit ingressusque eorum regionem Teuthrantem dominum locorum solitario certamine interficit ac post paucos dies expugnata atque incensa civitate magnam vim praedae trahit, abducens Tecmessam, filiam regis.

Dictys II.

II. 17.   But Achilles was by no means content with what he had already done. Therefore, he attacked the Cilicians and, within a few days, took Lyrnessos by storm. Having slain Eetion, the king of Lyrnessos, he filled his ships with much wealth and carried Astynome off, the daughter of Chryses and, at that time, Eetion's wife.

Then Achilles hastened to storm Pedasos, a city of the Leleges. When Brises, the king of the Leleges, saw the fierceness of the siege, he realized that there was no way the enemy could be resisted or his own people sufficiently defended. Despairing of both flight and safety, he returned to his palace and, while everyone else was busy fighting, hanged himself. Soon afterwards the city was taken; many people were killed, and, Hippodamia, the daughter of Brises, was carried off.

II. 18.   During the same time, Ajax the son of Telamon made a sweeping attack against the Thracian Chersonese. When Polymestor, the king of this region, learned of Ajax' prowess in war, he thought it was useless to fight and sought terms of surrender. First, he handed over Priam's son, Polydorus. (Priam, acting in complete secrecy, had sent this son, soon after birth, across for Polymestor to raise). Second, he gave gold and other such gifts, enough to satisfy his enemy's demands. Third, he promised a year's supply of grain for our entire army and filled the merchant ships Ajax had brought for this purpose. When, finally, he had denounced, with many curses, his treaty with Priam against us, his plea for peace was deemed acceptable.

After completing this campaign, Ajax turned toward the country of the Phrygians. He attacked them and slew their ruler Teuthras[7] in single combat. Within a few days he had stormed and fired their city and carried off a great amount of booty, including Tecmessa, the daughter of Teuthras.

---

7 This Teuthras is not to be confused with the father of Teuthranius (Dictys 2.3).

II. 19. Igitur ambo duces multis vastatis atque expugnatis regionibus ipsi clari atque magnifici ingenti nomine, per diversa loca quasi de industria eodem tempore ad exercitum remeavere. Dein per praecones conductis in unum cunctis militibus ducibusque progressi in medium singuli laborum atque industriae documenta in conspectu omnium exposuere. Quae ubi Graeci animadvertere, favore ingenti ac laudibus eos prosecuti mediosque statuentes ramis oleae coronavere. Dein consilium de dividenda praeda haberi coeptum Nestore et Idomeneo in decernendo optimis auctoribus. Itaque cunctorum sententia ex omni praeda, quam Achilles adportaverat, exceptam Eetionis coniugem Astynomen, quam Chrysi filiam supra docuimus, ob honorem regium Agamemnoni obtulere. Ipse etiam Achilles praeter Brisi filiam Hippodamiam Diomedeam sibi retinuit, quod eiusdem aetatis atque alimonii non sine magno dolore divelli poterant et ob id iam antea genibus Achillis obvolutae, ne separarentur, magnis precibus oraverant. Ceterum reliqua praeda viritim ob singulorum merita distributa est. dein quae Aiax adportaverat, Ulixes et Diomedes rogatu eius in medios intulere. ex quis auri atque argenti quantum satis videbatur Agamemnoni regi datur; ac deinde Aiaci ob egregia laborum eius facinora Teuthranti filiam Tecmessam concedunt. Ita divisis in singulos quae supererant, frumentum per exercitum dispertiunt.

DICTYS II.

II. 19. Then Achilles and Ajax, coming from different directions, returned to camp at the same time, as if by plan. Having sacked many cities and laid waste vast regions, they had won great renown for themselves. When the heralds had assembled all the soldiers and leaders, the two returning heroes entered the crowd, not together, but one at a time, and displayed, for everyone to see, the results of all their labours and pains. Seeing what they had brought, we shouted their praises, and crowned them, as they stood in our midst, with wreaths of olive.

In deciding how best to divide the booty, we followed the advice of Nestor and Idomeneus, the most judicious of men. First, from the booty that Achilles had brought, Astynome (the wife of Eetion and the daughter of Chryses, as we said above) was given, by unanimous decision, to Agamemnon in view of his kingly office. As for Achilles, he kept Diomedea and also Hippodamia, the daughter of Brises. It would have been cruel to separate these girls, for they were of the same age and from similar backgrounds; furthermore, they had fallen at Achilles' feet and begged him not to let them be parted. The rest of Achilles' booty was distributed among the men according to merit.

Then Ajax had Ulysses and Diomedes bring in the booty he had won. Agamemnon was given as much gold and silver as his station demanded. As for Ajax himself, he was allowed to keep Tecmessa, the daughter of Teuthras, a fitting reward for his valourous deeds. The rest of his things were fairly divided, and the grain was apportioned throughout the army.

II. 20. His actis fidem pacti, quod cum Polymestore intercesserat, traditumque Polydorum refert. Ob quae cunctis decernitur, ut Ulixes cum Diomede profecti ad Priamum Helenam cum abreptis recuperarent, atque ita Polydorum regi traderent. Igitur his pergentibus Menelaus, in cuius gratiam id negotium gerebatur, legationis officium eius pariter cum supradictis capit. Itaque habentes Polydorum ad Troianos veniunt. Sed ubi animadvertere populares electos ac magni nominis viros adventasse, propere senes omnes, quorum consilium haberi solitum erat, in unum conducunt Priamo a filiis domi retento. Igitur reliquis praesentibus Graecorum Menelaus verba facit: secundo iam se ob eandem causam venisse, cum multa alia adversum se domumque suam admissa, tum magno cum gemitu filiae orbitatem per absentiam coniugis conqueri, quae cuncta ab amico quondam et hospite non secundum meritum suum evenisse. Eam seniores lamentationem inmodicam cum lacrimis accipientes ad omnia, quae ab eo dicebantur, tamquam iniuriae eius participes adnuere.

DICTYS II.

II. 20.   When he had finished dividing the booty, Ajax told about the treaty he had made with Polymestor, and how Polydorus had been handed over to him. Thereupon we all agreed that Ulysses and Diomedes should go to Priam and, in return for surrendering Polydorus, recover Helen along with the things that had been carried off. While Ulysses and Diomedes were preparing to set out, Menelaus, this was his business, also joined in the mission. Thus these proceeded to Troy, with Polydorus' fate resting in their hands.[8]

When the Trojans beheld our envoys and saw that they were men of great renown, they hastened to assemble their elders, that is, those who were wont to hold council. Priam, however, was kept at home by his sons.

At the meeting of the council Menelaus said that now he had come a second time, but for the same reason. He complained about all the wrongs to himself and his house, and especially bewailed the fact that Helen's absence had made an orphan of his daughter.[9] A former friend, he said, a former guest, had done him all these wrongs, and he had ill deserved such treatment.

Seeing the depth of his sorrow, the Trojan leaders wept, and agreed with all he had said, as if they themselves shared in his wrongs.

---

8 This embassy (Dictys 2.20-26) is the one to which Homer refers: Ulysses makes the main speech (compare *Iliad* 3.204-224), and Antimachus urges that Menelaus should not be allowed to return to the Greek camp (compare *Iliad* 11.122-142). In the earlier embassy Palamedes made the main speech. See Dictys 1.4 (end), 6, and 10 (middle) - ll.

9 The daughter of Menelaus and Helen is Hermione (Dictys 6.4).

II. 21.   Post quem Ulixes medius adstans huiuscemodi is orationem habuit: *credo ego vos, Troiani principes, satis compertum habere, nihil temere Graecos, nihil inconsultum incipere solere, ac semper his iam tum a maioribus provisum atque elaboratum, uti facta gestaque eorum laus potius, quam culpa sequeretur. et ut praeterita a me consulta omittam, hoc iam licet recognoscere. Iniuriis contumeliisque Alexandri paulo ante laesa Graecia non ad vim neque ad arma decursum est, quod iracundiae refugium esse solet. Nam de consilii sententia legati ad recipiendam Helenam, ut meministis, cum Menelao venimus. quibus praeter superbas verborum minas et insidias occultas nihil a Priamo neque ab eius regulis remissum est. Imperfecta igitur re, ut opinor, consequens fuit arma capere hisque per vim extorquere, quod amice impetrari nequitum est. Itaque parato exercitu ac tot egregiis atque inclitis ducibus ne sic quidem proelium adversum vos inire consilium fuit, sed imitati morem modestiamque solitam iterato ad vos ob eandem causam oratum venimus. Cetera in manu vestra sita sunt, Troiani, neque nos pigebit concessisse vobis, si modo sana mens est, decretis salubribus priora male consulta corrigere.*

DICTYS II.

II. 21.   Next, Ulysses stood up in their midst and made a speech of this sort: 'Trojan lords, I believe that you know well enough that the Greeks are not accustomed to begin anything rashly or without proper consideration. From earliest times they have planned and laboured that praise rather than blame should attend whatever they do. Let me, without going into details, review that previous occasion when I had dealings with you. As soon as Alexander had attacked and insulted the Greeks, we did not yield to temptation and hasten to arms. This, to be sure, is the usual way for inflamed feelings to seek relief. Instead, as you remember, our council sent us, along with Menelaus, as envoys to seek the recovery of Helen; but we got nothing from Priam and his princes, nothing but haughty, threatening words and hidden treacheries. Therefore, with the failure of our mission, it was to be expected, I think, that we should take up arms and obtain by force what we had been unable to get by friendly means. Thus we have assembled an army with many excellent and famous leaders. But not even so have we determined on war. Rather, following our usual custom and showing our usual moderation, we have come again to implore you in the same cause. Trojans, the rest is in your hands. We will not think less of you for correcting your previously ill-advised actions. Consider only what is wise, and make a sound decision.

II. 22.   *Per deos immortales, reputate cum animis vestris, quanta clades et veluti contagio huiusce exempli orbem terrarum occupatura sit. Quis enim posthac, cui virile negotium est, recordatus Alexandri facinus non omnia suspecta atque insidiosa ab amico metuere cogetur? Aut quis frater fratri aditum patefaciet? Quis hospitem aut cognatum non tamquam hostem cavebit? Denique si haec, quod haud spero, probaritis, omnia foederis iura ac pietatis apud barbaros Graecosque clausa erunt. Quocirca, Troiani principes, bonum atque utile est Graecos receptis universis, quae per vim extorta sunt, amice atque uti par est domum mitti neque opperiri, quoad duo regna inter se amicissima manus conserant. Quae cum considero, dolendam hercule vicem vestram puto, qui innoxii et culpae eius vacui nati paucorum libidini paulo post alieni sceleris poenas subire cogemini. An vos soli ignoratis, ut affectae sint vicinae atque amicae vobis civitates, vel quae in dies residuis praeparentur? Nam captum Polydorum atque apud Graecos retineri cognitum vobis est. Qui, si Helena cum abreptis nunc saltem revocetur, inviolatus Priamo restitui poterit, alio pacto bellum differri non potest neque finis bellandi fiet, quin aut omnes Graeciae duces, qui singuli ad eruendam civitatem vestram satis idonei sunt, mortem obierint, aut, quod magis spero confore, capto Ilio crematoque igni posteris etiam exemplum impietatis vestrae relinquatur. Quapropter dum adhuc res integra in manibus vobis est, etiam atque etiam providete.*

II. 22.   'I beg you, by the immortal gods, to ponder what will happen if you make a wrong decision. The effect will be a disaster which will spread, like a plague, throughout the world. After this, when anyone is entering into an important negotiation, will he not, remembering Alexander's evil, find manifold reasons for being suspicious and fearing deceit? Friend will fear friend. Who will open his house even to his own brother? Who will not fear a guest or relative as if he were an enemy? Finally, if you make a wrong decision, and certainly I hope you will not, you will destroy every basis for agreement and mutual understanding between barbarians and Greeks. Therefore, Trojan leaders, do what is good and right, be truly friendly and just. Send the Greeks home with everything that was stolen from them. Do not wait until our two kingdoms, in spite of their friendship, actually come to hostilities.

'By Hercules, when I think of your plight, I have pity for you. Though you yourselves are innocent and free from fault, nevertheless you must bow to the desires of a few; and thus the injury of one man will cause you all to be punished. Surely you must know that the Greeks have attacked the cities nearby that are friendly to you and are planning, day after day, to make new attacks. Our success is shown by Polydorus' capture. We will give Polydorus to Priam unharmed when Helen, at long last, is returned with everything that was stolen. If this does not happen, there must be immediate war, continuous war, until one side is completely victorious. Either all the Greek leaders, any of whom could cause your city's destruction, must die or, as I hope, Troy must be captured and fired, and you must become an example of punished impiety for our descendants. I beg you, therefore, I implore you, have foresight, while matters are still in your hands'.

II. 23.   Postquam finem loquendi fecit, magno silentio cunctis, ut in tali negotio fieri solet, alienam sententiam expectantibus, cum se quisque minus idoneum auctorem crederet, Panthus clara voce: *apud eos,* ait, *Ulixe, verba facis, quibus praeter voluntatem mederi rebus potestas nulla est.* Dein post eum Antenor: *omnia, quae memorata a vobis sunt, scientes prudentesque patiemur neque voluntas consulendi abest, si potestas concederetur. sed, ut videtis, summae rei alii potiuntur, quibus cupiditas utilitate potior est.* quae ubi disseruit, mox per ordinem duces omnes, qui ob amicitiam Priami quique mercede conducti auxiliarem exercitum duxerant, introduci iubet. Quis ingressis Ulixes secundam exorsus orationem iniquissimos appellare universos neque dispares Alexandri, quippe qui a bono honestoque elapsi auctorem pessimi facinoris sequerentur. Neque ignorare quemquam, quin, si tam atrox iniuria probanda sit, fore, uti malo exemplo disseminato per mortales ipsos etiam, qui haud longe abessent, similia aut graviora hisce sequerentur. Ea, ut erant atrocia, cuncti taciti inter se reputare animo atque ita exemplum huiusmodi abhorrentes indignatione rerum permoveri. Dein solito more perrogatis seniorum sententiis pari consensu omnium Menelaum indigne passum iniuriam decernitur, solo omnium Antimacho in gratiam Alexandri adversum cunctos reclamante. Ac statim, qui de omnibus nuntiatum ad Priamum mitterentur, electi duo hique inter cetera, quae mandata erant, etiam de Polydoro docent.

DICTYS II.

II. 23. When Ulysses had finished speaking, there was a long silence. Everyone, as often happens, was waiting for someone else to speak, someone better than himself. Finally this silence was broken by Panthus, who said in a loud voice: 'Ulysses you are addressing people who are unable to do as they please. We are unable to remedy this situation'.

And next Antenor said: 'Since we are wise and prudent men, we grant you everything you say; and if we had the power, we would advise accordingly. But, as you see, others with whom personal greed counts more than the common welfare are in control of our state'.

Then Antenor ordered the leaders of the foreign forces to be introduced: those who had come because of their treaties with Priam, and those who were hired mercenaries.

When these had been introduced, Ulysses made a second speech. They were all, he said, the wickedest men. They were no different from Alexander, who was the worst of lawbreakers, for they had deserted the good and the true to follow him. Each of them knew that if they approved of this terrible injustice they would be setting an evil example which, being disseminated especially through the peoples nearby, would serve as a model for similar or even more sorrowful acts.

Then each of the elders silently pondered how terrible might be the results of this horrible evil. Being moved to disgust and shrinking from setting an evil example, they went on record, voting in their usual way, that Menelaus had suffered injustice. Only Antimachus, opposing everyone else, voted in Alexander's behalf. Thereupon they chose two men to go and tell Priam about all that had happened. And these reported, along with the other things they were ordered, also about Polydorus.

87

II. 24.   Ea ubi rex accepit, maxime consternatus filii nuntio ante ora omnium corruit. Dein a circumstantibus refectus paulisper erigitur; atque ire in consilium cupiens ab regulis cohibitus est. Ipsi namque relicto patre conventum inrumpunt ad id tempus, quo Antimachus multis in contumeliam Graecorum praeiactis probris tum demum dimitti Menelaum aiebat, si Polydorus redderetur, postremo eundem casum atque exitum utriusque custodiendum. Adversum quae cunctis silentibus Antenor resistere, ac ne quid huiusmodi decerneretur, magna vi repugnare. Sed postquam invicem multa consumpta oratione certamen eorum ad manus processerat, omnes qui aderant inquietum ac seditiosum Antimachum pronuntiantes e curia eiecere.

II. 24.   When Priam heard this report, he collapsed, utterly dumbfounded, in the presence of all. Soon, however, he got to his feet; those who were standing around helped to revive him. He wanted to go to the council, but the princes made him remain while they themselves went off.

Shortly before they burst into the council, Antimachus had been hurling reproaches against the Greeks. They had shown real effrontery, he said, and the Trojans should detain Menelaus until Polydorus was returned and treat Menelaus exactly as Polydorus was treated.

Everyone was silent to this suggestion with the exception of Antenor, who, using all the powers at his command, tried to prevent the council from such a course. He and Antimachus argued hotly, and finally their passions led them to blows. Then all the others who were present proclaimed Antimachus an unruly, seditious person, and drove him out of the council.

II. 25.   Sed ubi Priamidae ingressi sunt, Panthus Hectorem obsecrans, nam is inter regulos cum virtute tum consilio bonus credebatur, hortari, uti Helena nunc potissimum, cum Graeci supplices ob hanc causam venissent, cum amicitia redderetur; neque parum Alexandro ad explendum amorem, si quem circa Helenam habuerat, transactum. Quocirca versari ante omnium oculos oportere praesentiam regum Graecorum eorumque facta fortia ac recens partam gloriam erutis amicissimis Troiae civitatibus. Ob eam etiam causam Polymestorem exemplum admissi abhorrentem ultro Graecis Polydorum tradidisse, ex quo etiam verendum, ne quid tale commentae finitimae regiones perniciosa consilia adversum Troiam molirentur, nihil exploratum neque fidum, contra insidiosa cuncta atque adversa in obsidione fore. Quae si omnes, ita uti res est, animo reputarent neque ulterius differendos legatos paterentur et Helena cum gratia remissa maius atque artius amicitiae pignus inter duo regna coalesceret. Quae ubi accepit Hector, recordatione fraterni facinoris tristior aliquantum suffusisque cum macrore lacrimis Helenam tamen prodendam minime rebatur, quippe supplicem domus et ob id fide interposita tuendam. Si qua autem cum ea erepta docerentur, cuncta restituenda. Namque pro Helena Cassandram sive Polyxenam, quam legatis videretur, nuptum cum praeclaris donis Menelao tradendam.

DICTYS II.

II. 25. As soon as Priam's sons arrived, Panthus begged
Hector (who was believed to be the best of the princes in counsel
as well as in courage) to return Helen peacefully, now that the
envoys had come to regain her. Alexander, he said, had had time
enough to satisfy whatever love he had had for Helen. The Greek
kings, they should remember, were in their country and had
recently sacked cities which were friendly to Troy. Furthermore,
these Greek successes had caused Polymestor willingly to commit
the horrible act of giving the Greeks Polydorus. The Trojans should
learn from this example and fear that the neighbouring regions
might enter into similar schemes and plot the destruction of Troy.
Such an attack would catch the Trojans completely off guard;
bonds of faith would be broken; treachery would reign
everywhere; former pacts would be dashed. Therefore, they in
the council should see things as they really were and delay the
envoys no longer, but give Helen up. This act of good will would
bring about a stronger and closer bond of friendship between the
Greeks and the Trojans.

On hearing this, Hector was saddened and wept, remembering his
brother's violation. Nevertheless, he thought that Helen should by
no means be given up, for she was a suppliant at his home; good
faith intervened, and they must keep her. If, however, the envoys
would enumerate the various articles that had been carried off
with Helen, all of these things, he thought, should be returned.
And, to take Helen's place, Cassandra or Polyxena, whichever
seemed best to the envoys, should be given in marriage to
Menelaus, along with a handsome dowry.

II. 26.   Ad ea Menelaus iracunde atrox: *egregie hercules actum nobis est, siquidem proprio spoliatus commutare matrimonium pro arbitrio hostium meorum cogor.* adversum quem Aeneas: *Ac ne haec quidem,* ait, *concedentur contradicente ac resistente me reliquisque, qui adfines amicique Alexandro in rem eius consulimus. Sunt enim atque erunt semper, qui domum regnumque Priami tueantur neque amisso Polydoro orbitas Priamum insequetur tot talibusque filiis superstitibus. An solis qui ex Graecia sunt raptus huiusmodi concederetur, quippe Cretae Europam quidem a Sidona, Ganymedem ex hisce finibus atque imperio rapere licuerit? Quid Medeam? Ignoratisne a Colchis in Iolcorum fines transvectam? Et ne primum illud rapiendi initium praetermittam, Io ex Sidoniorum regione abducta Argos meavit. Hactenus vobiscum verbis actum, at nisi mox cum omni classe ex hisce locis aufugeritis, iam iamque Troianam virtutem experiemini, domi quippe iuventus perita belli abunde nobis est, atque in dies auxiliorum crescit numerus.* Postquam finem loquendi fecit, Ulixes placida oratione: *Et hercules ulterius,* ait, *differri inimicitias haud integrum vobis est. date igitur belli signum, atque ut in inferendis iniuriis, ita et in inchoando proelio fite auctores. nos sequemur lacessiti.* Talibus invicem consumptis verbis legati consilio abeunt. ac mox per populum disseminatis quae adversum legatos Aeneas dixerat, tumultus oritur scilicet per eum universam Priami domum odio regni eius pessimo intercedendi exemplo eversum iri.

Dictys II.

II. 26.   Menelaus was terribly angered at this and answered as follows: 'By Hercules, I am being treated in an excellent manner if I, who have been robbed of my wife, am forced to marry again according to the will of my enemies'.

Then Aeneas replied: 'You will not even be granted this favour since I and the other relatives and friends who advise Alexander strongly oppose it. Fortunately there are, and always will be, those who safeguard the house and kingdom of Priam.

The loss of Polydorus does not leave Priam bereft of children, for he still has many other such sons.

'Do you think that abductions, like that of Helen, should be allowed only to those who hail from Greece? The Greeks of Crete, as you know, successfully abducted Europa from Sidon and Ganymede from our kingdom. Medea is another example. She, as surely you know, was abducted from Colchis and carried off to Iolchus. And finally, not to omit your very first of abductions, Io was stolen from Sidon and taken to Argos.

'Up to this time we have merely been bandying words. Now, however, unless you flee our land within a reasonable time, and take your fleet, soon, very soon, you will be tasting Trojan valour and courage. Troy has more than enough young men who are ready for battle, and every day new allies are coming."

When Aeneas had finished this speech, Ulysses said calmly: 'Then, by Hercules, there is no need for you to put off hostilities any longer. Give the signal for war and, as you were the first to commit injustice, be also the first to begin the battle. Only provoke us and we will follow you example'.

After this exchange of taunts the envoys left the council and departed from Troy.

As soon as the Trojan people learned how Aeneas had answered the envoys, they raised a huge tumult. Aeneas, they thought, was without a doubt a diplomat of the very worst sort; he was the reason why Priam's kingdom was hated and Priam's whole house was headed for ruin.

II. 27.   Igitur ubi legati ad exercitum revenere, cunctis ducibus dicta gestaque Troianorum adversum se exponunt. Itaque decernitur, uti Polydorum in conspectu omnium atque ante ipsos muros necarent. Neque ulterius dilatum facinus. Quippe productus in medium visentibus ex muris plerisque hostium lapidibus ictus fraternae impietatis poenas luit. Ac mox unus ex praeconibus nuntiatum Iliensibus mittitur, uti Polydorum is sepeliendum peterent. Missusque ad eam rem Idaeus cum servis regiis foedatum ac dilaniatum lapidibus Polydorum matri eius Hecubae refert. interim Aiax Telamonius, ne quid quietum finitimis Troiae regionibus atque amicis relinqueretur, hostiliter eas ingressus Pityam Zeleamque, civitates divitiis nobiles, capit neque contentus his Gargarum Arisbam, Gergitham, Scepsim, Larissam admiranda celeritate depopulatur. Dein doctus ab incolis multa cuiuscemodi pecora in Idaeo monte stabulari, exposcentibus, qui cum eo erant, cunctis cito agmine montem ingressus interfectis gregum custodibus magnam vim pecorum abducit. Dein nullo omnium adversante, cunctis qua pergebat in fugam versis, ubi tempus visum est, cum magna praeda ad suos convertit.

II. 27.   The envoys, having returned to camp, told all our leaders what the Trojans had said and done to oppose them. Thereupon we determined to kill Polydorus within view of the wall where all the Trojans could easily see what was done. Delaying no further, we led him into the centre and stoned him to death in payment for his brother's impiety, while most of the enemy watched from the walls. Then we sent a herald to tell the Trojans to come and get the body for burial. Idaeus came and, with the help of some slaves of the king, took Polydorus, mangled and torn by the stones, back to his mother, to Hecuba.

Meanwhile Ajax the son of Telamon, in order to keep the enemy riled, attacked the regions nearby that were friendly to Troy. He captured Pitya and Zelia, notoriously wealthy cities, and, not being content with these, laid waste Gargarum, Arisba, Gergitha, Scepsis, and Larissa with marvellous swiftness. Then, having learned from the inhabitants that there were many herds of all sorts being grazed on Mount Ida, since all of his soldiers demanded it, he quickly attacked the mountain and, after killing the herdsmen, drove a large number of cattle away. Then no one opposed him; everyone fled wherever he went; and so, when the time seemed right, he returned to camp, laden with booty.

II. 28.   Per idem tempus Chryses, quem sacerdotem Zminthii
Apollinis supra docuimus, cognito filiam suam Astynomen cum
Agamemnone degere, fretus religione tanti numinis ad naves venit,
praeferens dei vultus ac quaedam ornamentorum templi eius, quo facilius
recordatione praesentis numinis veneratio sui regibus incuteretur. Dein
oblatis auri atque argenti donis plurimis redemptionem filiae deprecatur
obsecrans, uti magnificarent praesentiam dei, qui secum oratum eos ob
sacerdotem proprium venisset. Praeterea commemorat, quae in dies
adversum se ab Alexandro eiusque consanguineis ob exhibitam per se
paulo ante immolationem inimica hostiliaque pararentur. Quae ubi
accepere, reddendam filiam sacerdoti neque ob id accipiendum praemium
universis placet, quippe qui cum per se amicus fidelisque nobis tum
praecipue ob religionem Apollinis nihil non mereri crederetur. Namque
multis iam documentis ac fama incolarum obsequi numini eius per omnia
destinaverant.

II. 29.   Quae postquam Agamemnon accepit, obviam cunctorum
sententiis ire pergit. Itaque atroci vultu exitium sacerdoti comminatus, ni
recederet, perterritum senem atque extrema metuentem inperfecto negotio
ab exercitu dimittit. Hoc modo conventu dissoluto singuli reges ad
Agamemnonem adeunt eumque multis probris insecuntur, quippe qui ob
amorem captivae mulieris seque et, quod indignissimum videretur, tanti
numinis deum contemptui habuisset. Ac mox universi execrati deseruere ob
id et memores Palamedis, quem gratum acceptumque in exercitu haud sine
consilio eius Diomedes atque Ulixes dolo circumventum necavissent.
ceterum Achilles in ore omnium ipsumque et Menelaum contumeliis
lacerabat.

II. 28.   At the same time Chryses (who was the priest of the Sminthian Apollo, as we have said above), having learned that his daughter, Astynome, was with Agamemnon, came to the ships, trusting in the power of his awesome religion.[10] He brought with him a statue of the god and certain ornaments of the temple, hoping thereby the more easily to remind the kings of the god, and inspire them with awe. Praying for the release of his daughter, he offered gifts of gold and silver, countless ransom. We must, he implored, honour the presence of the god: Apollo was there, begging us in his behalf. Furthermore, because he had recently officiated at our sacrifice, he had incurred the enmity of Alexander and his brothers, who were daily plotting against him.

On hearing his plea, we all thought that the girl should be returned. Nor should we accept any ransom. We owed this to Chryses, not only because of his personal faithfulness to us but, what mattered more, because of his office as priest of Apollo. Having seen many evidences of Apollo's power and having learned of his popularity in the region nearby, we had made up our minds to serve this god devoutly.

II. 29.   When Agamemnon saw what was happening, he proceeded to take a stand opposite to that of everyone else. Scowling blackly and threatening death, he ordered the priest not to return. Accordingly, the old man departed, terrified and fearing for his life, his mission a failure.

When our assembly broke up, our leaders approached Agamemnon, one at a time, and taunted him with his manifold wickedness. Because of his love for a captive girl, he had treated his men, that is, themselves, with contempt and, what seemed a thing most shameful, had scorned a very powerful god.

When all had reviled him, they went away, thinking how he had shared in the plot by which Diomedes and Ulysses had treacherously slain Palamedes, the army's favourite. Achilles openly, in everyone's presence, abused both Agamemnon and Menelaus.

---

10 Sections 2.28-4.1 cover the events described in the *Iliad*.

II. 30.   Igitur Chryses ubi iniuriam perpessus ab Agamemnone domum discessit neque multi fluxerant dies, incertum alione casu an, uti omnibus videbatur, ira Apollinis morbus gravissimus exercitum invadit principio grassandi facto a pecoribus, dein malo paulatim magis magisque ingravescente per homines dispergitur. Tum vero vis magna mortalium corporibus fatigatis pestifera aegritudine infando ad postremum exitio interibat. Sed regum omnino nullus neque mortuus ex hoc malo neque adtemptatus est. Ceterum postquam nullus morbi modus et in dies plures interibant, cuncti duces converso iam in se quisque timore in unum coeunt ac dein flagitare Calchanta, quem futurorum praescium memoravimus, uti causam mali tanti ediceret. Ille enim perspicere se originem huiusce morbi, sed haud liberum esse cuiquam eloqui, ex quo accideret, uti potentissimi regis contraheret offensam. Post quae Achilles reges singulos adigit, ut interposita iurisiurandi religione confirmarent nequaquam se ob ea offendi. Hoc modo Calchas, ubi cunctorum animos in se conciliavit, Apollinis iram pronuntiat: eum namque ob iniuriam sacerdotis infestum Graecis poenas ab exercitu expetere. Dein perquirente Achille mali remedium restitutionem virginis pronuntiat.

II. 30.   Chryses, after Agamemnon had sent him away unjustly, returned to his home. And several days later a terrible plague invaded our army. Whether this was due to the wrath of Apollo, as everyone thought, or to some other cause, was uncertain. The disease attacked the cattle first and then, as it gradually gained momentum, spread among the men, a great number of whom suffered unspeakable deaths, their bodies slowly wasting away. Except for our leaders (the kings), none of whom died or was even attacked, the plague knew no bounds, and every day saw more men dying. Accordingly, our leaders, each of whom was afraid for himself, foregathered, and ordered Calchas (we have told about his knowledge of the future) to proclaim the cause of this terrible evil.

Although he admitted that he was able to do as they wished, he said that he was by no means free to speak out, for fear he would incur a most powerful king's displeasure. Thereupon Achilles forced all of our kings to swear that they would not be offended, no matter what Calchas might say.

Thus Calchas, feeling that everyone was favourably disposed, announced that the wrath of Apollo was the cause of the plague. Apollo, he said, was angry because of the unjust way we had treated his priest and was therefore exacting punishment from our army.

When Achilles asked what we must do to bring an end to the plague, the prophet said: 'Restore the girl'!

II. 31.   Tum Agamemnon coniectans, quod mox accidit, consilio tacitus egressus cunctos, quos secum habuerat, in armis esse iubet. Id ubi Achilles animadvertit, commotus rei indignatione simul pernicie defessi exercitus anxius defunctorum corpora miserandum in modum confecta undique in unum colligi iubet atque in conventu ante ora omnium proici. Quo spectaculo adeo commoti reges gentesque omnes, uti adversum Agamemnonem ab cunctis pergeretur duce atque auctore Achille et si perstaret suadente exitio vindicandum. Quae ubi regi nuntiata, pertinacia animi an ob amorem captivae cuncta extrema ratus experiri nihil remittendum de sententia destinaverat.

II. 32.   Ea postquam Troiani cognovere, simul ex muris conflagrationem corporum assiduam crebrasque sepulturas animadvertere doctique etiam reliquos incommodo cladis eius debiles agere, cohortati inter se arma capiunt ac propere cum manu auxiliari effusi portis pergunt advorsum. Ac dein per campos exercitu bipertito Troianis Hector, Sarpedon auxiliaribus duces facti. Tum nostri visis contra hostibus armati atque instructi pro negotio simplici fronte aciem composuere circa cornua divisis ducibus: dextrum Achilles cum Antilocho, alterum Aiax Telamonius cum Diomede curabant, medios accepere Aiax alter atque Idomeneus dux noster. Hoc modo exercitu utrimque composito pergunt obviam. At ubi in manus ventum est, cohortati suos quisque acie conflixere. Tum vero in aliquantum tracto certamine plurimi utriusque partis cadunt praecellentibus in ea pugna barbarorum Hectore et Sarpedone, Graecorum Diomede cum Menelao. dein nox communis amborum requies proelium diremit. igitur reducto exercitu corpora suorum cremata igni sepeliunt.

II. 31. Then Agamemnon, though he foresaw what was going to happen, said nothing but withdrew from the council and commanded everyone in his contingent to prepare for war. Achilles, on noticing this, being stirred to wrath and likewise vexed by the horrible way our men were dying, ordered that the bodies of everyone whom the plague had destroyed be collected and thrown out in the assembly for all to see. This was a sight which quickly moved all our leaders and men to desert Agamemnon and follow Achilles, who thereupon urged them to kill Agamemnon unless he repented. Agamemnon, however, when he heard about this, obstinately held to his first decision and refused to yield in the least. It is uncertain whether his inflexibility was due to his naturally stubborn character or to his love for the captive girl.

II. 32. The Trojans, looking from their walls, saw the many pyres of our dead burning continuously. They also were informed that those of us who were left were growing weak as the plague proceeded to rage. Accordingly, exhorting each other and taking up arms, they rushed from the gates along with their allies and made an attack. Their forces were arranged in the plain in two divisions: Hector was leading the Trojans, Sarpedon the allies.

When we saw them ready for attack, we armed ourselves and, forming an unbroken line of defence, drew up our forces to meet them. Achilles and Antilochus led our right wing; Ajax the son of Telamon and Diomedes led the left; and the other Ajax and Idomeneus, my leader, led the centre.

Then the two armies, drawn up in this way, advanced to attack. As soon as they had come within striking distance, everyone raised the war cry and joined in the battle. The conflict lasted some time, and the casualties on both sides were heavy. Hector and Sarpedon were the outstanding leaders among the barbarians; Diomedes and Menelaus shone among the Greeks. Finally night brought an end to the battle and rest to the armies. Then both sides, withdrawing, cremated and buried their dead.

II. 33.   Quis perfectis Graeci statuunt inter se Achillem, cuius in adversis Graecorum casibus sollicitudo praecipua videbatur, rem omnium confirmare. Sed Agamemnon anxius, ne decus regium amitteret, in consilio verba facit: sibi maxime cordi esse exercitus incolumitatem neque ulterius differre, quin Astynome parenti remitteretur, maxime si restitutione eius instantem perniciem subterfugerent nec quicquam deprecari amplius, si modo in locum eius Hippodamiam, quae cum Achille degeret, vicarium munus amissi honoris acciperet. Quae res, quamquam atrox omnibus et indigna videbatur, tamen conivente Achille, cuius id praemium pro multis et egregiis facinoribus fuerat, effectum habuit. Tantus amor erga exercitum curaque in animo egregii adulescentis insederat. igitur adversa cunctorum voluntate neque tamen quoquam palam recusante Agamemnon, tamquam ab omnibus concessa res videretur, lictoribus ut Hippodamia abstraheretur imperat; hique brevi iussa efficiunt. Interim Astynomen Graeci per Diomedem atque Ulixem cum magna copia victimarum ad fanum Apollinis transmisere. Dein perfecto sacrificio paulatim vis mali leniri visa, neque amplius adtemptari corpora et eorum, qui antea fatigabantur, tamquam sperato divinitus levamine relaxari. Ita brevi per universum exercitum salubritas vigorque solitus renovatus est. Mittitur etiam Philoctetae ad Lemnum portio praedae eius, quam Graeci per Aiacem atque Achillem advectam inter se viritim distribuerant.

DICTYS II.

II. 33. Now the Greeks were on the point of making Achilles commander-in-chief, for he was the one, so we thought, who seemed most troubled about our misfortunes. And this caused Agamemnon to fear he might lose his glorious position.

Speaking in the council, he said that he was deeply concerned for the welfare of the army and that Astynome, without any further delay, should be returned to her father, especially if thus we would rid ourselves of the plague. He asked only to be given Hippodamia, the bondmaid of Achilles, to take the place of the prize he was losing.

Although everyone thought his request was mean and dishonourable, nevertheless we were moved to grant it. As for Achilles, to whom Hippodamia had been given because of his many marvellous deeds, he showed no signs of his feelings; so great was the love and concern for our army in the heart of this excellent youth.

Thus Agamemnon was flouting everyone's wishes, but since no one openly opposed him, he thought that he had our unanimous approval. Accordingly, he ordered attendants to fetch Hippodamia; and they were prompt to obey.

At the same time we had Diomedes and Ulysses take Astynome, along with a great number of sacrificial victims, across to the shrine of Apollo. When these had completed the sacrifice, the force of the plague gradually seemed to abate. People were no longer becoming ill, and those who were already afflicted seemed to improve, as if their prayers had been divinely answered. Thus within a short time our entire army regained its usual strength and vigour.

During this period we also sent Philoctetes' share of the booty across to Lemnos, where he was. This was the booty which Ajax and Achilles had won and which we had divided up equally.

103

II. 34.   Ceterum Achilles memor iniuriae supra dictae abstinendum publico consilio decreverat odio maxime Agamemnonis abolitoque amore, quem circa Graecos habuerat, scilicet quod eorum patientia post tot bellorum victorias ac facta fortia Hippodamia concessum pro laboribus praemium per iniuriam abducta esset. Dein venientes ad se duces aditu prohibere neque cuiquam amicorum ignoscere, qui se, adversum Agamemnonis contumelias cum defendere liceret, deseruissent. Intus igitur manens Patroclum et Phoenicem, hunc morum magistrum, alterum obsequiis amicitiae carum, et aurigam suum Automedontem secum retinebat.

DICTYS II.

II. 34. Achilles, having (as we have described) been treated unjustly, stayed away from our councils. He hated Agamemnon especially; and now his love for the rest of the Greeks was also dead, since they had been silent when he had been robbed of Hippodamia, the reward which his many victories and many brave deeds had earned him. He refused to see any of the leaders who came to visit. Nor would he forgive any of his friends for having deserted him when they might have defended him against Agamemnon's outrageous action. He preferred to stay in his hut with only Patroclus, his closest friend, and Phoenix, his wise teacher, and Automedon, his charioteer.

II. 35. Per idem tempus apud Troiam exercitus sociorum quique mercede conducti auxiliares copias adduxerant, tempore multo frustra trito taedione an recordatione suorum domi seditionem occipiebant. quod ubi animadvertit Hector, coactus necessitate militibus, ut apud arma essent, iubet ac mox, ubi signum daretur, sequerentur sese. Igitur postquam tempus visum est et omnes in armis nuntiabantur, iubet egredi; ipse dux atque imperator militiae.

Res postulare videtur eorum reges, qui socii atque amici Troiae quique ob mercedem auxiliares ex diversis regionibus contracti Priamidarum imperium sequebantur, edicere. Primus igitur portis erumpit Pandarus Lycaone genitus ex Lycia, dein Hippothous ‡Pylei‡ ex Larissa Pelasgidarum, Acamas ‡...‡ Piros ex Thracia, post quos Euphemus Troezenius Ciconiis imperitans, Pylaemenes Paphlagonius patre Melio gloriosus, Odius et Epistrophus, filii Minui, Alizonorum reges, Sarpedon, Xantho genitus, rector Lyciorum ex Solemo, Nastes et Amphimachus Nomionis de Caria, Antiphus et Mesthles genitore Talaemene Maeonii, Glaucus Hippolochi Lycius, quem sibi Sarpedon, quod praeter ceteros regionis eius consilio atque armis pollebat, participem bellicarum rerum adsciverat, Phorcys et Ascanius Phryges, Chromius et Ennomus Mygdones ex Mysia, Pyraechmes Axii Paeonius, Amphius et Adrastus, Merope geniti, ex Adrestia, Asius Hyrtaci de Sesto. Dein alius Asius, Dymante genitus Hecubae frater, ex Phrygia. hos omnes, quos memoravimus, secuti multi mortales inconditis moribus ac dispari sono vocis, sine ullo ordine aut modo proelia inire soliti.

II. 35.   Meanwhile, at Troy, the allies and mercenaries who had come to help the Trojans began to mutiny. They were probably motivated either by boredom from spending a long time there to no purpose or by longing for those they had left behind in their homelands. Hector, noticing this, felt forced to call his troops to arms; they must be ready to follow whenever he signalled. Then, having been informed that the time looked favourable and that his men were in arms, he ordered them all to go forth, he himself taking command and leading the way.

This seems a good place to list the kings of the allied forces (those who were bound to the Trojans by treaties) and also of the mercenary forces (those who, coming from various regions, were serving Priam's sons for pay).[11] The first to rush from the gates was Pandarus, the son of Lycaon, from Lycia; then Hippothous and Pylaeus, the sons of Lethus,[12] from Pelasgian Larissa; then Acamas and Pirus[13] from Thrace; then Euphemus, the son of Troezenus, who led the Ciconians; Pylaemenes, the boasting Paphlagonian, whose father was Melius; Odius and Epistrophus, the sons of Minuus, who led the Alizonians; Sarpedon, the son of Xanthus, who led the Lycians, from Solymum; Nastes and Amphimachus, the sons of Nomion, from Caria; Antiphus and Mesthles, the sons of Talaemenes, from Maeonia; Glaucus, the son of Hippolochus, from Lycia, whom Sarpedon had summoned to share the command because he surpassed all other Lycians in counsel and arms; Phorcys and Ascanius from Phrygia; Chromius and Ennomus, who were Mygdonians, from Mysia; Pyraechmes, the son of Axius, from Paeonia; Amphius and Adrastus, the sons of Merops, from Adrestia; Asius, the son of Hyrtacus, from Sestos; and then the other Asius, the son of Dymas and the brother of Hecuba, from Phrygia. Many men followed each of the leaders we have listed; their different customs and different languages caused them to fight in disorder and turmoil.

---

11 This list is taken for the most part from Homer's catalogue of Trojan allies in *Iliad* 2.824-877.

12 The text, which is corrupt here, has been emended to agree with *Iliad* 2.842-843.

13 There is a lacuna in the text beween 'Acamas' and 'Pirus'.

II. 36. Quod ubi nostri animadvertere, in campum progressi more militiae aciem ordinant magistro ac praeceptore componendi Menestheo Atheniensi, ordinant autem per gentes atque regiones singulas seorsum manente Achille cum Myrmidonum exercitu. Is namque, quamquam ob inlatam ab Agamemnone iniuriam et abductam Hippodamiam nihil animi remiserat, tamen maxime indignatus, quod reliquis ducibus ad cenam deductis solus contemptui habitus intermitteretur. Ceterum ordinato exercitu ac tunc primum omnibus copiis adversum se instructis hostibus, ubi neutra pars committere audet, paulisper in loco retentis militibus tamquam de industria utrimque receptui canitur.

II. 36.   When our men saw what was happening, we proceeded onto the plain and drew up our forces in battle array. Menestheus, the Athenian, who was in charge of our deployment, set us in order according to our different clans and regions. Only Achilles and his Myrmidons stayed behind. Achilles continued to be angry with Agamemnon for unjustly depriving him of Hippodamia; also the fact that Agamemnon had not invited him to dinner along with the other leaders seemed insulting to him.[14] When our army had been drawn up, we were facing the full force of the enemy for the first time. But neither side dared to begin; both held their ground for a while and then retreated at signals given as if by common consent.

---

14 According to Aristotle (*Rhetoric* 2.24), Achilles was terribly angry with the Greeks on Tenedos because he had not been invited to dinner.

II 37. Iamque Graeci regressi ad naves arma deponere ac singuli per loca solita corpus cibo curare occeperant, cum Achilles ultum ire cupiens iniurias ignaros consilii sui nostros et ob id otiose agentes clam invadere temptat. at ubi Ulixes a custodibus, qui eruptionem eius praesenserant, rem comperit, propere duces circumcursans magna voce monet atque hortatur, uti armis arreptis tuerentur sese, dein consilium inceptumque Achillis singulis aperit. Quo cognito clamor ingens oritur festinantibus ad arma cunctis ac seorsum sibi singulis consulentibus. Ita Achilles praeverso de se nuntio, ubi omnes in armis sunt neque conata procedere queunt, intemptato negotio ad tentoria regreditur. Ac mox duces nostri rati repentino suorum clamore moveri Ilienses et ob id novi quid negotii incepturos, augendae custodiae causa mittunt duos Aiaces, Diomedem atque Ulixem, hique inter se regionem, qua aditus hostibus erat, dispertiunt. Quae res non frustra eos habuit. Namque apud Troiam Hector causam tumultus eorum cupidus persciscere filium Eumedi Dolonem multis praemiis promissisque inlectum ad postremum, uti exploratum res Graecorum egrederetur, mittit isque non longe a navibus avidus ignara cognoscendi, dum cupit suscepti negotii fidem complere, in manus Diomedis, qui eum locum cum Ulixe custodiebat, devenit ac mox ab his comprehensus refert cuncta atque occiditur.

Dictys II.

II. 37.   Having returned to the ships, we put down our arms and prepared to enjoy our dinners as usual. We were relaxing, fearing no trouble, when Achilles tried to catch us off guard. There were, however, guards who heard of his plans and told Ulysses. And Ulysses, running around to all of the leaders, exhorted and warned them, shouting that Achilles was going to attack. They must, he said, be ready; they must be armed. A great commotion arose, with everyone rushing to arms and striving to save himself. Thus Achilles' plot was disclosed, and he, being foiled, returned to his hut, despairing of any success against our alerted army.

Then our leaders, fearing that this sudden commotion might cause the Trojans to make a new attack, increased the number of the advanced guard. The two Ajaxes, Diomedes, and Ulysses were sent forth. They took up positions where they thought, quite rightly, as it happened, that the enemy would be most likely to come.

Hector, desiring to learn the reason for the uproar in the camp of the Greeks,[15] had persuaded Dolon, the son of Eumedes, with promises of a huge reward, to go and spy. While Dolon, trying to fulfil his mission, was eagerly gathering information, he fell into Diomedes' hands. Diomedes and also Ulysses, who were guarding the area near the ships, made him tell whatever he knew. Then they killed him.

---

15 According to Euripides (*Rhesus* 41-146), Hector sent Dolon to find out why the Greeks had lit their fires and gathered, in an uproar, around Agamemnon's hut. Compare *Iliad* 10.

II. 38.   Dein diebus aliquot in otio tritis productio utriusque exercitus praeparatur. Divisoque inter se campo, qui medius inter Troiam atque naves interiacet, ubi tempus bellandi videbatur, magna cura universus miles instructus armis utrimque procedere. Dein signo dato densatis frontibus conflixere acies, composite Graecis ac singulis per distributionem imperia ducum exsequentibus, contra sine modo atque ordine barbaris ruentibus. Ceterum in ea pugna interfecti utriusque partis multi mortales, cum neque instantibus cederetur et exemplo strenuissimi cuiusque, qui iuxta steterat, aequiperare gloriam festinaret. Interim vulnerati graviter ex ducibus bello decedere coacti sunt barbarorum Aeneas, Sarpedon, Glaucus, Helenus, Euphorbus, Polydamas, nostrorum Ulixes, Meriones, Eumelus.

II. 39.   Ceterum Menelaus forte conspicatus Alexandrum magno impetu inruit, quem evitans neque diutius sustinere ausus Alexander fugam capit. At ubi procul animadvertit Hector concurrens cum Deiphobo comprehendere fratrem, eum verbis maledictisque acrioribus insecuti ad postremum cogunt, uti progressus in medias acies eundem Menelaum conquiescentibus reliquis solitario certamine lacesseret. Igitur reducto ad bellandum Alexandro progressoque ante aciem, quod signum lacessentis videbatur, postquam procul animadvertit Menelaus, nunc demum oceasionem invadendi inimicissimum sibi maxime oblatam ratus et iam iamque confidens omnium iniuriarum poenas lui sanguine eius, omnibus animis advorsum pergit. Sed ubi eos contra se tendere paratos armis atque animis uterque exercitus animadvertit, signo dato recedunt cuncti.

Dictys II.

II. 38. Several days passed without any outbreak of hostilities. Then Greeks and Trojans prepared to lead their armies onto the plain between Troy and the ships. When everything seemed ready for battle, both sides, in full force, cautiously advanced. At given signals the front lines clashed in dense formation. The Greeks fought in good battle order, everyone following the commands of the leader in charge of his division. The barbarians, however, rushed on without any order or discipline. Nevertheless, many on both sides fell in this battle. There was no retreating; everyone attacked and strove to rival the valour of the heroes fighting around him. Among the barbarian leaders who were seriously wounded and forced to withdraw from the battle were Aeneas, Sarpedon, Glaucus, Helenus, Euphorbus, and Polydamas. Among those on our side who were similarly afflicted were Ulysses, Meriones, and Eumelus.

II. 39. Then Menelaus happened to catch sight of Alexander and rushed, with all his might, to meet him. Alexander, however, not daring to stay where he was, soon took to flight and escaped. But Hector, having noticed this from a distance, ran forward, along with Deiphobus, and caused Alexander to halt. They reproached him bitterly and finally persuaded him to go out between the battle lines and, when everyone else had grown quiet, challenge Menelaus to single combat.

Thus these brought Alexander back into battle; and he (apparently this was the way to make a challenge) went out in front of the Trojan line. Menelaus, noticing this from a distance, felt that at long last he was being given an opportunity to attack the man he most hated. Right here and now, he thought, Alexander is going to pay with his life for all his crimes. And so he rushed against him again. Signals were given, and everybody on both sides drew back as they saw these two rushing head-on, armed and eager to fight.

II. 40.   Iamque uterque pleno gradu advorsum cedens intra iactum teli pervenerant, cum Alexander, praevenire cupiens simulque ratus primo iaculi eventu locum vulneri inventurum, praemittit hastam eaque inlisa clipeo facile decussa est. Dein Menelaus magno impetu iaculatur, haud sane dissimili casu; namque parato iam ad cavendum ictumque declinante hoste telum humi figitur. at ubi novis iaculis manus utriusque redarmatae sunt, pergunt. tum demum Alexander ictus femur cadit ac ne mox hosti ultionem cum summa gloria concederet, pessimo exemplo intercessum est. Namque cum ad interficiendum eum educto gladio prorueret Menelaus, ex occulto sagitta Pandari vulneratus in ipso impetu repressus est. Igitur ab nostris clamore orto simulque cum ira indignantibus, quod duobus seorsum adversum se hisque maxime, quorum gratia bellum conflatum esset, decernentibus repente a Troianis pessimo more intercederetur, rursus globus barbarorum ingruens Alexandrum e medio rapit.

II. 40.   Soon the two fighters, taking full strides, had advanced to where they could use their spears. Alexander, hoping to get the start and wound Menelaus, was the first to make a cast. His spear, however, struck against Menelaus' shield, and thus was deflected. Then Menelaus, throwing with all his might, met, alas, with the same result, his spear stuck in the earth; Alexander had been on his guard and dodged the blow. But soon they were armed with new spears, and the fight was on again. Finally, Alexander fell, wounded in the thigh; and Menelaus, hoping to take complete vengeance and win greatest glory, rushed forward to kill him, but Pandarus, committing an act of the blackest treachery by shooting his bow from a hidden spot, wounded Menelaus and caused him to halt. This stirred our men to wrath, and they raised a huge cry, feeling cheated because the Trojans had ended the fight in this treacherous way, especially this fight between the two men who had caused the whole war. During this general confusion, a group of barbarians rushed in and saved Alexander from danger.

II. 41. Interim in ea permixtione, dum nostri haesitant, Pandarus procul adstans multos Graecorum sagittis configit. Neque prius finis factus, quam Diomedes atrocitate rei motus progressusque comminus telo hostem prosterneret. Hoc modo Pandarus certaminis foedere violato atque ob id interemptis multis ad postremum poenas scelestissimae militiae luit. Ceterum corpus eius liberatum ex acie Priamidae igni cremant; reliquiasque socii traditas sibi Lyciam in solum patrium pertulere. Interim utriusque exercitus signo dato manus conserunt pugnantesque vi summa atque ancipiti fortuna bellum ad occasum solis producunt. Sed ubi nox adventabat, utrimque reges subducta haud longe acie custodibus idoneis exercitus communivere. Ita per aliquot dies tempus bellandi opperientes militem frequentem apud arma frustra habuere. Namque ubi hiems adventare et imbribus crebris compleri coepere campi, barbari intra muros abeunt. at nostri nullo palam hoste digressi ad naves munia hiemis disponunt moxque bipertito campo, qui reliquus non pugnae opportunus erat, utraque pars aratui insistere, frumenta aliaque, quae tempus anni patiebatur, parare. interim Aiax Telamonius instructo milite, quem secum adduxerat, habens etiam nonnullos de exercitu Achillis, ingressus Phrygiae regionem multa hostiliter vastat, capit civitates, ac post paucos dies praeda auctus ad exercitum victor revenit.

II. 41.   At the same time, Pandarus was taking advantage of our irresolution. Standing at a distance, he was finding many of our men with his arrows. He continued his slaughtering until Diomedes, stirred by this barbarous action, advanced upon him and cut him down at close quarters. Thus Pandarus, who had killed many men in violation of the treaty (that is, the agreement according to which Menelaus and Alexander should fight), paid with his life for his heinous method of fighting. His body was carried from the battle and duly cremated by Priam's sons; the ashes were given to his companions to take to Lycia for burial in his native soil.

Meanwhile the two armies had given the signal for battle and joined in combat. They fought until sundown with all their might, but neither side could claim a victory. With the coming of night, the commanders-in-chief withdrew their forces a short distance and posted sufficient guards along the facing battle lines.

They kept their men fully armed in these positions and waited for an opportunity to make a successful attack. But this opportunity never came, for winter began to set in, soaking the battlefield with frequent rains. The barbarians retreated within their walls, and our men, left with no enemy to fight, returned to the ships and took up winter duties. Dividing the portion of the plain that was unfit for battle into two parts, they cultivated the soil and grew whatever crops the time of year permitted.

During the same period, Ajax the son of Telamon, with a force consisting of his own men and some from the army of Achilles, made an attack against Phrygia, capturing cities and causing general destruction. Within a few days, he returned to camp, victoriously laden with booty.

II. 42.   Isdem fere diebus barbari nostris per condicionem hiemis quietis nihilque hostile suspicantibus paravere eruptionem, quis Hector dux atque audendi auctor factus. is namque omnes copias instructas armis cum luce simul porta educit ac protinus cursu pleno ad naves tendere atque invadere hostes iubet. At Grai infrequentes tum incuriosique ab armis turbari simul et fugientibus, quos primus hostis incesserat, quominus arma caperent, impediri, tum caesi multi mortales. iamque fusis qui in medio fuerant, Hector ad naves progressus ignem in proras iacere ac saevire incendiis coeperat nullo nostrorum auso resistere. Qui territi atque improviso tumultu exsangues genibus Achillis auxilium renuentis tamen obvolvebantur. tanta repente mutatio animorum nostros atque hostes incesserat.

II. 42.   Just before his arrival, the barbarians made a sneak attack upon our men, who were relaxing in winter quarters and suspected no hostilities. Hector, the instigator of this rash expedition, was chosen as leader. At daybreak, after calling all of his men to arms, he led them through the gates, with orders to move at double-time straight for the ships, and fall upon us. Our forces, which were scattered hither and yon, were caught off guard. The flight of those who were attacked first increased the confusion of the others and made it difficult for them to arm. A great slaughter ensued. As soon as our men in the centre gave way, Hector was at the ships, raging with firebrands and setting fire to the prows. None of us dared to oppose him. Our unforeseen plight frightened us almost to death, and we begged Achilles for help; but even now he refused. How suddenly and radically the spirit had changed in us and our enemies!

II. 43.   Interea Aiax Telamonius adveniens cognito apud naves Hectore magna armorum specie ibidem apparuit ac dein mole sua urgens hostem multo sudore ad postremum navibus extra vallum detrudit. Tum iam cedentibus acrior insistens Hectorem, qui adversus eum promptius steterat, ictum inmani saxo ac mox consternatum deicit. Sed eum concurrentes undique plurimi multitudine sua tectum bello atque Aiacis manibus eripiunt, seminecemque intra muros ferunt male prospera eruptione adversus hostes usum. Ceterum Aiax saevior ob ereptam e manibus gloriam adsumptis iam Diomede et cum Idomeneo Aiace altero territos dispersosque sequi ac fugientes nunc telo eminus prosternere, modo adprehensos obterere armis prorsus nullo, qui in ea parte fuerat, intacto. Inter quae tam trepida Glaucus Hippolochi, Sarpedon atque Asteropaeus ad morandum hostem paulisper ausi resistere mox vulneribus gravati locum amisere. Quis versis barbari nullam spem reliquam salutis rati sine rectoribus neque usquam certo ordine palantes effusique ruere ad portas eoque arto et properantium multitudine impedito ingressu, cum super alium alius ruinae modo praecipitarentur, supervenit cum supra dictis ducibus Aiax. tum magna vis barbarorum trepida impeditaque inter se caesa extinctaque, in quis Priami filiorum Antiphus et Polites, Pammon Mestorque atque Euphemus Troezenius, dux egregius Ciconum.

II. 43.   But when Ajax the son of Telamon returned and learned where Hector was at the ships, he presented himself at this spot, dressed in his marvellous armour. There he was, streaming with sweat, his great bulk pressing against the enemy, as he drove them away from the ships and thrust them outside the rampart. The more they retreated, the more he pressed his attack.

Hector, however, stood his ground, too bold for his own good, for Ajax struck him with a huge rock and sent him sprawling. Then, from every direction, a large number of Trojans rushed up and, crowding around, rescued Hector out of the battle and carried him into the city, a hero half dead, his expedition a failure.

Ajax, being thus deprived of honour and glory, was all the more savage. Accompanied by Diomedes, Idomeneus, and the other Ajax, he pursued the Trojans, who fled pellmell in terror. He was using his spear to hit those in the distance, his shield to crush those he met at close quarters. No one in that part of the battlefield escaped without wounds. Glaucus, the son of Hippolochus, Sarpedon, and Asteropaeus tried to stem their fearful route but, after briefly resisting, soon gave way, seriously wounded. The loss of these leaders caused the barbarians to lose all hope and, breaking ranks, they rushed for the gates in confusion. The passageway, however, was too narrow for the great number of men who tried to enter; they stumbled and fell, like a landslide, over each other. Ajax and the Greeks we just mentioned were soon upon them, and great numbers of barbarians, being terrified and confused, were cut down and killed. Among those who were slain were the sons of Priam, Antiphus and Polites, Pammon and Mestor, and the son of Troezenus, Euphemus, the Ciconians' glorious leader.

II. 44.   Ita Troiani paulo ante victores, ubi adventu Aiacis fortuna belli mutata est, versis ducibus poenas luere militiae inconsultae. At postquam adventante vespera signum nostris receptui datum est, victores laetique ad naves regressi mox ab Agamemnone cenatum deducuntur. Ibi Aiax conlaudatus a rege donis egregiis honoratur. Neque reliqui duces facta gestaque viri silentio remittunt, quippe singuli extollentes virtutem memorare fortia facta, eversas ab eo tot Phrygiae civitates abductasque praedas et ad postremum in ipsis navibus adversum Hectorem egregiam pugnam liberatasque igni classes. Neque cuiquam dubium, quin ea tempestate tot egregiis ac pulcherrimis eius facinoribus spes omnes atque opes militiae in tali viro sisterentur. Ceterum proras duarum navium, quibus inlatus ignis eam partem tantum modo consumpserat, Epios brevi restituit. Tumque Graeci rati post malam pugnam Troianos ulterius nihil hostile ausuros quieti ac sine terrore egere.

DICTYS II.

II. 44.   Thus the arrival of Ajax caused the fortunes of war to change; the Trojans, until then victorious, lost their leaders, and were forced to pay for their ill-considered aggression. When evening came and the signal was given for retreat, our men returned to the ships, rejoicing in victory.

Then Agamemnon gave a dinner in honour of Ajax, at which time he praised this hero most highly and gave him beautiful gifts. Our other leaders, too, praised the courage of Ajax. No one was silent. They told of his valourous deeds, how he had captured and plundered many Phrygian cities, and how he had fought with Hector at the very ships, a battle to be remembered, and freed the ships from fire. There was no one who doubted that at that time, because of his many excellent and glorious deeds, all of our hopes for a successful campaign rested with him.

Within a short time Epeus repaired the two ships that had caught fire; only their prows had been destroyed.

Then the Greeks felt free to relax without fear, thinking that the Trojans, in view of the attack that had recently failed, would refrain from another attempt.

II. 45.   Per idem tempus Rhesus, Eione genitus, haud alienus a Priami amicitia pacta mercede cum magnis Thracum copiis adventabat. is incedente iam vespera paulisper moratus apud paeninsulam, quae anteposita civitati continenti eius adiungitur, secunda circiter vigilia ingressus Troianos campos explicitisque tentoriis ibidem opperiebatur. Quod ubi Diomedes cum Ulixe vigilias in ea parte curantes procul animadvertere, rati Troianos a Priamo exploratum missos arreptis armis mox presso gradu circumspicientesque omnia pergunt ad eum locum. tum fatigatis ex itinere custodibus et ob id somno pressis eosque et interius progressi in ipsis tentoriis regem interficiunt. Dein nihil ultra audendum rati currum eius et cum egregiis insignibus equos ad naves ducunt. Ita reliquum noctis in suis quisque tabernaculis requiescentes transigunt. At lucis principio reliquos duces conveniunt, eos facinus ausum expletumque docent. ac mox rati barbaros incensos caede regis adire iubent omnes frequentes apud arma agere opperirique hostem.

Dictys II.

II. 45.   During this time Rhesus, the son of Eion, arrived with a large army of Thracians; he had had some dealings with Priam who had promised him pay for his aid. On the day of his arrival, he waited until nightfall on the peninsula which adjoined his kingdom in Thrace. Then, about the time of the second watch, he advanced onto the Trojan plain, spread out his tents, and set up camp.

Diomedes and Ulysses, who were guarding this sector, having noticed the commotion from afar, thought that Priam was sending some Trojans on a reconnaissance mission. Accordingly, they seized their arms and, moving stealthily and looking all around as they went, soon arrived at the spot. There they discovered the Thracian guards, who, being wearied by their long journey, had fallen asleep. After killing these, they entered Rhesus' tent and slew the king himself. They were, however, afraid to press their luck any further, and so returned to the ships, taking along Rhesus' chariot and richly caparisoned horses. Then, having gone to their huts, they slept for the rest of the night.

At daybreak they went to all of our leaders and told about their successful adventure. The consensus was that the death of Rhesus would anger the Thracians and that they would make an attack. Therefore, everyone was ordered to stand by his arms and be ready for battle.

II. 46. Neque multo post Thraces, ubi expergefacti e somno regem interemptum, foedam faciem intra tentoria animadvertere et vestigia abducti currus manifesta sunt, raptim ac sine ullis ordinibus, ut quemque fors conglobaverat, ad naves evolant. Quibus procul visis nostri conferti inter se atque imperia servantes eunt obviam. Sed Aiaces duo in aliquantum progressi primos Thracum invadunt atque opprimunt. Dein reliqui duces, ut quisque locum ceperat, caedere singulos et ubi conferti steterant, bini aut amplius congregati impetu suo dissolvere ac mox dispersos palantesque interficere, uti nullus reliquus caedis fieret. Ac statim Grai exstinctis qui adversum ierant signo dato ad tentoria eorum pergunt. At illi, qui custodes castris relicti soli supererant, visis contra hostibus terrore ipso miserandum in modum effeminati omnibus omissis ad moenia confugiunt. Tum undique versus nostri inruentes arma, equos, regias opes et ad postremum uti quidque fors dederat praeripiunt.

II. 47. Hoc modo victores Grai deletis cum imperatore Thracibus onusti praeda atque victoria ad naves digrediuntur, cum interim Troiani ex muris respectantes nequiquam pro sociis intra moenia tamen trepidarent. Igitur barbari tot iam adversis rebus fracti legatos indutias postulantes ad Graecos mittunt ac mox nostris condicionem adprobantibus interposito sacrificio fidem pacti firmavere. Eodem fere tempore Chryses, quem sacerdotem Zminthii Apollinis supra memoravimus, ad exercitum venit actum gratias super his, quae in se recepta filia benigne ab nostris gesta erant, ob quae tam honorifica, simul quod Astynomen liberaliter habitam cognoverat, reductam secum Agamemnoni tradit. Neque multo post Philocteta cum his, qui partem praedae ad eum portaverant, Lemno regreditur invalidus etiam tum neque satis firmo gressu.

Dictys II.

II. 46. We had not long to wait, for the Thracians, when they awoke, discovered that their king had been foully slain within his tent and saw the telltale traces the stolen chariot had left. Immediately, undisciplined and disorganised bands of men began rushing toward the ships. As soon as our men caught sight of the Thracians, they advanced, following their leader's commands, in a solid front. The two Ajaxes led the way; they were the first to meet and slay the enemy. Then our other leaders, in their various positions, cut down those who opposed them. Sometimes several of them united their strength to break the power of the attacking bands, and thus they slaughtered them, scattered and leaderless; no one survived.

As soon as these attackers had been wiped out, our men, obeying the signal to advance, hastened to the Thracian tents. The only Thracians still alive were those who had been left to guard the camp. When these saw our men advancing, they were terrified and, abandoning everything, fled to the walls for safety. It was really pathetic. Our men moved in from all sides and seized the armour, horses, and royal wealth that fate had kindly left us.

II. 47. Thereupon, with Rhesus and his Thracians completely destroyed, our forces returned to the ships, victoriously laden with booty. Meanwhile the Trojans were frightened, as they watched from their battlements, but to no avail for their ally, and stayed within their walls. Their spirits broken by recent reverses, they sent us envoys begging for peace. And thus a treaty was made which both sides, making due sacrifice, swore to uphold.

At about the same time, Chryses (who was the priest of the Sminthian Apollo, as we have said above) came to the Greeks to thank them for returning his daughter, Astynome. Because of this kindness, and because he knew that his daughter had been properly treated, he was now bringing her back for Agamemnon to have.

The next event was the return of Philoctetes from Lemnos, along with those who had gone to take him his share of the booty. He was still rather sick and walked with difficulty.

II. 48.   Interea consilium Graecis agentibus Aiax Telamonius in medium progressus docet opportere mitti ad Achillem precatores, qui eum imperatorum verbis atque exercitus peterent remittere iras ac repetere solitam cum suis gratiam; minime quippe aspernandum talem virum, nunc vel maxime, cum secundis rebus Graeci et paulo ante victores non ob utilitatem sed honoris merito gratiam eius peterent. Inter quae deprecari etiam Agamemnonem, daret operam simul voluntatemque agendo negotio adhiberet; namque tali tempore in commune ab omnibus consulendum, praesertim procul ab domo locis alienis atque hostilibus, neque se aliter inter tam gravia bella undique versus inimicis regionibus quam concordia tutos fore. At ubi finem loquendi fecit, cuncti duces laudare consilium viri simulque praedicantes ad caelum tollere, scilicet quod cum virtute corporis, tum ingenio universos anteiret. Post quae Agamemnon docere se et ante ad reconciliandum Achillem multos misisse et nunc nihil aliud cordi esse. Ac mox Ulixem atque ipsum Aiacem orare, susciperent negotium atque ad eum nomine omnium irent, maxime quod Aiax cognatione fretus impetraturus veniam facilius credebatur. Igitur his operam suam pollicentibus iturum se una Diomedes sponte ait.

II. 48.   Then our leaders held a meeting of the council, at which Ajax the son of Telamon, having gone to the centre, delivered a speech. He advised us to send suppliants to Achilles to beg him, on behalf of the officers and common soldiers, to give up his wrath and resume his position of honour among us. We should, he felt, act now, for now, in view of our recent victory and the favourable treaty we had made, we would be seeking him out, not because of our need, but merely to honour him as he deserved; we wanted him with us, simply because of his greatness. Furthermore, Ajax implored, Agamemnon should show his willingness to be reconciled with Achilles. In their present circumstances, fighting, as they were, this terrible war in a far-off country, everyone should think only of the common cause.

When he had finished speaking, all of our leaders agreed unanimously with what he had said and praised him largely. He was, they said, not only stronger but also more intelligent than anyone else.

Then Agamemnon told how he had already sent many suppliants to try to reconcile Achilles. There was nothing he would more desire. Accordingly, he asked Ajax (whose relationship with Achilles should add to his persuasiveness) and Ulysses to undertake this mission and go to Achilles in behalf of them all.

Ajax and Ulysses promised to do what they could. And Diomedes offered to go with them.

II. 49.   His actis Agamemnon adferre hostiam lictores iubet ac mox sublata super terram, cum duo, quibus imperatum erat, suspensam retinerent, gladium vagina educit eoque bifariam excisam hostiam in conspectu, uti diviserat, collocat. dein ferrum sanguine oblitum manu retinens inter utramque sacri partem medius vadit. Interim Patroclus cognito quod parabatur in consilium supervenit. At rex sicut supra diximus transgressus ad postremum iurat inviolatam a se in eum diem Hippodamiam mansisse; neque cupiditate ulla aut desiderio lapsum, sed ira, qua plurima mala conficiuntur, eo usque processisse. his addit cupere se praeterea, si ipsi etiam videretur, filiarum, quae ei cordi esset, in matrimonium dare decimamque regni omnis ac talenta quinquaginta doti adiungit. Quae ubi accepere qui in consilio erant, admirari magnificentiam regis maximeque Patroclus, qui cum oblatione tantarum opum, tum praecipue laetus, quod intacta Hippodamia adfirmaretur, ad Achillem venit eique universa gesta atque acta refert.

II. 49.   Thereupon Agamemnon ordered two attendants to bring a sacrificial victim. These brought the victim and held it above the ground while he, drawing his sword, cut it in half; the pieces fell to earth where all could see. This done, he walked through the middle, smearing his sword with blood. It was at this time that Patroclus, who had learned that the council was meeting, arrived. When Agamemnon had passed through the sacrifice, he swore that he had never violated Hippodamia; he had never been prone to lust or sensual pleasures; it was, rather, his inability to control his temper that had caused him countless troubles and brought him to this pass. Now he wanted to make the following offer: he would give Achilles one of his daughters to marry, whichever one he desired, besides a tenth of all his kingdom and fifty talents as dowry.

Those at the council, on hearing this, were amazed at his magnanimity. Patroclus was especially impressed by the offer of so much wealth, and he was also happy that Hippodamia had not been violated. Thus he returned to Achilles and told him all that had happened at the council.

II. 50.   Dein ubi rex ea, quae audierat, volutare animo ac deliberare
secum ipse occepit, supervenit cum supradictis Aiax. Tum ingressos eos ac
iam benigne salutatos sedere hortatur iuxtaque se Aiacem. Qui tempus
loquendi nactus familiariter et ob id liberius incusare atque increpare, quod
in magnis discriminibus suorum nihil iracundiae remiserit, potueritque
cladem exercitus perpeti, cum eum multi amici, plurimi etiam adfinium
obvoluti genibus deprecarentur. Post quem Ulixes illa quidem deorum esse
ait, eorum autem, quae in consilio acta essent, ordine exposito, quae etiam
Agamemnon pollicitus quaeque iurasset, ad postremum orat, ne preces
omnium neve oblatas nuptias aspernaretur; moxque eorum omnium, quae
una offerebantur, enumerationem facit.

DICTYS II.

II. 50.   Achilles was pondering Agamemnon's offer, trying to decide what he should do, when Ajax and the other leaders entered his hut. He received them hospitably and offered them seats.

Ajax, having taken the seat that was next to Achilles, began, when the time seemed right, to chide and admonish him. Since they were relatives, he could speak more freely than the others. He blamed Achilles for nursing his wrath when many of his friends and most of his relatives, they, his people, were in serious danger, were begging him to relent.

Ulysses was next to speak. First, he said that the gods were to blame for what had happened so far. Then he told about the meeting of the council, about the promises Agamemnon had made and the oath Agamemnon had taken. Finally, urging Achilles not to scorn the prayers of the Greeks and not to spurn such a marriage, he ended by listing all of the dowry that Agamemnon was offering.

II. 51.   Tunc Achilles longam exorsus orationem primum omnium acta gestaque sua exponere. Ac dein admonere, quantas aerumnas pro utilitate omnium pertulerit, quas civitates adgressus ceperit cunctis interim requiescentibus ipse anxius ae dies noctesque bello intentus et, cum neque militibus suis neque sibi ipse parceret, asportatas nihilominus praedas in commune solitum redigere. pro quis solum omnium se electum, qui tam insigni iniuria dehonestaretur, solum ita contemptum, a quo Hippodamia tot laborum pretium per dedecus abstraheretur neque in ea culpa solum esse Agamemnonem sed maxime ceteros Graecos, qui immemores benificiorum contumeliam suam silentio praeterierint. postquam finem loquendi fecit, Diomedes: *praeterita,* ait, *omittenda sunt neque oportet prudentem meminisse transactorum, quando ea, etsi maxime cupias, nequeas revocare.* Interea Phoenix et cum eo Patroclus circumstantes genas atque omnem vultum iuvenis, manus adosculari, contingere genua, rediret in gratiam atque animos remitteret cum propter praesentes, qui eum oratum venissent, tum praecipue ob bene de se meritum reliquum exercitum.

DICTYS II.

II. 51. Then Achilles, in a long speech, began by expounding upon his deeds and accomplishments, reminding them of the many labours he had borne for the common good, of the cities he had stormed. While everyone else was relaxing, he had spent his days and nights anxiously and zealously committed to war, sparing neither himself nor his soldiers; and, furthermore, he had allowed the booty he had carried off to be distributed among the entire army. In return for these services, he had received the unique honour of being deprived of his just reward. Only he had been treated with such contempt, such dishonour, for he had been robbed of Hippodamia, his prize, the symbol of his success. Agamemnon was not entirely to blame. What was even worse, all the other Greek leaders, forgetful of past kindnesses, had, by keeping silent, ignored the fact that he was being insulted.

When Achilles had finished speaking, Diomedes said: 'What is past is past, and a wise man does not dwell upon it. Try as you may, you can not call it back'.

Meanwhile Phoenix and Patroclus were standing around Achilles in the position of suppliants, taking hold of his knees and, without restraint, kissing his hands and face, begging him to give up his wrath and return to his place of honour. Do this, they said, not so much for these representatives but, as is right, for all of the army.

II. 52.   Igitur Achilles praesentia talium virorum praecibus familiarium ac recordatione innoxii exercitus tandem flexus ad postremum facturum se quae vellent respondit. dein hortatu Aiacis tum primum post malam iracundiam Graecis mixtus consilium ingreditur atque ab Agamemnone regio more salutatur. Interea reliquis ducibus favorem attollentibus gaudio laetitiaque cuncta completa sunt. igitur Agamemnon manum Achillis retentans eumque et reliquos duces ad cenam deducit. Ac paulo post inter epulas, cum laeti inter se invitarent, rex Patroclum quaesiit, ut Hippodamiam cum ornamentis, quae dederat, ad tentoria Achillis deduceret; isque libens mandata efficit. Ceterum per id tempus hiemis saepe Graeci atque Troiani singuli pluresve, ut fors evenerat, inter se sine ullo metu in luco Thymbraei Apollinis miscebantur.

II. 52. Finally Achilles yielded.[16] He would do what they wanted. The sight of the representatives, the prayers of his closest friends, and the realisation that the army was not to blame had made him change his mind.

Then for the first time after his wrath, at the suggestion of Ajax, Achilles went to a meeting of the council. Agamemnon greeted him in a royal manner, and the other leaders were happy to welcome him back. On every side there was joy, unbounded joy. And then Agamemnon, taking Achilles by the hand, led him off, along with the other leaders, to dinner.

A little later, during the dinner, when they were enjoying themselves, Agamemnon commanded Patroclus to take Hippodamia to Achilles' hut, and also the jewellery he had given to her. This was an order Patroclus was glad to obey.

During this winter, Greeks and Trojans mingled in the grove of the Thymbraean Apollo.[17] They went freely, whether singly or in groups, without any fear of each other.

---

16 How different is this Achilles from the Achilles of *Iliad* 9!

17 The temple of the Thymbraean Apollo was located in a grove east of Troy where the Thymbrius River emtpied into the Scamander. See Strabo *Geography* 13.1.35.

LIBER TERTIVS

Interim per totam hiemem dilato condicionibus in tempus bello Graeci cuncta, quae in tali otio militia exposcebat, intenti animo summis studiis festinabant. namque pro vallo multitudo universa variis bellandi generibus per duces populosque instructa et ob id more optimo diversis ad officia sua quibusque, hinc iaculis hastarum vice fabricatis neque ponderis aut mensurae inferioribus, et quibus ea non erant praeustis sudibus, illinc sagittis certantes inter se invicem ad multum diem exercere, alii saxis utebantur. Sed inter sagittarios maxime anteibant Ulixes, Teucer, Meriones, Epios, Menelaus. neque dubium, quin inter hos tamen praecelleret Philocteta, quippe Herculis sagittarum dominus et destinata feriundi arte mirabilis. At Troiani cum auxiliaribus laxiores militia neque circa exercitum solliciti socordius agitare ac saepe sine ullo insidiarum metu hi aut illi multis immolationibus Thymbraeo Apollini supplicabant. Isdem fere diebus nuntius adportatur universas prope Asiae civitates descivisse a Priamo atque eius amicitiam execrari. namque facinoris exemplo suspectis iam per universos populos gentesque circa hospitium omnibus, simul quia omnibus proeliis Graecos victores cognitum et eversio multarum in ea regione civitatum in animis haeserat et ad postremum grave odium filiorum regnique eius incesserat.

Book Three

III. 1.   Both Greeks and Trojans kept the truce and refrained from hostilities throughout the whole winter. The Greeks took advantage of the break and spent all their time and energies preparing for battle. They would assemble in front of the rampart, under their various leaders, each in the contingent that practiced his specialty. One group would practice throwing the spear, using, as a rule, pikes of exactly the right weight and length, or else pointed stakes. Others would practice hurling the sling or shooting the bow. Among those excelling in archery were Ulysses, Teucer, Meriones, Epeus, and Menelaus; but Philoctetes was the best: he owned the bow of Hercules, and always hit the mark with amazing skill.

The Trojans and their allies were, in comparison with the Greeks, almost carefree. They feared no treachery, and therefore neglected their military duties, spending their time making frequent sacrifices to the Thymbraean Apollo.

At about the same time they were informed that almost all of the cities of Asia had turned against Priam and were breaking off diplomatic relations with Troy. These cities blamed Priam for upholding Alexander's cause: he was setting a bad example which would undermine the laws of friendship in their region. Also, they were well aware that the Greeks had won all their battles to date and had conquered many of the neighbouring cities. Last but not least, they hated Priam's sons and Priam's kingdom.

III. 2.   At apud Troiam forte quadam die Hecuba supplicante Apollini Achilles adveniens visere cerimoniarium morem eum paucis comitibus supervenit. Erant praeterea cum Hecuba matronae plurimae, coniuges principalium filiorumque eius, partim honorem atque obsequium reginae tribuentes, reliquae tali obtentu pro se quaeque rogaturae supplicabant. Etiam Hecubae filiae nondum nuptae Polyxena et Cassandra, Minervae atque Apollinis, antistites novo ac barbaro redimitae ornatu effusis hinc atque inde crinibus precabantur suggerente sibi Polyxena apparatum sacri eius. Ac tum forte Achilles versis in Polyxenam oculis pulchritudine virginis capitur. Auctoque in horas desiderio, ubi animus non lenitur, ad naves discedit. Sed ubi dies pauci fluxere et amor magis ingravescit, accito Automedonte aperit ardorem animi; ad postremum quaesiit, uti ad Hectorem virginis causa iret. Hector vero daturum se in matrimonium sororem mandat, si sibi universum exercitum proderet.

III. 2.   One day at Troy, when Hecuba was praying to Apollo, Achilles and a few of his men came to watch the religious ceremonies. Many other women were there besides Hecuba: her daughters-in-law, for instance, and the wives of the leading Trojans; some of these, in pure devotion to their queen, attended upon her, while others, pretending to be so devoted, had really come to pray for something for themselves. There were also the daughters of Hecuba, Polyxena and Cassandra, as yet unmarried. They were the priestesses of Minerva and Apollo. Their hair was disheveled, their fillets strange and barbarous. Polyxena was the one who had set them to these duties.

When Achilles by chance turned his gaze on Polyxena, he was struck by the beauty of the girl. The longer he remained there, the deeper his passion grew. Finding no relief, he returned to the ships and, after several days of increasing torment, sent for Automedon and laid bare his heart. Automedon, he finally begged, must go to Hector and plead his suit for the girl.

As for Hector, he, to be sure, would give him his sister to marry if he would betray the whole army to him.

III. 3.　　　　Dein Achilles soluturum se omne bellum pro Polyxena tradita pollicetur. Tum Hector: aut proditionem ab eo confirmandam, aut filios Plisthenis atque Aiacem interficiendos, alias de tali negotio nihil se auditurum. ea ubi Achilles accepit, ira concitus exclamat: se, cum primum tempus bellandi foret, primo proelio interempturum. Dein animi iactatione saucius huc atque illuc oberrans interdum tamen, quatenus praesenti negotio utendum esset, consultare. At ubi eum Automedon iactari animo atque in dies magis magisque aestuare desiderio ac pernoctare extra tentoria animadvertit, veritus, ne quid adversum se aut in supradictos reges moliretur, Patroclo atque Aiaci rem cunctam aperit. Hique dissimulato quod audierant cum rege commorantur. Ac forte quodam tempore recordatus sui convocatis Agamemnone et Menelao negotium, ut gestum erat, desideriumque animi aperit: a quis omnibus ut bono animo ageret respondetur, brevi quippe dominum eum fore eius, quam deprecando non impetraverit. Quae res eo habere fidem videbatur, quoniam iam summa rerum Troianarum prope occasum erat. Omnes namque Asiae civitates execratae amicitiam Priamidarum ultro nobis auxilium societatemque belli offerebant. quis ab ducibus nostris benigne respondebatur: satis sibi esse praesentium copiarum neque auxiliorum egere, amicitiam sane, quam offerent; ultro suscipere voluntatemque erorum fore gratam omnibus. Scilicet quia fluxa fides et animi parum spectati neque tam subita mutatio sine dolo credebatur.

III. 3.　　　Accordingly, Achilles promised that he would bring the whole war to an end if Polyxena were given to him.

Then Hector said that Achilles must either swear an oath to this betrayal or kill the sons of Plisthenes and Ajax, and that otherwise he was going to hear of no agreement.

Achilles, on hearing this, became terribly angry and shouted that, in the first battle, as soon as fighting was resumed, he was going to kill Hector. Then, his heart being wounded by his violent emotion, he wandered around, now here, now there; sometimes, nevertheless, he considered how far he should go in meeting Hector's demands.

But when Automedon saw how violently he was disturbed and that, as the days went by, he was becoming more and more distraught with longing, and spending the nights outside his hut, he feared that Achilles might harm himself or the leaders mentioned above, and thus he revealed the whole matter to Patroclus and Ajax. These kept a careful watch on their friend, without disclosing that they knew anything.

As it happened, in time Achilles came to his senses. Having summoned Agamemnon and Menelaus, he told them about his love for Polyxena and about his dealings with Hector. Then everyone tried to console him by pointing out that the girl would be his soon enough, for, before very long, force would succeed where entreaty had failed.

What they said seemed reasonable, since the fall of Troy was already imminent: all the cities of Asia had broken off diplomatic relations with Priam and had willingly offered their aid and alliance to us. Our leaders had answered politely: Our present forces were quite sufficient, and we had no need of auxiliaries; though, to be sure, we willingly accepted the friendship they offered, and their good will would be pleasing to us. This we said, no doubt, because their faith was not to be trusted, their courage was too little tested, and their sudden change of allegiance was probably made with guile.

III. 4. Iamque exactis hibernis mensibus ver coeperat, cum Grai edicto prius, uti omnis miles in armis esset, mox signo belli edito exercitum in campis productum ordinant; neque ea a Troianis segnius agebantur. Igitur ubi utrimque instructae acies adversum processere atque infra teli iactum ventum est, cohortati suos quisque manus conserunt in medio locatis equitibus et ob id primis congressis. Tumque primum reges nostri atque hostium ascensis curribus bellum ineunt adscito sibi quisque auriga ad regendos equos. Sed primus omnium Diomedes invectus Pyraechmem, regem Paeonum, hasta fronte ictum interficit, dein ceteros, quos ob virtutem rex secum stipatores habuerat, conglobatos inter se atque ausos resistere partim telo eminus fundit, alios curru per medios concito humi obterit. Dein Idomeneus adhibito equis Merione Acamanta Thracum regem deicit, ruentique telo occurrit atque ita interficit. Sed ubi Hector situs in parte alia medios suorum fundi accipit, dispositis satis strenuis, ubi pugnabat, accurrit auxilio laborantibus Glaucum secum ac Deiphobum et Polydamanta habens. Neque dubium, quin deleta a praedictis regibus ea pars hostium foret, ni adventu suo Heetor nostrosque ulterius progredi ac suos fugere cohibuisset. Ita Graeci prohibiti caede reliquorum represso gradu adversum eos, qui supervenerant, constitere.

III. 4.   Winter came to an end and, with the beginning of spring, both Greeks and Trojans were ready for war. They called their forces to arms and, giving the signal, led them onto the plain. When they had advanced, in formation, close enough to use their spears, they raised the war cry and joined in battle. The cavalry on both sides held the centre and were therefore first to clash: the kings ascended their chariots and entered the fray, each beside the charioteer he had chosen to guide his horses.

Diomedes was in the van. Bearing down upon Pyraechmes, the king of the Paeonians, he slew him with a spear thrust in the face. The retainers of Pyraechmes, men he had chosen because of their courage, banded together and tried to resist. But Diomedes, riding through their midst at full gallop, ran some of them down with his chariot and put the others to flight with his spear.

Then Idomeneus (Meriones was his charioteer) killed Acamas, the king of the Thracians. Thrusting him out of his chariot, he caught him, as he fell, on the tip of his spear.

When Hector, who was fighting in another part of the plain, heard that the Trojan horsemen in the centre were fleeing, he ran to their rescue, leaving his command in the hands of worthy fighters, and taking along Glaucus, Deiphobus, and Polydamas. Without a doubt, the Trojans in the centre would have been completely destroyed if Hector had not arrived and checked their flight. Now we were no longer able to pursue them up, our offensive was dead; nevertheless, we held our ground and refused to retreat before Hector and the other recent arrivals.

III. 5.   Ac mox cognito per universum exercitum proelio in ea parte reliqui duces confirmati, ubi quisque pugnaverat, undique eo confluunt. Densatur utrimque acies et proelium renovatum est. Igitur Hector ubi plurimos suorum adesse et satis tutum se intellegit, tollit animos. Dein clamore magno singulos suorum nomine appellans confidentius in hostem pugnare hortatur; ac progressus intra aciem Diorem et Polyxenum Alios satis impigre pugnantes vulnerat. at ubi eum Achilles ita in hostem promptum animadvertit, simul subvenire his, quos adversum bellabat, cupiens et memor paulo ante repulsae in Polyxena contra tendit; progressusque in medio Pylaemenem Paphlagonum regem impedimento sibi oppositum comminus fundit non alienum sanguinis Priamidarum. Perhibebatur quippe hic etiam ex his, qui a Phineo Agenoris originem propriam memoria repetebant, a quo etiam Olizonen genitam, postquam adoleverit deductam in matrimonium Dardani.

III. 6.   Ceterum Hector postquam ad se agmine infesto tendi videt, causas odii recordatus non ulterius impetum viri experiri ausus ex acie subterfugit. Tumque Achilles insecutus quantum acies hostium patiebatur, ad postremum iaculatus aurigam eius interfecit, postquam Hector per aliam partem relicto curru aufugerat. Dein ereptum sibi e manibus inimicissimum omnium dolens rursus vehementius saevire extractoque ex corpore aurigae iaculo fundere obvios ac prostratos, cum alios invaderet, desuper proculcans obterere. Inter quae tam trepida cunctis fugientibus Helenus quaesitum ex occulto vulneri locum ubi nactus est, manum Achillis procul atque improvisus sagitta transfigit. Ita vir egregius bellandi, cuius adventu territus fugatusque Hector, multi mortales cum ducibus extincti, clam atque ex occulto vulneratus eo die finem bellandi fecit.

III. 5.   Soon news of this battle spread throughout the army, and the other leaders, having entrusted their positions to worthy subordinates, rushed toward the centre. The battle lines, on both sides, were closed up, and the battle was renewed. Hector felt greatly encouraged, seeing that a large number of Trojans were present and thinking himself sufficiently safe. Then he urged on his men to fight with more daring, shouting in a loud voice and calling them each by name; and he himself entered the battle and wounded the two brave leaders of the Elians, Diores and Polyxenus.

As soon as Achilles saw Hector attacking like this, he came to the aid of the embattled Greeks, his spirit moved by the thought of how Hector had rejected his suit for Polyxena. He was forced, however, to stop in midcourse and slay Pylaemenes, the king of the Paphlagonians, who stood in his way. Pylaemenes, so they say, claimed to be related to Priam through Phineus, the son of Agenor, for Phineus' daughter, Olizone, on coming of age, had been married to Dardanus.[1]

III. 6.   Then Achilles continued his raging drive against Hector, but Hector, who knew very well how hateful he was to Achilles, refused to stay where he was and, mounting his chariot, fled from the battle. Achilles pursued as far as the enemy lines and, throwing his spear, mortally wounded Hector's charioteer, after Hector had abandoned his horses and escaped to another sector. Achilles was terribly vexed when he thought how the man he most hated had eluded his grasp. After extracting his spear from the charioteer, he raged all the more violently, slaying all who opposed him, trampling, as he advanced, over the dead.

The Trojans fled, terrified, until Helenus, who had found a distant hiding place from which to shoot his arrow, put an end to Achilles' attack. Achilles was caught off guard. His hand was hit, and thus the great champion of the Greeks, he who had caused Hector to flee in fear, he who had slain many men and their leaders, was forced from the field, treacherously wounded.

---

1 For Phineus' relationship with Priam, see Dictys 4.22.

III. 7.   Interim Agamemnon et cum eo Aiaces duo inter ceteram stragem ignotorum nacti plurimos Priami filiorum interficiunt, atque Agamemnon Aesacum cum Deiopite, Archemachum, Laudocum et Philenorem, Aiax Oilei et Telamonius Mylium, Astynoum, Doryclum, Hippothoum atque Hippodamanta. At in alia belli parte Patroclus et Lycius Sarpedon locati in cornibus nullis propinquorum praesentibus signo inter se dato solitarii certaminis extra aciem processere, moxque telis adversum iactis, ubi uterque intactus est, curru desiliunt atque arreptis gladiis pergunt obviam. Iamque crebris adversum se ictibus congressi, neque vulneratus quisquam, multum diei consumpserant, cum Patroclus amplius audendum ratus colligit sese in arma et cautius contectus ingressusque hostem complectitur, manu dextra poplitem succidens, quo vulnere debilitatum atque exsectis nervis invalidum propulsat corpore ruentemque interficit.

III. 7.   Meanwhile Agamemnon and the two Ajaxes, amidst their general slaughter of insignificant opponents, caught and slew many of Priam's sons. Agamemnon slew Aesacus and Deiopites and also Archemachus, Laudocus, and Philenor. The Ajaxes, both the son of Oileus and the Telamonian Ajax, slew Mylius, Astynous, Doryclus, Hippothous, and Hippodamas.

In another part of the field Patroclus and Sarpedon the Lycian had withdrawn from their men and were trying to protect the flanks of their respective armies. Driving out beyond the battle lines, they challenged each other to fight in single combat. First, they threw their spears, but neither hit the mark. Then, leaping from their chariots and drawing their swords, they came face to face and fought for much of the day, exchanging blows fast and furious, but neither could wound the other. Finally, Patroclus, realizing that he must act with greater boldness, crouched behind the protection of his shield and came to close quarters. With his right hand he dealt Sarpedon a crippling blow along the back sinews of the leg and then, pressing his body against him, Sarpedon was faint and beginning to totter, pushed him over and finished him off as he fell.

III. 8.   Quod ubi animadvertere Troiani, qui iuxta steterant, gemitu magno clamorem tollunt, relictisque ordinibus signo dato arma in Patroclum vertunt, scilicet Sarpedonis interitu publicam cladem rati. At Patroclus praeviso hostium agmine telum positum humi propere rapit compositusque in armis audentius resistit. Tunc ingruentem Deiphobum hasta comminus tibiam ferit atque excedere ex acie coegit interfecto prius Gorgythione fratre eius. Neque multo post adventu Aiacis fusi reliqui, cum interim Hector edoctus quae acciderant, supervenit ac mox conversam suorum aciem pro tempore restituit increpatis ducibus ac plerisque ex fuga reductis. Ita praesentia eius animi tolluntur et proelium incenditur. tum vero inclitis ex utraque parte ducibus confirmato exercitu confligunt acies, nunc hinc, nunc inde cedentibus instantes et, ubi acies nutaverat, praesidiis accurrentibus. Interea utriusque exercitus cadunt plurimi neque fortuna belli mutatur. sed postquam miles per multum diem bello intentus magis magisque fatigabatur et diei vesper erat, utrisque cupientibus pugna decessum.

III. 8.   The Trojans, seeing what had happened, cried aloud and abandoned their battle formation, and, at a given signal, made a concerted attack against Patroclus. They felt, no doubt, that Sarpedon's death was a general disaster for their side. Patroclus, however, had seen the enemy coming. Protected by his armour and holding a spear he had snatched from the ground, he resisted more boldly. He slew Gorgythion and drove off Deiphobus, Gorgythion's brother, wounding him in the leg with his spear. Soon afterwards Ajax arrived and put the other Trojans to flight.

At about the same time Hector, who had also learned what was happening, came to the rescue. He rebuked the Trojan officers and stopped most of the men from retreating. He made them turn and resume, for the time, their battle formation. Thus by his presence he restored the spirits of his people and caused the battle to be renewed. The battle lines clashed, both sides being inspired by marvellous leaders. Now these were attacking, now those. Wherever the lines seemed about to give way, reinforcements came up. Meanwhile both armies were losing great numbers of men, and victory was favouring neither. When evening came, after a long and increasingly wearisome day of intensive fighting, the soldiers on both sides were glad to depart from the battle.

III. 9.   Tum apud Troiam circa Sarpedonis cadaver cunctis deflentibus ac praecipue feminis luctu atque gemitu omnia completa sunt, quis non alii casus acerbissimi, ne interitus quidem Priamidarum, prae desiderio eius cordi insederant. Tantum in eo viro praesidium et interfecto spes ablata credebatur. At Graeci in castra regressi primum omnium Achillem revisunt eumque de vulnere percontati, ubi sine dolore agere vident, laeti ad postremum narrare occipiunt Patrocli facta fortia, dein reliquos, qui vulnerati erant, per ordinem circumeunt; ita inspectatis omnibus ad tentoria sua quisque digreditur. Interim Achilles regressum Patroclum extollere laudibus, dein monere, uti reliquo quoque bello memor rerum, quas gesserat, hostibus vehementius ingrueret. Hoc modo nox consumitur. At lucis principio corpora suorum quisque collecta igni cremant, dein sepeliunt. Sed postquam dies aliquot triti et vulnerati convaluerant, arma expedire et producere militem placet.

III. 9. Then Troy was filled with cries of grief. All the Trojans, especially the women, were weeping and wailing around the body of Sarpedon. They felt that no other disaster, however bitter, could be compared with this, not even the deaths of Priam's sons. They had believed in Sarpedon. They had hoped that he would protect them. But now their hopes were dashed.

The Greeks, for their part, returning to camp, immediately went to Achilles. After inquiring about his wound and learning, to their joy, that he was not suffering, they told him about the brave deeds of Patroclus. Then, before scattering to their different huts, they visited and inspected all the others who were wounded.

When Patroclus returned, Achilles praised him and urged that the memory of what he had done that day should spur him to fight more fiercely in future battles.

Thus Trojans and Greeks spent this night. When dawn arrived, they collected, cremated and buried their dead. Then, after some days, when the wounded were well, they readied their arms and drew up their forces for battle.

III. 10.   Sed barbari more pessimo nec quicquam compositum, nihil aliud quam turbata atque insidiosa cupientes clam atque ante tempus egressi proelium praevertere. Tuncque effusi ruinae modo clamorem inconditum simul et tela in hostes coniciunt semermes etiam tum atque incompositos. Caesi itaque nostrorum multi, in quis Arcesilaus Boeotius et Schedius Crissaeorum uterque duces optimi; ceterum vulnerata pars maxima, Meges etiam et Agapenor, alter Echinadibus imperator, Agapenor Arcadiae. Inter quae tam foeda tanta inclinatione rerum Patroclus fortunam belli vincere adgressus, dum hortatur suos simul atque instat hostibus promptiore quam bellandi mos est, telo Euphorbi ictus ruit. Statimque Hector advolans opprimit ac desuper vulneribus multis fodit; moxque enititur abstrahere proelio, scilicet insolentia gentis suae inludere cupiens per universa genera dehonestamenti. Quod ubi Aiaci cognitum est, relicto ubi pugnaverat propere accurrit, iamque eripere cadaver occipientem proturbat hasta. interim Euphorbus a Menelao et Aiace altero summo studio circumventus scilicet auctor interempti ducis morte poenas luit. Deinde occipiente vespera proelium dirimitur male et cum dedecore plurimis nostrorum interfectis.

III. 10.   The barbarians, in accordance with their utter lack of principles, began hostilities with a sneak attack. Pitched battles were not to their liking; nothing else than treachery and turmoil would do. They fell upon us like a landslide, hurling their javelins with barbarous war cries. Many of our men, being caught off guard and half armed, were killed, including Arcesilaus, the Boeotian, and Schedius, the Crissaean, both of whom were the best of leaders. The number of the wounded, however, was even greater; among whom were Meges, the ruler of the Echinades, and Agapenor, ruler of Arcadia.

During this terrible conflict, Patroclus, seeing our side being beaten, hoped he could turn the tide of battle. Thus, having exhorted our men, he entered the fray and attacked the enemy fiercely, more fiercely than anyone ever. Euphorbus, however, found him with a javelin. And soon Hector rushed up and, straddling the fallen body, dealt it many piercing thrusts and then tried to drag it from the battle. No doubt, in keeping with his people's total lack of human decency, Hector wanted to mock and mangle this victim in every way.

When Ajax, who was fighting in another part of the field, saw what was happening, he came up quickly; using his spear, he drove off Hector, who was already beginning to drag the body away. Meanwhile Menelaus and the other Ajax were pouncing upon Euphorbus and making him pay with his life for having been the cause of Patroclus' death. When evening finally came and the battle was broken off, a great number of our men were dead, treacherously and barbarously slain.

III. 11. Sed postquam reductae utrimque acies et iam in tuto miles noster erat, cuncti reges Achillem conveniunt deformatum iam lacrimis atque omni supplicio lamentandi. Qui modo prostratus humi, nunc cadaveri superiacens adeo reliquorum animos pertemptaverat, ut Aiax etiam, qui solandi causa adstiterat, nihil luctui remitteret. Nec Patrocli tantum mors gemitum illum cunctis incusserat, sed praecipue recordatio vulnerum per loca corporis pudibunda, quod exemplum pessimum per mortales tum primum proditum est numquam antea a Graecis solitum. Igitur reges multis precibus atque omni consolationis modo tandem Achillem flexum humo erigunt. Dein Patrocli corpus elutum mox veste circumtegitur maxime ob tegenda vulnera, quae multimodis impressa haud sine magno gemitu cernebantur.

III. 12. His actis monet, uti custodes vigilias agere curarent, ne qua hostes detentis circa funus nostris more solito inruerent. ita per distributionem officia sua quisque procurantes igni plurimo in armis pernoctant. At lucis principio placet, uti ex omni ducum numero quinque in montem Idam vaderent silvam caesum, qua Patroclus cremaretur, decretum quippe ab omnibus erat, funus eius publice uti curaretur. Iere igitur Ialmenus, Ascalaphus, Epios et cum Merione Aiax alter. Moxque Ulixes et Diomedes busto locum dimetiuntur quinque hastarum longitudine totidemque in transversum. Advecta deinde ligni copia bustum extruitur impositumque desuper cadaver igni supposito cremant exornatum iam decore omni pretiosae vestis; id namque Hippodamia et Diomedea curaverant, quarum Diomedea nimium iuveni et omni affectu dilecta fuerat.

DICTYS III.

III. 11.   Now that the two armies had withdrawn, we were free to relax. Our leaders went to Achilles. He was showing every sign of unbearable grief, for his face was distorted with weeping as he lay stretched out on the ground or over the body. He stirred everyone's heart. Even Ajax, who was standing by and trying to console him, broke down and wept. All of our leaders bewailed the death of Patroclus and, even more, the terrible way he had been mutilated; this was the first instance of such a shameful and inhuman act, a thing that the Greeks had never practiced before. Thus our leaders, with many prayers, consoling Achilles in every way, finally persuaded him to arise. Then, having washed the body of Patroclus, they covered it with a robe, being especially careful to hide the wounds, which to behold caused them to weep.

III. 12.   When this had been done, Achilles exhorted the guards to keep careful watch in case the enemy should make an attack in their usual way, while we were detained with the burial. Accordingly, the guards, each of whom was dedicated to his duty, armed themselves and spent the night keeping the watchfires burning brightly.

At daybreak, since we had decided to hold a public funeral, we chose five of the leaders, Ialmenus, Ascalaphus, Epeus, Meriones, and the other Ajax, to go to Mount Ida for wood. Then we built a huge pyre with the wood which they brought, in a place five spears long and five spears wide, which Ulysses and Diomedes had measured off. After the body had been arranged, we lit the fire. Patroclus was clothed in the most beautiful and costly garments; Hippodamia and Diomedea (he had loved her especially) had seen to this.

III. 13.   Ceterum paucis post diebus refectis ex labore vigiliarum ducibus cum luce simul exercitus in campum productus per totum diem in armis agit opperiens barbarorum adventum. Qui muris despectantes postquam nostros paratos proelio vident, eo die certamen distulere. Ita occasu solis Graeci ad naves regressi. At vix principio diei Troiani rati etiam nunc incompositos Graecos, armati portis evolant temere et cum audacia, uti antea soliti, instantesque circa vallum certatim tela iaciunt crebra magis quam cum effectu nostris ad evitandos tantum ictus compositis. Igitur ubi ad multum diem barbari intenti iaculis fessi iam neque is ita vehementes animadvertuntur, ex parte una nostri erumpunt, incursantesque sinistrum latus fundunt fugantque; neque multo post ex alio adnuentibus iam barbaris ac sine ulla difficultate versis.

III. 13.   After spending a few days of restoration, our leaders early one morning led forth our army onto the plain. We waited and waited, but the barbarians, looking from their walls and seeing us armed, would not come out and fight. Therefore, at sunset we returned to the ships.

The next day, however, had hardly begun when the Trojans armed themselves and rushed from their gates, hoping, as was their custom, to catch us off guard with a wild and sudden attack. But we were organized well enough to protect ourselves, and, therefore, their javelins, which they, as they came against our fortifications, hurled in great numbers with energy and spirit, usually failed of their mark. Towards the end of the day we noticed that they were showing signs of strain and losing some of their fierceness. Accordingly, those of our men who were facing their left flank went on the offensive and thus scattered and put them to flight. Soon afterwards the other flank, which was already wavering, was driven off without any trouble.

III. 14.　Ita plurimi barbarorum, ubi vertere terga, foede et vice inbellium ab insequentibus proculcati ad postremum dispereunt, in quis Asius, Hyrtaco genitus, et cum Hippothoo Pylaeus, hi Larisaeis, Asius Sesto regnantes. Eodem die vivi a Diomede capiuntur duodecim, ab Aiace quadraginta. Captus etiam Pisus et Euander Priamidae. In ea pugna Graecorum Guneus interfectus rex Cyphius, vulneratus etiam Idomeneus dux noster. Ceterum ubi Troiani muros ingressi clausere portas et finis instandi factus est, nostri spoliata armis hostilia cadavera adportataque in flumine praecipitant memores paulo ante in Patroclo insolentiae barbarorum; dein captivos omnes, uti quem ceperant, in ordine Achilli offerunt. Isque vino multo sopita iam favilla reliquias in urnam collegerat, decretum quippe animo gerebat, secum in patrium solum uti adveheret vel, si fortuna in se casum mutaret, una atque eadem sepultura cum carissimo sibi omnium contegi. Itaque eos, qui oblati erant, deduci ad bustum, una etiam Priami filios ibique seorsum aliquantum a favilla iugulari iubet, scilicet inferias Patrocli manibus. Ac mox regulos canibus dilaniandos iacit confirmatque se non prius desinere pernoctando humi, quam in auctorem tanti luctus sui sanguine vindicasset.

III. 14. Turning tail, most of them fled like shameless cowards; and we, pursuing and treading them down, slew great numbers; among whom were the rulers of Larissa, Pylaeus and Hippothous, and the ruler of Sestos, Asius, the son of Hyrtacus. On the same day, Diomedes took twelve captives; Ajax took forty. Two of the captives, Pisus and Evander, were sons of Priam. As for the casualties on our side in this battle, Guneus, the king of the Cyphians, was slain, and my leader, Idomeneus, was wounded.

When the Trojans had reached the safety of their walls and shut the gates, we were no longer able to pursue. Remembering the outrage that had been committed against the body of Patroclus, we stripped the enemy corpses of their armour and dumped them into the river. Then we gave all the captives to Achilles, one after the other, as we had captured them.

Achilles, having doused the ashes of Patroclus with wine, gathered the remains into an urn. He intended to carry them, whenever he went, to his native soil, or be buried with them, with his dearest friend, there in the selfsame tomb if fate decreed his death. He ordered the captives we had given him, including the sons of Priam, to be led off to the pyre and slaughtered not far from the ashes, no doubt as a sacrifice to the departed spirit of Patroclus.

Then he threw the bodies of the sons of the king to the dogs to be torn apart. He swore that he would spend his nights under the open sky until he had taken vengeance, blood for blood, on the man who was the cause of his unspeakable grief.

III. 15.   Sed nec multi transacti dies, cum repente nuntiatum
Hectorem obviam Penthesileae cum paucis profectum. Quae regina
Amazonibus incertum pretio an bellandi cupidine auxiliatum Priamo
adventaverat, gens bellatrix et ob id ad finitimos indomita, specie armorum
inclita per mortales. Igitur Achilles paucis fidis adiunctis secum insidiatum
propere pergit atque hostem securum sui praevortit, tum ingredi flumen
occipientem circumvenit. Ita eumque et omnes, qui comites regulo dolum
huiusmodi ignoraverant, ex improviso interficit. At quendam filiorum
Priami comprehensum mox excisis manibus ad civitatem remittit
nuntiatum quae gesta erant ipse cum caede inimicissimi, tum memoria
doloris ferox spoliatum armis hostem, mox constrictis in unum pedibus
vinculo currui postremo adnectit, dein ubi ascendit ipse, Automedonti
imperat, daret lora equis. Ita curru concito per campum, qua maxime visi
poterat, praevolat hostem mirandum in modum circumtrahens, genus
poenae novum miserandumque.

DICTYS III.

III. 15.   After a few days news was suddenly brought that
Hector and a few other men had set out to meet Penthesilea, the
queen of the Amazons.[2] Why she was coming to Priam's aid,
whether for money or simply because of her love of war, was
uncertain; her race, being naturally warlike, was always conquering
the neighbouring peoples and carrying the Amazon standards far
and wide. Accordingly, Achilles chose a few faithful comrades and
hastened to lay an ambush for the Trojans. He caught them off
guard, they were trying to cross a river, and surrounded and slew
them before they knew what had occured. Hector and all those
who were with him were killed; with the single exception of one of
Priam's sons, whom Achilles captured and, having cut off his
hands, sent back to Troy to tell what had happened. Achilles was
being driven to bestial acts, first by the slaughter of his most hated
enemy, and then by his lasting grief for Patroclus. Having stripped
Hector of armour, he tied the body, feet bound together, behind his
chariot, then mounted and ordered Automedon, his charioteer, to
give the horses free reins. And so he went galloping over the plain
where he could be most easily seen dragging his enemy. A new
and terrible kind of revenge.

---

2 Penthesilea does not arrive until Dictys 4.2.

III. 16. At apud Troiam ubi spolia Hectoris desuper ex muris animadvertere, quae Graeci praecepto regis ante ora hostium praetulerant, et filius Priami praemissus ab Achille rem ut gesta erat disseruit, tantus undique versus per totam civitatem luctus atque clamor editur, ut aves etiam consternatae vocibus alto decidisse crederentur nostris cum insultatione reclamantibus. Ac mox portis ex omni parte urbs clauditur. Foedatur regni habitus atque in modum lugubrem funestumque obducta facies civitatis. Cum sicut in tali nuntio adsolet, repente cursus trepidantium fieret in eundem locum ac statim sine ulla certa ratione per diversum fuga. Nunc planctus crebri, modo urbe tota silentium ex incerto. inter quae et spes extremas multi credidere cum nocte simul Graecos moenia invasuros excisurosque urbem securos interitu tanti ducis, nonnulli etiam pro confirmato habere Achillem exercitum eum, qui duce Penthesilea Priami rebus auxilio venerat, partibus suorum adiunxisse, postremo omnia adversa hostilia fractas ablatasque opes, nullam salutis spem interempto Hectore in animo habere, quippe is solus omnium in ea civitate adversum tot milia imperatoresque hostium varia semper victoria certaverat. Cui fama bellandi inclito per gentes numquam tamen vires consilio superfuerant.

DICTYS III.

III. 16.   But at Troy, the Trojans, looking down from their walls, saw the armour of Hector, which Achilles had ordered the Greeks to carry within sight of the enemy. And the son of Priam whom Achilles had sent back told what had happened. Throughout the whole city there was weeping and wailing; in answer to which our men shouted insults. The noise was so loud that even the birds seemed to fall from the sky, dumbfounded, confused. All the gates of the city were closed. The kingdom, dressed in mourning, hid its face in woe. As often happens in such circumstances, the frenzied people would suddenly rush to one place and then, for no apparent reason, rush off again in all directions. Now there was shrieking everywhere; now an uncanny and total silence. Many of the Trojans were losing all hope. They thought that, with the coming of night, the Greeks, elated at the death of Hector, would make an attack against the walls and take the city by storm. Some of them believed that the army which Penthesilea had brought to aid Priam was now joined with Achilles; everything was adverse and hostile, all their power was broken and destroyed. They had no hope of safety, for Hector was dead. He alone had ever been an equal match for the countless hordes, for the many leaders of the enemy. His valour in battle was famed throughout the world and, nevertheless, it had not surpassed his wisdom.

III. 17.   Interim apud Graecos, ubi Achilles ad naves redit et cadaver Hectoris in ore omnium est, dolor, quem ob Patrocli interitum paulo ante perceperant, nece metuendi hostis et ob id praecipua laetitia circumscribitur. Ac tum universis placet, uti in honorem eius, quoniam abesset hostilis metus, certamen ludis solitum celebraretur. Neque minus tamen reliqui populi, qui non certaturi spectandi gratia convenerant, instructi armis paratique adessent, ne qua scilicet hostis quamvis fractis rebus solito tamen insidiandi more inrueret. Igitur Achilles victorum praemia, quae ei videbantur maxima, statui imperat. Et postquam nihil reliquum erat, reges omnes ad considendum hortatur, ipse medius atque inter eos excelsior. Tum primum quadriiugis equis Eumelus ante omnes victor declaratur, bigarum praemia Diomedes meruit, secundo post eum Menelaus.

III. 18.   Ceterum ad certandum qui sagittarum arte maxime praevalebant Meriones atque Ulixes duos erexere malos, quis religatum linum tenuissimum atque ex transverso extentum utriusque capiti adnectebatur, media columba sparto dependebat; eius contingendae certamen maximum. Tum reliquis incassum tendentibus Ulixes cum Merione destinatum confixere. Quibus cum a reliquis favor attolleretur, Philocteta non columbam se, verum id, quo religata esset, sagitta excisurum promittit. Admirantibus deinde difficultatem regibus, fidem promissi non felicius quam sollertius confirmavit; ita dirupto vinculo columba cum maxima populi adclamatione decidit. Praemia certaminis eius Meriones atque Ulixes tulere. Achilles duplici extra ordinem munere Philoctetam donat.

III. 17.   Meanwhile, among the Greeks, Achilles had brought the body of Hector back to the ships and shown it to everyone; the sorrow that we had recently felt for the death of Patroclus was replaced by exuberant joy over the slaughter of our formidable enemy. Since now there was nothing to fear from the Trojans, everyone was eager to hold games, as is customary at funerals, in honour of Patroclus.[3] The other peoples, moreover, who had come to watch and not participate, stood ready in arms to meet any attack the enemy, though broken in strength, might make in the usual treacherous way. Then Achilles ordered prizes to be set for the victors, things that he deemed of highest value. When everything was ready, he took a position in the midst of the kings, a little higher than the rest, and urged them all to take their seats. In the first contest, the four-horse chariot race, Eumelus was victor. No one could beat him. Diomedes won the prize in the two-horse chariot race. Menelaus came in second.

III. 18.   Next was the contest in archery. Ulysses and Meriones erected two masts between which, tied to the tops, they stretched a very thin cord, from the middle of which they hung a dove attached by a string. This was the target. Then all the contestants took their turns. But only Ulysses and Meriones hit the mark. They were congratulated by everyone, except Philoctetes who boasted that he could do better: he would cut the string by which the dove was suspended. Our leaders marvelled at the difficulty of what he was trying to do. Nevertheless, he, trusting in his skill more than in luck, made good his boast. The string was snapped and the dove fell to earth. A loud shout of approval arose from our men. Meriones and Ulysses received the prizes for this contest, but Achilles rewarded the exceptional feat of Philoctetes with a double prize.

---

3 Sections 17-19, which describe the funeral games in honour of Patroclus, should be compared with *Iliad* 23.

III. 19.   Cursu longo certantibus Oilei Aiax victor excipitur, post quem secundus Polypoetes. duplici campo Machaon, singulari Eurypylus, saltu Tlepolemus, disco Antilochus victores abeunt. Praemia luctandi intacta permansere, quippe Aiax arripiens medium Ulixem deicit, qui ruens pedibus eius circumvertitur, atque ita praepedito obligatoque nixu Aiax paene iam victor ad terram ruit. Caestibus reliquoque manuum certamine idem Aiax Telamonius palman refert. Cursu in armis postremo Diomedes praevaluit. Dein ubi praemia certaminis persoluta sunt, Achilles primum omnium Agamemnoni donum, quod ei honoratissimum videbatur, offert, secundo Nestori, Idomeneo tertio, post quos Podalirio et Machaoni, dein reliquis pro merito ducibus, ad postremum eorum sociis, qui in bello occiderant; hisque mandatum, uti, cum tempus fuisset, domum ad necessarios eorum perferrent. Postquam certandi praemiorumque finis factus et iam diei vesper erat, ad sua quisque tentoria discessere.

III. 19.   Ajax the son of Oileus won the long distance race. Polypoetes came in second. Machaon won the double-lap race, Eurypylus the single lap, Tlepolemus the high jump, and Antilochus the discus.

The prizes for wrestling went un-awarded. Ajax had almost beaten Ulysses, gripping him by the waist and throwing him down. But Ulysses, even while falling, had entangled the feet of his opponent and knocked him off balance. Thus both men were sprawled on the ground.

The same Ajax, the son of Telamon, carried off the palm in all of the boxing matches, including the fight with the cestus.

Diomedes won the last contest, the race in full armour.

After Achilles had awarded the prizes, he gave gifts; first, the gift he thought was most valuable to Agamemnon; then to Nestor, to Idomeneus, to Podalirius and Machaon, and to all the other leaders in order of their merit; and finally, to the comrades of those who had fallen in battle, commanding them to take the gifts home, when time allowed, to the relatives of the deceased. By the time that the games were completed and the prizes awarded, it was already evening and everyone went to his hut.

III. 20. At lucis principio Priamus lugubri veste miserabile tectus, cui dolor non decus regium, non ullam tanti nominis atque famae speciem reliquam fecerat, manibus vultuque supplicibus ad Achillem venit, quocum Andromacha, non minor quam in Priamo miseratio. Ea quippe deformata multiplici modo Astyanacta, quem nonnulli Scamandrium appellabant, et Laodamanta parvulos admodum filios prae se habens regi adiumentum deprecandi addiderat, qui maeroribus senioque decrepitus filiae Polyxenae umeris innitebatur. Dein sequebatur vehicula plena auri atque argenti pretiosaeque vestis, cum super murum despectantes Troiani comitatum regis oculis prosequerentur. Quo viso repente silentium ex admiratione oritur ac mox reges avidi noscere causas adventus eius procedunt obviam. Priamus ubi ad se tendi videt, protinus in os ruit pulverem reliquaque humi purgamenta capiti aspargens. Dein orat, uti miserati fortunas suas precatores secum ad Achillem veniant. Eius aetatem fortunamque recordatus Nestor dolet, contra Ulixes maledictis insequi et commemorare, quae ad Troiam in consilio ante sumptum bellum ipse adversum legatos dixerat. ea postquam Achilli nuntiata sunt, per Automedontem eum accersi iubet, ipse retinens gremio urnam cum Patrocli ossibus.

III. 20.   At daybreak Priam came to Achilles, a wretched sight, dressed in clothes of mourning, with suppliant face and suppliant hands, a king to whom grief had left no signs of royal majesty or former power and glory.[4] With him came Andromache, no less wretched than himself, her features marred in every way. To aid the king in his request, she brought her sons, leading them before her, two little boys, Astyanax (some called him Scamandrius) and Laodamas. Polyxena also came, supporting her father, as he tottered beneath the burden of his years and sorrows. Carts followed, filled with gold and silver and costly clothing. This is the picture of king and retinue that caused a sudden silence among the astonished Trojans watching from their walls.

Soon our leaders were going to meet Priam, eager to discover why he was coming. When Priam saw them advancing, he fell on his face and threw dust, and whatever filth he could find, over his head. He begged them to pity his fortunes and plead his case with Achilles.

His old age and ruined life evoked the sympathy of Nestor. Ulysses, however, cursed him, reminding him of how he had spoken against the envoys at Troy before the war had begun.

When Achilles learned of Priam's arrival, he sent Automedon to summon the king. He himself waited, holding the urn that contained the bones of Patroclus.

---

4 Sections 20-27, which describe the return of Hector's body, should be compared with *Iliad* 24.

III. 21.   Igitur ingressis ducibus nostris cum Priamo rex genua Achilli manibus complexus: *non tu mihi,* inquit, *causa huiusce fortunae, sed deorum quispiam, qui postremam aetatem meam, cum misereri deberet, in hasce aerumnas deduxit confectam iam ac defatigatam tantis luctibus filiorum. Quippe hi fisi regno per iuventutem, cum semper cupiditates animi quoquo modo explere gestiunt, ultro sibi mihique perniciem machinati sunt. Neque dubium cuiquam, quin contemptui sit adulescentiae senecta aetas. Quod si interitu meo reliqui huiusmodi facinoribus temperabunt, me quoque, si videtur, exhibeo poenae mortis, cui misero confectoque maeroribus omnes aerumnas, quibus nunc depressus infelicissimum spectaculum mortalibus praebeo, cum hoc exiguo spiritu simul auferes. Adsum en ultro, nihil deprecor, vel si ita cordi est, habe in custodia captivitatis. Neque enim mihi quicquam iam superioris fortunae reliquum est, quippe interfecto Hectore cuncta regni concidere. Sed si iam Graeciae universae ob meorum male consulta satis poenarum filiorum sanguine et meis aerumnis persolvi, miserere aetatis ac deos recordatus retorque animos ad pietatem: concede parvulis saltem non animam parentis, sed cadaver deprecantibus. Veniat in animum recordatio parentis tui omnes curas vigiliasque in te tuamque salutem impendentis. Sed illi quidem cuncta secundum sua vota proveniant longeque aliter neque mei similem senectam degat.*

III. 22.   Interea dum haec commemorat, paulatim animo deficere ac dissolvi membris, dein obmutescere occipit, quod spectaculum longe miserrimum omnibus, qui tum aderant, dolori fuit. Dein Andromacha parvulos Hectoris filios ante Achillem prosternit, ipsa fletu lamentabili orans, uti sibi cadaver coniugis intueri saltem concederetur. Inter haec tam miseranda Phoenix Priamum sustollere atque uti animum reciperet hortari. Tum rex ubi in aliquantum refovit spiritum, nixis genibus atque utraque manu caput dilanians: *ubi nunc illa est,* ait, *quae apud Graecos praecipue erat iusta misericordia? An solum in Priamum circumscribitur?*

172

III. 21. Accordingly, Priam, along with our leaders, entered the hut of Achilles. Then, clasping Achilles' knees, he said: 'You are not to blame for my misfortunes. It is one of the gods who, instead of pitying me, has brought the end of my life to ruin. Now I am overwhelmed and worn out with grief for my sons. They, confident in their youth and the resources of their kingdom, and always desiring to fulfil the desires of their hearts, have devised, contrary to their expectations, destruction both for themselves and for me. It is their maxim that old age should be despised by youth. Nevertheless, if my death will prevent those of my sons who are left from committing other crimes of this sort, I also offer myself, if thus it is pleasing, for capital punishment. Do as you wish. With one stroke take away my little life and all those tribulations which have made me a sorrowful wretch, a most miserable spectacle among men. Here I am. I ask no mercy. Take me captive, if you wish. Nothing remains of my former fortune; my kingdom fell when Hector died. But if I have already paid with my personal sorrows, with the blood of my sons, a sufficient penalty to all Greece for the ill-considered acts of my people, pity my age, consider the gods, remember piety. At least grant the petition of these young boys for the body, not the life, of their father, Hector. Remember your own father who is spending all of his waking hours thinking of you, wondering if you are safe. May all his prayers be answered. May he enjoy a good old age, one far different from mine'.

III. 22. While he was talking, his spirit was failing. Then, as he lost his power of speech, his legs gave way. Everyone who was present was pained at this very pitiable sight.

Then Andromache prostrated the small sons of Hector before Achilles. She herself was weeping; with a voice full of sorrow, she begged for permission only to look at the body of her husband.

During this pitiable scene, Phoenix was raising Priam and encouraging him to recover. When the king had revived somewhat, he spoke, while kneeling and pulling his hair with both hands: 'Where is that righteous mercy for which the Greeks were famous? Is it denied to Priam alone?'

III. 23.   Iamque omnibus dolore permotis Achilles decuisse ait filios eum suos initio ab eo, quod admiserint, facinore cohibere neque ipsum concedendo tanti delicti participem fieri. Ceterum ante id decennium non ita defessum senecta fuisse, ut suis despectui esset, sed obsedisse animos eorum desiderium rerum alienarum, neque ob mulieren solum unam, sed Atrei atque Pelopis divitiis inhiantes raptum res more incondito perrexisse; pro quis aequissimum esse eiusmodi poenas vel etiam graviores pendere. Namque ad id tempus Graecos secutos morem in bellis optimum, quoscumque hostium pugna conficeret, sepulturae restituere solitos, contra Hectorem supergressum humanitatis modum, Patroclum eripere proelio ausum, scilicet ad inludendum ac foedandum cadaver eius, quod exemplum poenis ac suppliciis eorum eluendum, ut Graeci ac reliquae posthac gentes memores ultionis eius moremque humanae condicionis tuerentur. non enim Helenae neque Menelai gratia exercitum relictis sedibus parvulisque procul ab domo, cruentum suo hostilique sanguine inter ipsa belli discrimina huiusmodi militiam tolerare, sed cupere dinoscere, barbarine Graecine summa rerum potirentur, quamquam iustam causam fuisse inferendi belli etiam pro muliere. Namque uti ipsi raptu rerum alienarum laetarentur, ita maxime dolori esse his, qui amiserint. Ad haec multa infausta detestandaque imprecari confirmareque se capto Ilio ante omnes tanti admissi poenas sanguine eius expetere, ob quam patria parentibusque carens Patroclum etiam solitudinis suae levamen maximum amiserit.

III. 23.   Everyone was deeply moved. Achilles, however, said that Priam should have prevented his sons from their inhuman acts in the beginning. By acquiescing, he had become their accomplice in treachery. Ten years ago he was not so old that they would have refused to listen to him, but, as it was, their greed, their lust for the property of others, had driven them to monstrous acts; they had carried off not only a woman but also the wealth of Atreus and Pelops. It was simple justice that they should receive their present punishments, or even worse. Until now, the Greeks had obeyed civilised rules of war and returned the bodies of their enemies for burial, but Hector had acted contrary to the laws of human nature when he dragged the body of Patroclus from the battle, with the evident intent of abusing and defiling it. Now the Trojans must bear their punishments in expiation of this crime. Thus, in future time, the Greeks and other peoples, remembering what had happened in this case, would keep the natural law. The Greeks had not left their homes and children and come to fight this bloody, toilsome war just for Helen's sake, or Menelaus'. What they really wanted to decide was who would rule the world, themselves or the barbarians. Nevertheless, the abduction of a woman was cause enough for an invasion: those who are plundered grieve over their losses no less than the plunderers delight in their gains. So saying, Achilles called down curses upon Helen, swearing that when Troy was taken he would slay her in public, a fitting reward for her crime. He blamed her for his loss of native land and parents and, also, of the greatest consolation of his homesick heart, Patroclus.

III. 24.   Dein consiliatum cum supradictis ducibus surgit. quis omnibus una atque eadem sententia est, scilicet uti acceptis quae allata essent corpus exanime concederet. Quod ubi satis placuit, singuli ad sua tentoria discedunt. moxque Polyxena ingresso Achille obvoluta genibus eius sponte servitium sui pro absolutione cadaveris pollicetur. Quo spectaculo adeo commotus iuvenis, ut, qui inimicissimus ob mortem Patrocli Priamo eiusque regno esset, tum recordatione filii ac parentis ne lacrimis quidem temperaverit. Itaque manu oblata Polyxenam erigit praedicta prius mandataque cura Phoenici super Priamo. Sed rex nil se luctus neque praesentium miseriarum remissurum ait. tum Achilles confirmare non prius cupitis eius satis futurum quam mutato in melius habitu cibum etiam secum sumeret. Ita rex veritus, ne quae concessa videbantur, ipse recusando impediret, demisse omnia quaeque imperarentur facienda decrevit.

III. 24.   Then Achilles stood up and went out to consult with the leaders mentioned above. He was persuaded to follow their unanimous advice; he would accept the gifts that were being offered and hand over the body of Hector. When this had been decided, the leaders departed to their different huts, and he returned to his.

Upon his reentry, Polyxena fell at his feet and promised to be his willing slave if he would return the body. This sight, and also the thought of father and son, moved him to tears, in spite of all of his hatred for Priam and Troy because of Patroclus' death. Thus he gave Polyxena his hand and helped her to rise; but first he showed his concern for Priam and commanded Phoenix to comfort him. When, however, Priam refused to be consoled and continued to lament, Achilles swore that Priam's wishes would not be satisfied until he had changed into better clothes and dined with him. And so the king, fearing to refuse, lest he lose what seemed to have been granted, decided humbly to submit to the will of Achilles.

III. 25.　　　Igitur ubi excussus comis pulvis totusque lautus est, mox a iuvene ipseque et qui cum eo venerant, cibo invitantur. Dein ubi satias omnes tenuit, hoc modo Achilles disseruit: *refer nunc iam mihi, Priame, quid tantum causae fuerit, cur deficientibus quidem vobis in dies copiis militaribus, ingravescentibus autem calamitatibus atque aerumnis Helenam tamen in hodiernum retinendam putetis neque velut contagionem infausti ominis reppuleritis? Quam prodidisse patriam parentesque et, quod indignissimum omnium est, fratres sanctissimos cognoveritis. Namque hi execrati facinus eius ne in militiam quidem nobiscum coniuraverunt, scilicet ne, quam audiri incolumem nollent, ei per se reditum in patriam quaererent. Eam igitur, cum cerneretis malo omnium civitatem intravisse vestram, non eiecistis? Non cum detestationibus extra muros prosecuti estis? Quid illi senes, quorum filios pugna in dies conficit? Nonne adhuc persenserunt eandem causam extitisse tantorum funerum? Itane ergo divinitus vobis eversa mens est, ut nullus in tanta civitate reperiri possit, qui fortunam labentis patriae dolens de pernicie publica cum exitio eius transigat? Ego quidem aetatis tuae contemplatione atque horum precum cadaver restituam neque umquam committam, ut, quod in hostibus reprehenditur crimen malitiae, ipse subeam.*

III. 25.   After shaking the dust from his hair, he took a bath; and then he and his retinue went to dine with Achilles. When everyone had had enough to eat, their host spoke as follows: 'Now tell me, Priam, what was the real reason you thought Helen should be kept so long, even when your military efforts were failing and your troubles and tribulations were steadily mounting? Why did you not drive her out, like an ill-omened plague? You knew that she had betrayed her native land and parents and, what was most disgraceful, her godlike brothers.[5] These brothers cursed her crime and refused even to join with us in this campaign, lest, to be sure, they should be responsible for obtaining her return. Why, when she had come to Troy to be a bane to everyone, why did you not cast her out? Why did you not drive her from your walls with curses? Why did the elders of Troy acquiesce when their sons were dying every day in battle? Could it be that they did not know that she alone was causing all those deaths? Is everyone in Troy so demonically infatuated that no one can be found to pity the failing fortunes of his country and try to save her with the death of Helen? For my part, I honour both your old age and your prayers. I shall return the body. Never shall I allow myself to be guilty of crimes I condemn in my enemies'.

---

5 Helen's godlike brothers were Castor and Pollux. See *Iliad* 3.236-242.

III. 26. Ad ea Priamus renovato fletu quam miserabili non sine decreto divum adversa hominibus inruere ait, deum quippe auctorem singulis mortalibus boni malique esse neque quoad beatum esse licitum sit, cuiusquam in eum vim inimicitiasque procedere. Ceterum se diversi partus quinquaginta filiorum patrem beatissimum regum omnium habitum ad postremum Alexandri natalem diem, quem evitari ne dis quidem praecinentibus potuisse. Namque Hecubam foetu eo gravidam facem per quietem edidisse visam, cuius ignibus conflagravisse Idam ac mox continuante flamma deorum delubra concremari omnemque demum ad cineres conlapsam civitatem intactis inviolatisque Antenoris et Anchisae domibus. Quae denuntiata cum ad perniciem publicam expectare aruspices praecinerent, inter necandum editum partum placuisse. Sed Hecubam more femineae miserationis clam alendum pastoribus in Idam tradidisse. Eum iam adultum, cum res palam esset, ne hostem quidem quamvis saevissimum, ut interficeret, pati potuisse, tantae scilicet fuisse eum pulchritudinis atque formae. Quem coniugio deinde Oenonae iunctum cupidinem cepisse visendi regiones atque regna procul posita. Eo itinere abductam Helenam urgente atque instigante quodam numine cunctorum civium animis, sibi etiam laetitiae fuisse, neque cuiquam, cum orbari se filio aliove consanguineo cerneret, non acceptam tamen, solo omnium adversante Antenore, qui initio post Alexandri reditum filium suum Glaucum, quod eius comitatum secutus erat, abdicandum a penatibus suis decreverit, vir domi belloque prudentissimus. Ceterum sibi, quoniam ita res ruerent, optatissimum adpropinquare naturae finem omissis iam regni gubernaculis atque cura; tantum se in Hecubae filiarumque recordatione cruciari, quas post excidium patriae captivas incertum cuius domini fastus manerent.

III. 26.   These words made Priam begin to weep again. He said that it had been the will of the gods for him to go to war. The gods were the authors of good and evil for every mortal; so long as he had been permitted to be happy, the might of none of his enemies had succeeded against him. He who had fathered fifty sons by different mothers had been considered the most blessed of all kings, until the birth of the youngest, Alexander. He had been unable to avoid the future, even though the gods had revealed the events that Alexander would cause. When Hecuba was pregnant, she had told him how she had dreamt of a torch in whose flames Mount Ida and then, as the fire continued, the shrines of the gods and finally the whole state had been consumed, excepting only the homes of Antenor and Anchises. The interpreters had said that this dream portended the fall of Troy. Accordingly, they had decided to kill the baby at birth, but Hecuba with a woman's tenderness toward her child, had given him secretly to shepherds to rear on Mount Ida. When he was grown, and they knew what had happened, he was so handsome that no one, not even his fiercest enemy, could bear to kill him. Then he had married Oenone. Soon, however, having been seized with a desire of seeing faraway regions and kingdoms, he had gone on that journey on which he carried off Helen; some god was urging him, driving him on. As for Helen, all the Trojans, including Priam himself, loved her. Not even the thought of the deaths of their sons and relatives could persuade them to reject her. Only Antenor, his wisest counsellor in peace and war, was for this; Antenor, in the beginning, when Alexander returned from Greece, even disowned his own son, Glaucus, because he had gone along on that journey. Now Troy was being destroyed and he, the king, was near to death. In fact, he longed to die and give up the burden of being king. He was tortured only by the thought that when his country fell, Hecuba and his daughters would be enslaved. What masters, what shame, would they have to endure?

III. 27.　　　Dein omnia, quae ad redimendum filium advectaverat, ante conspectum iuvenis exponi imperat. Ex quis quicquid auri atque argenti fuit tolli Achilles iubet, vestis etiam quod ei visum est; reliquis in unum collectis Polyxenam donat et cadaver tradidit. Quo recepto rex in gratiamne impetrati funeris an si quid Troiae accideret securus iam filiae, amplexus Achillis genua orat, uti Polyxenam suscipiat sibique habeat. Super qua iuvenis aliud tempus atque alium locum tractatumque fore respondit; interim cum eo reverti iubet. Ita Priamus recepto Hectoris cadavere ascensoque vehiculo cum his, qui se comitati erant, ad Troiam redit.

III. 27.   When Priam had finished this speech, he ordered that everything be displayed which he had brought to ransom his son. Achilles commanded the gold and silver to be removed, and also the clothes he liked best. Having gathered together what was left, he gave it to Polyxena. Then he handed over the body to Priam. The king, whether desiring to show his gratitude for being able to hold the funeral, or hoping to insure the safety of his daughter if Troy should fall, fell at the knees of Achilles and begged him to take Polyxena and keep her for himself. The young man answered that she should return with her father; they would see about her at some other time and in some other place.

Thus Priam recovered the body of Hector and, mounting his chariot, returned to Troy along with the others.

LIBER QUARTVS

IV. 1.   Sed postquam Troianis palam est regem perfecto negotio inviolatum atque integro comitatu regredi, admirati laudantesque Graeciae pietatem ad caelum ferunt, quippe quis animo ita haeserat nulla spe impetrandi cadaveris ipsumque et qui cum eo fuissent retineri ab Graecis, maxime ob Helenae, quae non remitteretur, recordationem. Ceterum viso Hectoris funere cuncti cives sociique adcurrentes fletum tollunt, divellentes comam foedantesque ora laniatibus, neque in tanta populi multitudine quisquam in se virtutis aut spei bonae fiduciam credere illo interfecto, qui inclita per gentes fama rerum militarium, in pace etiam praeclara pudicitia, ex qua haud minorem, quam reliquis artibus gloriam adeptus erat. Interea sepelivere eum haud longe a tumulo Ili regis quondam. Dein exorto quam maximo ululatu postrema funeri peragunt, hinc feminis cum Hecuba deflentibus, hinc reclamantibus Troianis viris et ad postremum sociorum gentibus. Quae per dies decem concessa bellandi requie ab ortu solis ad usque vesperam per Troianos gesta nullo usquam remisso lugendi officio.

Book Four

IV. 1.   On learning that the king had accomplished his mission and returned unharmed along with the others, the Trojans praised the Greeks' compassion. Priam, they had thought, would never obtain the body; the Greeks would feel justified in holding him prisoner since they, the Trojans, had refused to give Helen up.

When they saw Hector's body, everyone, including the allies, ran forward. They were weeping and pulling their hair and scratching their faces. The city was ruled by despair. Hector, whose deeds in war and peace alike were known throughout the world, his fame being due to his righteous character no less than to his martial spirit, Hector was dead. They buried him close to the tomb of their former king Ilus;[1] and, gathering around, on this side the women with Hecuba, on that the Trojan men and their allies, they raised the mournful dirge. For ten days from sunrise until sunset, the time of the truce, everyone, without ceasing, wailed for Hector, as was his due.

---

1 The tomb of Ilus is mentioned in *Iliad* 10.415 and 11.372.

IV. 2.   Interim per eosdem dies Penthesilea, de qua ante
memoravimus, cum magna Amazonum manu reliquisque ex finitimo
populis supervenit. Quae postquam interemptum Hectorem cognovit,
perculsa morte eius regredi domum cupiens ad postremum multo auro
atque argento ab Alexandro inlecta ibidem opperiri decreverat. Dein exactis
aliquot diebus copias suas armis instruit. At seorsum ab Troianis ipsa suis
modo bellatoribus satis fidens in pugnam pergit: cornu dextro sagittariis,
altero peditibus instructo, medios equites collocat; in quis ipsa. contra ab
nostris ita occursum, ut sagittariis Menelaus atque Ulixes et cum Teucro
Meriones, peditibus Aiaces duo, Diomedes, Agamemnon, Tlepolemus et
cum Ialmeno Ascalaphus opponerentur, in equites ab Achille et reliquis
ducibus pugnaretur. Hoc modo instructo utrimque exercitu conflixere acies.
Cadunt sagittis reginae plurimi neque ab Teucro secus bellatum. Interim
Aiaces et qui cum his erant pedites, contra quos steterant, caedere ac
restantes detrudere umbonibus, moxquo repulsos obtruncare. neque, quoad
deletae peditum copiae, finis fit.

Dicrys IV

IV. 2.   During the funeral Penthesilea (whom we have mentioned above) arrived. She brought a huge army of Amazons and other neighbouring peoples. On being informed of Hector's death, she was very upset and desired to go home. But Alexander gave her much gold and silver, and finally prevailed upon her to stay.

Several days later she drew up her forces and made an attack, without any help from the Trojans, so great was her trust in her people. She arranged the archers on the right flank, the foot soldiers on the left, and the cavalry, to which she herself belonged, in the centre. Our men were drawn up to meet her, with Menelaus, Ulysses, Meriones, and Teucer against the archers, the two Ajaxes, Diomedes, Agamemnon, Tlepolemus, Ascalaphus, and Ialmenus against the foot soldiers, and Achilles, along with the others, against the cavalry. Thus the two armies, having drawn up their forces, joined battle. The queen slaughtered many, using her bow; as did Teucer for us. Meanwhile the Ajaxes were leading the foot soldiers; advancing with their shields before them and pushing back any who got in their way, they wreaked general havoc; no one, it seemed, could stop them from destroying the enemy.

IV. 3.　　　Achilles inter equitum turmas Penthesileam nactus hasta petit, neque difficilius quam feminam equo deturbat manu comprehendens comam atque ita graviter vulneratam detrahens. quod ubi visum est, tum vero nullam spem in armis rati fugam faciunt. Clausisque civitatis portis nostri reliquos, quos fuga bello exemerat, insecuti obtruncant, feminis tamen abstinentes manus parcentesque sexui. Dein uti quisque victor, interfectis quos adversum ierant, regrediebatur, Penthesileam visere seminecem etiam nunc admirarique audaciam. Ita brevi ab omnibus in eundem locum concursum placitumque, uti, quoniam naturae sexusque condicionem superare ausa esset, in fluvium reliquo adhuc ad persentiendum spiritu aut canibus dilanianda iaceretur. Achilles interfectam eam sepelire cupiens mox a Diomede prohibitus est. Is namque percontatus circumstantes, quidnam de ea faciendum esset, consensu omnium pedibus adtractam in Scamandrum praecipitat, scilicet poenam postremae desperationis atque amentiae. Hoc modo Amazonum regina deletis copiis, quibuscum auxiliatum Priamo venerat, ad postremum ipsa spectaculum dignum moribus suis praebuit.

IV. 3. Achilles found Penthesilea among the cavalry and, hurling his spear, hit the mark. Then, no trouble now that she was wounded, he seized her by the hair and pulled her off her horse. Her followers, seeing her fallen, became disheartened and took to flight. We pursued and cut down those who were unable to reach the gates before they closed; nevertheless, we abstained from touching the women because of their sex.

Then we returned, all of us victors, our enemies slain. Finding Penthesilea still half-alive, we marvelled at her brazen boldness. Almost immediately a meeting was held to determine her fate, and it was decided to throw her, while still alive enough to have feeling, either into the river to drown or out for the dogs to tear apart, for she had transgressed the bounds of nature and her sex. Achilles favoured just letting her die and then giving her burial. Diomedes, however, prevailed: going around, he asked everyone what to do and won a unanimous vote in favour of drowning. Accordingly, dragging her by the feet, he dumped her into the Scamander. It goes without saying that this was a very cruel and barbarous act. But thus the queen of the Amazons, having lost the forces she had brought to aid Priam, died in a way that befitted her foolhardy character.

IV. 4. At sequenti die Memnon, Tithoni atque Aurorae filius, ingentibus Indorum atque Aethiopum copiis supervenit, magna fama, quippe in unum multis milibus armatis vario genere spes etiam votaque de se Priami superaverat. Namque omnia circum Troiam et ultra, quae visi poterant, viris atque equis repleta splendore insignium refulgebant. Eos omnes iugis Caucasi montis ad Troiam duxit, reliquos neque numero inferiores imposito Phala duce atque rectore mari misit. Qui adpulsi Rhodum, ubi animadvertere insulam Graecis sociam, veriti, ne re cognita incenderentur naves, ibidem opperiebantur; ac mox divisi in Camirum et Ialysum, urbes opulentas. neque multo post Rhodii Phalam incusare, quod paulo ante eversa ab Alexandro Sidona, patria sua, auxilium ei, a quo laesus sit, ferre cuperet. quo animos exercitus permoverent, confirmare haud dissimiles barbarorum videri eos, qui tam indignum facinus defenderent. Multa praeterea, quae accensura vulgum et pro se facturi essent, disserere. quae res haud frustra fuit. Phoenices namque, qui in eo exercitu plurimi aderant, permoti querelis Rhodiorum an cupidine diripiendarum rerum, quas secum advexerant, Phalam lapidibus insecuti necant distributique per supradictas urbes aurum ac reliqua praedae inter se dispertiunt.

190

IV. 4. On the following day, Memnon, the son of Tithonus and Aurora, arrived with a large army of Indians and Ethiopians, a truly remarkable army which consisted of thousands upon thousands of men with various kinds of arms, and surpassed the hopes and prayers even of Priam. All the country around and beyond Troy, as far as eye could see, was filled with men and horses, and glittered with the splendour of arms and standards. Memnon had led these forces to Troy by way of the Caucasus mountains.

At the same time he had sent another group of equal size by sea, with Phalas as their guide and leader. These others had landed on the island of Rhodes, which they soon discovered to be an ally of Greece. At first, fearing that when the purpose of their mission was known, their ships might be fired, they stayed in the harbour. Later, however, dividing their strength, they went to the wealthy cities of Camirus and Ialysus.

Soon the Rhodians were blaming Phalas for trying to aid Alexander, the same Alexander who had recently conquered Phalas' country, Sidon.[2] In order to stir up the army, they said that whoever defended this crime was in no way different from a barbarian; and they added many such things as would incense the common soldiers and make them take their side. Nor did they fail in their intent, for the Phoenicians, who composed a majority of Phalas' army, whether influenced by the accusations of the Rhodians, or wishing to gain control of the wealth their ships were carrying, made an attack against Phalas and stoned him to death. Then, dividing their gold and whatever booty they had, they dispersed to the cities we mentioned above.

---

2 See Dictys 1.5.

IV. 5.   Interim exercitus, qui cum Memnone venerat, positis per locos patulos castris – nam intra moenia haud facile tanta vis hominum retineri poterat – diversi suo quisque genere exercebantur. Neque in eadem arte simplex atque idem modus, sed ut quemque regionis suae mos adsuefecerat, ita telis aliis in alium modum formatis, scutorum etiam et galearum multiformi specie horrendam belli faciem praebuerant. At ubi triti aliquot dies et miles bellum cupit, simul cum luce exercitus omnis signo dato in proelium ducitur cumque his Troiani et qui intra moenia socii fuerant. At contra Graeci instructi pro tempore opperiri, debilitati aliquantum animos metu ingentis atque incogniti hostis. Igitur ubi intra teli iactum ventum est, tum vero barbari clamore ingenti ac dissono ruinae in modum inrumpunt, nostri confirmati inter se satis impigre vim hostium sustentavere. Sed postquam acies renovatae atque in ordinem reformatae sunt et iaci hinc atque inde tela coepere, cadunt utriusque exercitus plurimi, neque finis fit, quoad Memnon curru vectus adhibito secum fortissimo quoque medios Graecorum invadit, primum quemque obvium fundens aut debilitans. Ita iam plurimis nostrorum interfectis duces, ubi fortuna belli eversa neque spes reliqua nisi in fuga est, victoriam concessere. eo die incensae deletaeque naves omnes forent, ni nox, perfugium laborantium, ingruentes hostes ab incepto cohibuisset. Tanta in Memnone bellandi vis peritiaque et nostris adversae res.

IV.5.   Meanwhile the army that had come with Memnon had set up camp in a wide area (the walls of the city could not have easily contained so great a number of men), and everyone, each in his own particular group, was training for combat. These groups differed in their fighting methods and skills according to the regions from which they came. Their different kinds of weapons, their different kinds of shields and helmets, gave them a terrifying warlike appearance.

Then at dawn, after several days, when his soldiers were ready to fight, Memnon gave them the signal and led them to battle. And the Trojans, along with their allies, left the protection of their walls and also advanced. We, for our part, drew up our forces to meet them, being somewhat awed by the size of our unknown enemy. When they had come within a spear's throw of our side, they fell upon us with a huge and dissonant clamour. It was like a landslide. Our men, standing together, were able to break their attack. But soon their lines were renewed and reformed, and weapons were flying this way and that, and many on both sides were dying. Nor was there any end in sight, so long as Memnon, accompanied by all of his bravest men, was attacking our centre, riding in his chariot, and slaying or wounding whomever he met. Our casualties were mounting terribly, and our leaders conceded defeat; they felt that we were destined to lose and that our only hope was in flight. However night, the refuge of the oppressed, kept the enemy off. Otherwise, that day would have seen our ships destroyed by fire; so great was Memnon's power and martial skill, so grievous our predicament.

IV. 6.   Igitur Graeci, postquam requies est, perculsi inter se ac summae rerum diffidentes per universam noctem quos in bello amiserant sepelivere. Dein consilium futuri certaminis adversum Memnonem ineunt; ac placet sorte eligi nomen ducis cum eo bellaturi. Tunc Agamemnon Menelaum excipit, Ulixem, Idomeneum; reliquorum sors agi coepta Aiacem Telamonium votis omnium deligit. Ita refectis cibo corporibus reliquum noctis cum quiete transigunt. At lucis principio armati instructique pro negotio egrediuntur. Neque segnius a Memnone actum, cum quo Troiani omnes. Ita hinc atque inde ordinato exercitu proelium initum. Plurimi utriusque partis, ut in tali certamine, cadunt aut icti graviter proelio decedunt. In quo bello Antilochus Nestoris obvius forte Memnoni interficitur. moxque Aiax, ubi tempus visum est, inter utramque aciem progressus lacessit regem, praedicto prius Ulixi et Idomeneo, ab ceteris uti se defenderent. Igitur Memnon ubi ad se tendi videt, curru desilit confligitque pedes cum Aiace magno utriusque partis metu atque expectatione, cum dux noster summa vi umbonem scuti eius telo in aliquantum foratum gravis atque summis viribus ingruens impulit vertitque in latus. Quo viso regis comites adcurrere Aiacem exturbare nitentes. Tum Achilles, ubi barbaris intercedi videt, pergit contra et nudatum scuto hostis iugulum hasta transfigit.

IV. 6.   When the fighting had stopped, we, being broken in spirit and fearing the war's final outcome, spent the night burying those we had lost in battle. Then we thought of a plan; one of our men should challenge Memnon to fight in single combat. Accordingly, we proceeded to choose a champion by lot. The lots of all were shaken, excepting only, as Agamemnon requested, those of Menelaus, Ulysses, and Idomeneus; and Ajax, the son of Telamon, in answer to everyone's prayers, was chosen. Then we ate and renewed our strength and spent the rest of the night in sleep.

At daybreak we armed, drew up our forces in order, and went out to battle. Memnon, no less alert, also advanced, and with him all the Trojans. When both of the armies were ready, the battle was joined. As might be expected, a great number of men fell dead on both sides, or withdrew mortally wounded. It was in this battle that Antilochus, the son of Nestor, ran into Memnon, and thus met his death.

When Ajax thought that the time was right, he went out between the lines and challenged the king. First, however, he called on Ulysses and Idomeneus to defend him in case any others attacked. Memnon, seeing Ajax advance, leaped from his chariot and met him on foot. Among both armies fear and hope were running high. Finally Ajax thrust his spear into the centre of Memnon's shield and, using all his weight and force, shoved it through and into Memnon's side. The companions of Memnon, when they saw what had happened, rushed to his aid and tried to push Ajax away. But this interference on the part of the barbarians stirred Achilles to act; he entered the fray and drove his spear through Memnon's throat, where the shield gave no protection.

IV. 7.   Ita praeter spem interfecto Memnone animi hostium commutantur et Graecis aucta fiducia. Iamque Aethiopum versa acie nostri instantes caedunt plurimos. Tum Polydamas renovare proelium cupiens circumventus ad postremum atque ictus inguina ab Aiace interficitur, Glaucus Antenoris adversum Diomedem adstans Agamemnonis telo cadit. Tum vero cerneres hinc Aethiopas cum Troianis per omnem campum sine ordine atque imperio fugientes multitudine ae festinatione inter se implicari cadere ac mox palantibus equis proculcari, hinc Graecos resumptis animis sequi caedere impeditosque dissolvere atque ita confodere laxatos. Redundant circa muros campi sanguine et omnia, qua hostis intraverat, armis atque cadaveribus completa sunt. In ea pugna Priami filiorum Aretus et Echemmon ab Ulixe interfecti, Dryops, Bias et ‡Chorithan ab Idomeneo, ab Aiace Oilei Ilioneus cum Philenore, itemque Thyestes et Telestes a Diomede, ab Aiace altero Antiphus, Agavus, Agathon atque Glaucus et ab Achille Asteropaeus. Neque prius finis factas, quam Graecos satias et ad postremum fatigatio incessit.

IV. 7. Memnon's unexpected death, while breaking the enemy's spirit, bolstered ours. Now the Ethiopians had turned and were fleeing; now our men were pursuing, wreaking great slaughter. Polydamas tried to renew the battle, but soon was surrounded and fell, hit in the groin by Ajax and Glaucus, the son of Antenor, was killed; he was fighting Diomedes when Agamemnon struck him down with a spear. One might see Ethiopians and Trojans fleeing everywhere over the field in disorder, without leaders, crowding and rushing, hindering each other, falling where unguided horses were trampling them down. Our men, their spirits renewed, were attacking and slaughtering the enemy, scattering those who had been entangled and then picking them off with their spears. The field near the walls was flowing with blood; armour and corpses abounded wherever the enemy went. It was in this battle that Priam lost the following sons: Aretus and Echemmon were killed by Ulysses; Dryops, Bias, and Chorithan[3] were killed by Idomeneus; Ilioneus and Philenor by Ajax the son of Oileus; Thyestes and Telestes by Diomedes; Antiphus, Agavus, Agathon, and Glaucus by the other Ajax; and Asteropaeus by Achilles. There was no end to the slaughter until our men were finally thoroughly sated, thoroughly tired.

---

3 The spelling of this name is doubtful.

IV. 8.   At ubi ab nostris in castra recessum est, missi ab Troianis, qui peterent eorum, qui in bello ceciderant, humandi veniam. Collectos suos quisque igni cremant et more patrio sepeliunt seorsum ab ceteris cremato Memnone, cuius reliquias urnae conditas per necessarios regis remisere in patrium solum. At Graeci lautum bene cadaver Anticholi iustisque factis Nestori tradunt eumque orant, ferret animo aequo fortunae bellique adversa. Ita ad postremum corpora sua quisque curantes vino atque epulis per multam noctem Aiacem simulque Achillem laudibus celebrant atque ad caelum ferunt. At apud Troiam, ubi requies funerum est, non iam dolor in casu Memnonis, sed metus summae rerum et desperatio incesserat, cum hinc Sarpedonis interitus, inde secuta paulo post Hectoris clades spes reliquas animis abstulissent neque, quod postremum in Memnone fortuna obtulerat, reliquum iam existeret. Ita confluentibus in unum tot adversis curam omnem exsurgendi omiserant.

IV. 8.   When we had returned to camp, the Trojans sent envoys to obtain permission to bury their dead. Thus the dead were gathered, each by his own, and cremated and buried according to ancient custom. Memnon, however, was cremated apart from the others; his remains were put in an urn and given to relatives to take to his native land.[4]

When we had duly washed the body of Antilochus, we handed it over to Nestor for proper burial and begged him to bear the adversities of war with courage. Then, finally, each of us spent much of the night honouring his dead with wine and funeral feasts, and praising both Ajax and Achilles in highest terms.

The Trojans, with the completion of their funerals, ended their grief over Memnon's disaster. But now they were gripped by despair; they feared the war's final outcome. The death of Sarpedon and, soon afterwards, the slaughter of Hector, had taken away their remaining hopes; and now what fortune had for the last time offered in the person of Memnon no longer remained. Thus, with so many adversities conspiring against them, their will to recover was utterly gone.

---

4 In the *Aethiopis* (frag. 1, p. 507, ed. Evelyn-White), Aurora obtains immortality for her son from Jupiter.

IV. 9.   At post paucos dies Graeci instructi armis processere in campum lacessentes, si auderent, ad bellandum Troianos. Quis dux Alexander cum reliquis fratribus militem ordinat atque adversum pergit. Sed priusquam ferire inter se acies aut iaci tela coepere, barbari desolatis ordinibus fugam faciunt. Caesique eorum plurimi aut in flumen praeceps dati, cum hinc atque inde ingrueret hostis atque undique adempta fuga esset. capti etiam Lycaon et Troilus Priamidae, quos in medium productos Achilles iugulari iubet indignatus nondum sibi a Priamo super his, quae secum tractaverat, mandatum. Quae ubi animadvertere Troiani, tollunt gemitus et clamore lugubri Troili casum miserandum in modum deflent recordati aetatem eius admodum immaturam, qui in primis pueritiae annis cum verecundia ac probitate, tum praecipue forma corporis amabilis atque acceptus popularibus adolescebat.

IV. 10.   Deinde transactis paucis diebus solemne Thymbraei Apollinis incessit et requies bellandi per indutias interposita. Tum utroque exercitu sacrificio insistente Priamus tempus nactus Idaeum ad Achillem super Polyxena cum mandatis mittit. Sed ubi Achilles in luco ea, quae inlata erant, cum Idaeo separatim ab aliis recognoscit, cognita re apud naves suspicio alienati ducis et ad postremum indignatio exorta. Namque antea rumorem proditionis ortum clementer per exercitum in verum traxerant. Ob quae simul uti concitatus militis animus leniretur, Aiax cum Diomede et Ulixe ad lucum pergunt hique ante templum resistunt opperientes, si egrederetur, Achillem, simulque uti rem gestam iuveni referrent, de cetero etiam deterrerent in colloquio clam cum hostibus agere.

IV. 9. After a few days the Greeks took up arms and, having gone onto the field, challenged the Trojans to come out and fight, if they dared. Alexander and his brothers, in answer to this challenge, set their army in order and led it forth, but before the battle lines could meet or spears be thrown, the barbarians broke formation and took to flight. We rushed upon them, from this side and that, slaughtering great numbers, or hurling them headlong into the river; they had no way to escape. And two of Priam's sons were captured, Lycaon and Troilus, the throats of whom, when they had been brought forth into the centre, were cut, by order of Achilles, who was angry with Priam for not having seen to that business they had discussed. The Trojans raised a cry of grief and, mourning loudly, bewailed the fact that Troilus had met so grievous a death, for they remembered how young he was, who, being in the early years of his manhood, was the people's favourite, their darling, not only because of his modesty and honesty, but more especially because of his handsome appearance.

IV. 10. After a few days, the religious festival of the Thymbraean Apollo began; a truce was made and hostilities ceased. Then, while both armies were preoccupied with sacrificing, Priam found time to send Idaeus to Achilles with instructions concerning Polyxena. While, however, Achilles was examining these instructions, alone in the grove with Idaeus, word of this meeting was brought to the ships. Our men were angered, suspecting Achilles of being disloyal, for the rumour that he was a traitor had gradually grown and now was accepted as truth throughout the whole army. Therefore, in order to placate the enraged emotions of the soldiers, Ajax, Diomedes and Ulysses went to the grove and stood in front of the temple, waiting for Achilles to leave. They likewise wanted to tell him what had happened at the ships and hoped to deter him from further secret dealings with Trojans.

IV. 11.   Interim Alexander compositis iam cum Deiphobo insidiis pugionem cinctus ad Achillem ingreditur confirmator veluti eorum, quae Priamus pollicebatur moxque ad aram, quo ne hostis dolum persentisceret aversusque a duce, adsistit. Dein ubi tempus visum est, Deiphobus amplexus inermem iuvenem quippe in sacro Apollinis nihil hostile metuentem exosculari gratularique super his, quae consensisset, neque ab eo divelli aut omittere, quoad Alexander librato gladio procurrensque adversum hostem per utrumque latus geminato ictu transfigit. At ubi dissolutum vulneribus animadvertere, e parte alia, quam venerant, proruunt, re ita maxima et super vota omnium perfecta, in civitatem recurrunt. Quos visos Ulixes: *non temere est,* inquit, *quod hi turbati ac trepidi repente prosiluere.* Dein ingressi lucum circumspicientesque universa animadvertunt Achillem stratum humi exsanguem atque etiam tum seminecem. tum Aiax: *fuit,* inquit, *confirmatum ac verum per mortales nullum hominum existere potuisse, qui te vera virtute superaret, sed, ut palam est, tua te inconsulta temeritas prodidit.* Dein Achilles extremum adhuc retentans spiritum: *dolo me atque insidiis,* inquit, *Deiphobus atque Alexander Polyxenae gratia circumvenere.* Tum exspirantem eum duces amplexi cum magno gemitu atque exosculati postremum salutant. denique Aiax exanimem iam umeris sublatum e luco effert.

IV. 11. Meanwhile Alexander and Deiphobus, having formed a plot, approached Achilles, as if to confirm the agreement of Priam. In order to incur no suspicion, Alexander (he was wearing a dagger) stopped near the altar and faced away from our leader. Achilles was carrying no weapon, thinking there was nothing to fear in the temple of Apollo. Then Deiphobus, when the time seemed right, came up to Achilles and, with flattering congratulations for the terms he had made, embraced him and, hanging upon him, refused to let go until Alexander, with sword drawn, rushed forward and thrust two blows in the victim's sides. When they saw that he dying, they departed in haste and returned to the city, their very important mission accomplished beyond their best hopes.

Ulysses, who had seen them leave, said: 'Something is wrong. Why are these men so excited? Why are they frightened and rushing like this?' And thereupon he and the others entered the grove and, looking around, discovered Achilles stretched on the ground, already half-dead with the loss of much blood.

Then Ajax said: 'We know that no one could have defeated you in a fairly fought contest but, as is clear, you are undone by your own ill-advised rashness'.

And Achilles, breathing his last, said: 'Deiphobus and Alexander overpowered me. They came in the matter concerning Polyxena, deceitfully, treacherously'.

As he lay there dying, our leaders embraced him and kissed him farewell. Great was their grief. And when he was dead, Ajax shouldered the body and carried it from the grove.

IV. 12.   Quod ubi animadvertere Troiani, omnes simul portis proruunt eripere Achillem nitentes atque auferre intra moenia scilicet more solito inludere cadaveri eius gestientes. Contra Graeci cognita re arreptis armis tendunt adversum, paulatimque omnes copiae productae, ita utrimque certamen brevi adolevit. Aiax tradito his, qui secum fuerant, cadavere eius infensus Asium Dymantis, Hecubae fratrem, quem primum obvium habuit, interficit. dein plurimos, uti quemque intra telum, ferit, in quis Nastes et Amphimachus reperti Cariae imperitantes. iamque duces Aiax Oilei et Sthenelus adiuncti multos fundunt atque in fugam cogunt. quare Troiani caesis suorum plurimis nusquam ullo certo ordine aut spe reliqua resistendi dispersi palantesque ruere ad portas neque usquam nisi in muris salutem credere. Quare magna vis hominum ab insequentibus nostris obtruncantur.

IV. 12.   The Trojans, having seen what had happened, rushed from their gates all together. Following their usual custom, they wanted, no doubt, to mangle the body and thus were eager to snatch it away and carry it into the city. But the Greeks were also alerted and, taking up arms, advanced to meet them. Soon after they had led forth all of their forces, both sides clashed in battle.

Ajax, having handed the body of Achilles to those who were with him, went on the attack and slew Asius (the son of Dymas and the brother of Hecuba) whom he encountered first. Then he cut down a great number of others, as they came, one by one, within reach of his spear. Among these were Nastes and Amphimachus, the rulers of Caria.

And now our leaders, Ajax the son of Oileus and Sthenelus, joined together and killed and put great numbers to flight.

Finally this general destruction caused the Trojans to rush for their gates. They abandoned all hope of resisting and scattered and fled in utter disorder, believing that only their walls could protect them. Behind them the Greeks were pursuing, piling slaughter on slaughter.

IV. 13.   Sed ubi clausis portis finis caedendi factus est, Graeci Achillem ad naves referunt. Tuncque deflentibus cunctis ducibus casum tanti viri plurimi militum haud condolere, neque, uti res exposcebat, tristitia commoveri, quippe quis in animo haeserat Achillem saepe consilia prodendi exercitus inisse cum hostibus; ceterum interfecto eo summam militiae orbatam et ademptum complurimum; et viro egregio bellandi ne honestam quidem mortem aut aliter quam in obscuro oppetere licuerit. Igitur propere ex Ida adportata ligni vis multa atque in eodem loco, quo antea Patroclo, bustum extruunt. Dein imposito cadavere subiectoque igni iusta funeri peragunt Aiace praecipue insistente, qui per triduum continuatis vigiliis labore non destitit, quam reliquiae coadunarentur. Solus namque omnium paene ultra virilem modum interitu Achillis consternatus est, quem dilectum praeter ceteros animo summis officiis percoluerat, quippe cum amicissimum et sanguine coniunctum sibi, tum praecipue plurimum virtute ceteros antecedentem.

IV. 14.   Contra apud Troianos laetitia atque gratulatio cunctos incesserat interfecto quam metuendo hoste; hique Alexandri commentum laudantes ad caelum ferunt, scilicet cum insidiis tantum perfecerit, quantum ne in certamine auderet quidem. Inter quae nuntius Priamo supervenit Eurypylum Telephi ex Mysia adventare, quem rex multis antea inlectum praemiis, ad postremum oblatione desponsae Cassandrae confirmaverat. Sed inter cetera, quae ei pulcherrima miserat, addiderat etiam vitem quandam auro effectam, et ob id per populos memorabilem. Ceterum Eurypylus virtute multis clarus Mysiacis modo Ceteiisque instructus legionibus summa laetitia a Troianis exceptus spes omnes barbaris in melius converterat.

IV. 13.   When the gates were closed and the slaughter had ended, the Greeks took Achilles back to the ships. All of our leaders bewailed the loss of this hero. Many of the soldiers, however, believing that Achilles had often tried to betray them, were grieved not in the least and refused to mourn as they should. Nevertheless, he had been their greatest military asset and now, by his death, all was lost. They had to admit that, for a man so outstanding in battle, he had met a dishonourable death, or at least an obscure one. Accordingly, they hastened to bring plenty of wood from Mount Ida and built a pyre in the place where that of Patroclus had been. Then, having put the body in place, they lit the fire, and thus performed the rites of the funeral. Ajax acted with special devotion, keeping watch for three continuous days until the remains were gathered together. He was grieved by the death of Achilles more than any one else, grieved almost beyond his powers of endurance. He had loved Achilles above all others and had served him with highest allegiance, for Achilles was not only his relative and closest friend but also, what especially mattered, the most courageous man there was.

IV. 14.   The Trojans, for their part, abounded in joy and thanksgiving, for the enemy whom they had feared the most was dead. They lavished praises on Alexander's trickery; he had, to be sure, done by devious means what he would never have dared to do in combat.

Meanwhile a messenger arrived to tell Priam that Eurypylus, the son of Telephus, was arriving from Mysia. (The king had enticed him with many beautiful gifts, and had finally won his support by offering Cassandra in marriage. Among the other very beautiful things he had sent to him was a staff which, being made of gold, was talked of far and wide). Eurypylus, the illustrious warrior, had come with his Mysian and Ceteian forces. The Trojans welcomed him joyously, for in him their every hope was revived.

IV. 15. Interim Graeci ossa Achillis urna recondita adiunctaque simul Patrocli in Sigeo sepelivere. Cui sepulchrum etiam extruendum ab his, qui in eo loco habebant, mercede Aiax locat indignatus iam de Graecis, quod nihil in his dignum doloris iuxta amissionem tanti herois animadverteret. Per idem tempus Pyrrhus, quem Neoptolemum memorabant, genitus Achille ex Deidamia Lycomedis superveniens offendit tumulum extructum iam ex parte maxima. Dein percontatus exitum paternae mortis Myrmidonas gentem fortissimam et inclitam bellandi armis atque animis confirmat, impositoque faciendo operi Phoenice ad naves atque ad tentoria parentis vadit. ibi custodem rerum Achillis Hippodamiam animadvertit. Moxque adventu eius cognito in eundem locum a cunctis ducibus concurritur; hique, uti animum aequum haberet, deprecantur. Quis benigne respondens nec sibi ait ignoratum esse omnia, quae divinitus confierent, forti pectore patienda, neque cuiquam super fatum vivendi concessam legem, turpem namque ac detestandam viris fortibus condicionem senectae, contra imbellibus optabilem. Ceterum sibi eo leviorem dolorem esse, quod non in certamine neque in luce belli Achilles interfectus esset, quo fortiorem ne optasse quidem quemquam existere nunc vel in praeteritum excepto uno illo Hercule. addit praeterea: solum virum dignum ea tempestate, sub cuius manibus excindi Troiam deceret, neque tamen abnuere, quod imperfectum a patre relictum esset, a se atque a circumstantibus perfici.

IV. 15.   Meanwhile the Greeks placed the bones of Achilles in an urn with those of Patroclus and buried the urn at Sigeum.[5] Then Ajax hired some Sigeans to build a tomb for Achilles; he was angry with the Greeks, for he thought that their grief was in no way equal to the loss of so great a hero.

When the tomb was almost finished, Pyrrhus arrived. He was called Neoptolemus and was the son of Achilles by Deidamia, the daughter of King Lycomedes. After being informed how his father had died, he reinforced the Myrmidons and bolstered their spirits; they were the bravest of men and famous in war. Then, leaving Phoenix in charge of this work, he went to the ships and there, at his father's hut, found Hippodamia guarding the property.

Soon his arrival was known, and all the leaders convened. When they begged him to keep control of himself, he, answering calmly, said that he knew well enough that men must bravely endure whatever the gods caused to happen. Everyone's life must come to an end; only the weak wanted old age, the strong shunned and despised it. Moreover, his grief was mitigated by the fact that Achilles had been killed neither in single combat nor in the blaze of war; Achilles could never have been beaten, it was unthinkable, by anyone, living or dead, with the single exception of Hercules. Though the time called for Achilles, under whose hands it was fitting that Troy should fall, nevertheless, he affirmed, they, with his help, would finish the task that his father had left uncompleted.

---

5 Sigeum was located at the mouth of the Scamander River. Strabo tells of a temple and a monument of Achilles in this area, and also of monuments of Patroclus and Antilochus. See his *Geography* 13.1.31-32.

IV. 16. Postquam finem loquendi fecit, in proximam diem certamen pronuntiatum. Duces omnes, ubi tempus visum est, solito ad Agamemnonem cenatum veniunt, in quis Aiax cum Neoptolemo, Diomedes, Ulixes et Menelaus hique inter se eundem locum cenandi capiunt. Interim inter epulas plurima iuveni patris fortia facinora numerare virtutemque eius commemorando efferre laudibus. Quis Pyrrhus non mediocriter laetus accensusque industria enisurum se omni opere respondit, quo ne indignus patris meritis existeret. Dein ad sua quisque tentoria quietum abeunt. At postero die simul cum luce iuvenis castris egressus offendit Diomedem cum Ulixe. Quos salutatos quid causae foret; hique aiunt interponendam dierum moram ad reficiendos militum eius animos, longo itinere maris torpentibus etiam nunc membris et ob id nequaquam satis firmo nisu, ut solitis viribus agerent.

IV. 16.   After he had finished this speech, they decided to fight on the following day.

All of our leaders, when the time seemed right, went, as usual, to Agamemnon's to dine. Among them were Ajax and Neoptolemus, and Diomedes, Ulysses, and Menelaus; these took places of equal honour at dinner. While they were eating, they praised the prowess of Achilles and told Neoptolemus about the numerous brave deeds of his father. Their words delighted him and moved him to say that he would strive, with might and main, to prove himself a worthy son. After the dinner was over, they left to spend the night in their huts.

At dawn of the next day Neoptolemus, on leaving camp, was met by Diomedes and Ulysses. Having given them greeting, he asked if something was wrong. They answered that we should delay our attack a few days, until his soldiers recovered from their long journey by sea: their legs were still shaky, their feet were unsteady.

IV. 17. Itaque ex eorum sententia biduum interpositum, quo transacto omnes duces regesque suis quisque militibus instructis exercitum ordinant atque ad pugnam vadunt. in quis Neoptolemus regens medios circum se Myrmidonas statuit atque Aiacem, quem adfinitatis merito parentis loco percolebat. Interim Troiani vehementer moventur, maxime quod suis in dies deficientibus auxiliis novus adversum se miles pararetur cum memorando duce. Tamen Eurypyli hortatu arma capiunt; is namque adiunctis secum regulis copias suas Troianis mixtas porta educit. Atque ita ordinata acie medium sese locat. Tum primum Aeneas parato certamine intra muros manet execratus quippe Alexandri facinus commissum in Apollinem, cuius sacra is praecipue tuebatur. Sed ubi signum bellandi datum est, manus conserunt magna vi utrimque decertantes caduntque plurimi. Interim Eurypylus obvium forte nactus Peneleum proturbat hasta atque interficit; inde multo saevior Nirea adgressus moxque obtruncat. Iamque deturbatis, qui in acie steterant, medios adgrediebatur, cum Neoptolemus re cognita comminus advolat deiectumque curru hostem et ipse desiliens gladio impigre interficit. Tum ablatum propere cadaver atque ad naves iussu eius perlatum. Quod ubi animadvertere barbari, quibus spes omnis in Eurypylo fuerat, sine certo ordine aut rectore fuga proelium deserunt atque ad muros revolant; tum plurimi eorum in fuga interfecti.

IV. 17.   And so, in accordance with this advice, our attack was delayed for two days. Then all our leaders and kings, having armed our men and set them in order, went out to battle. Neoptolemus commanded the centre. With him were the Myrmidons and also Ajax (whom Neoptolemus, as befitted their close relationship, honoured in place of his father).

The Trojans were very upset, for they saw that, while their own allies were daily defecting, a new contingent, led by an illustrious leader, had come to the aid of the Greeks. Nevertheless, they took up arms, as Eurypylus urged them to do. He, having gained the support of the princes, created a combined force consisting of his own men and those of the Trojans and leading them out of the gate, deployed them for battle; he himself commanded the centre. (Aeneas stayed behind in the city and, for the first time, refused to fight; he was a devoted worshiper of Apollo and detested the crime Alexander had committed against this god).

When the signal for battle was given, the two sides clashed and fought with all their might; great numbers were slain. Eurypylus, chancing upon Peneleus, drove him back and pinned him with his spear; then he attacked Nireus even more savagely, and cut him down; and finally, having put to flight our men in front, he was fighting in the very midst of our forces. But Neoptolemus, on seeing this, drove up close and knocked Eurypylus out of his chariot; then he dismounted himself and, sword in hand, quickly finished Eurypylus off. Thereupon our men, as Neoptolemus ordered, carried the body out of the battle and back to the ships. When the barbarians, they had placed all their hopes in Eurypylus, saw this sight, they deserted the battle and fled for the walls, leaderless, without any definite order. And as they fled, great numbers were killed.

IV. 18.   Igitur postquam fusis hostibus ad naves revertere Graeci, ex consilii sententia Eurypyli cremata ossa atque urnae condita patri remittunt, scilicet memores beneficiorum atque amicitiae. Cremati etiam per suos Nireus atque Peneleus, seorsum singuli. at postero die per Chrysem cognoscitur Helenum Priami fugientem scelus Alexandri apud se in templo agere. Moxque ob id missis Diomede et Ulixe tradidit sese deprecatus prius, uti sibi partem aliquam regionis, in qua reliquam vitam degeret semotam ab aliis concederent. Dein ad naves ductus ubi consilio mixtus est, multa prius locutus non metu, ait, se mortis patriam parentesque deserere, sed deorum coactum aversione, quorum delubra violari ab Alexandro neque se neque Aeneam quisse pati. Qui metuens Graecorum iracundiam apud Antenorem agere senemque parentem. De cuius oraculo imminentia Troianis mala cum cognovisset, ultro supplicem ad eos decurrere. Tunc nostris festinantibus secreta dinoscere, Ohryses nutu uti silentium ageretur significat atque Helenum secum abducit. A quo doctus cuncta Graecis uti audierat refert, addit praeterea tempus Troiani excidii idque administris Aenea atque Antenore fore. Tum recordati eorum, quae Calchas edixerat, eadem cuncta congruentiaque animadvertunt.

IV. 18.   Thus the enemy was put to flight, and the Greeks returned to the ships. Then, the council so willing, we cremated Eurypylus and sent his bones, in an urn, back to his father, for we remembered his father's kindness and friendship.[6] Also, there were separate funerals for Nireus and Peneleus; each was cremated by his own people.

On the next day Chryses reported to the Greeks that Priam's son Helenus had fled from Troy because of Alexander's crime and was now at the temple nearby. Accordingly, we sent Diomedes and Ulysses to fetch him. After these had promised him leave to spend the rest of his life somewhere in seclusion, he placed himself in their power.

When he had been brought to the ships, he made a long speech at a meeting of the council, in which he told his reason for leaving his parents and people: he feared not death but the gods, whose shrines Alexander had desecrated, a crime which neither Aeneas nor himself was able to bear. As for Aeneas, he, fearing our anger, had stayed behind with Antenor and old Anchises, his father. It was from an oracle of Anchises, Helenus said, that he had learned of Troy's imminent fall, and thus had made up his mind to come to us as a suppliant.

We were eager to know the contents of this oracle. Accordingly, Chryses, having nodded for us to keep silent, took Helenus aside and learned everything, which then he reported to us. Thus we were informed of the very time of Troy's fall and how Aeneas and Antenor would help us. And we saw that this oracle was entirely consistent with what we remembered Calchas had already told us was going to happen.

---

6 See Dictys 2.10 and 12.

IV. 19.   Dein postero die egresso utrimque milite ad bellandum plurimi Troianorum cadunt, sed ex sociis pars maxima. At ubi vehementius ab nostris instatur et omni ope bellum finire in animo est, signo dato dux duci occurrit atque in se proelium convertunt. Tunc Philocteta progressus adversus Alexandrum lacessit, si auderet, sagittario certamine. Ita concessu utriusque partis Ulixes atque Deiphobus spatium certaminis definiunt. Igitur primus Alexander incassum sagittam contendit, dein Philocteta insecutus sinistram manum hosti transfigit, reclamanti per dolorem dextrum oculum perforat ac iam fugientem tertio consecutus vulnere per utrumque pedem traicit fatigatumque ad postremum interficit, quippe Herculis armatus sagittis, quae infectae Hydrae sanguine haud sine exitio corpori figebantur.

IV. 19. On the next day both armies went out to battle and many were killed on the Trojan side, their allies suffering the greatest losses. But as our men were attacking more vehemently and striving with all their might to end the war, our leaders, at a given signal, attacked those of the enemy and centred the battle around themselves.

Philoctetes advanced against Alexander and challenged him to fight, if he dared, a duel with the bow. Alexander agreed, and thus Ulysses and Deiphobus marked off a place for the contest. Alexander was the first to shoot and missed. Thereupon Philoctetes hit Alexander in the left hand, and then, he was howling with pain, struck his right eye, and then, he was trying to flee, pierced both his feet, and finally finished him off. Philoctetes' arrows had once been Hercules', and the Hydra's lethal blood had stained their points.[7]

---

7 See Sophocles *Philoctetes*.

IV. 20.   Quod ubi animadvertere barbari, magna vi inruunt, eripere Alexandrum cupientes, multisque suorum interfectis a Philocleta negotium tamen peragunt, atque in civitatem reportant. Tumque Aiax Telamonius insecutus fugientes ad usque portam pergit. Ibi caesa vis multa hostium, cum festinantibus inter se et singulis evadere inter primos cupientibus magis in ipso aditu multitudine sua detinerentur. Interim multi eorum, qui primi evaserant, super muros siti collecta undique cuiuscemodi saxa super clipeum Aiacis deicere congestamque quam plurimam terram desuper volvere, scilicet ad depellendum hostem. Cum supra modum gravaretur egregius dux, facile scuto decutiens haud segnius imminere. Denique Philocteta eos, qui in muris locati erant, eminus sagittis proturbat multosque interficit. neque secus ab reliquis in parte alia res gestae. Atque eo die excisa eversaque moenia hostium forent, ni nox iam ingruens nostros ab incepto cohibuisset. Qui ubi ad naves regressi sunt, laeti Philoctetae facinoribus et ob id maximam animo fiduciam gestantes, summo favore ac laudibus ducem celebrant. Qui simul cum luce adiunctis sibi reliquis ducibus in proelium egressus hostes metu sui adeo deterruit, ut vix se moenibus defensarent.

IV. 20. The barbarians, seeing that their leader was dead, rushed in and tried to snatch his body away. Philoctetes killed many of them, but they kept pressing on, and eventually got the body into the city. Ajax the son of Telamon pursued them as far as the gate, and there the slaughter was huge. Many were unable to enter; the crowd was frantic, with everyone shoving, everyone striving to get in first. Those who had entered went to the walls and hurled down rocks of every description, rolled down earth collected from everywhere, onto the shield of Ajax, hoping to drive him off, but our illustrious leader, shaking his shield whenever it grew too heavy, relented not in the least. And Philoctetes, shooting from a distance, killed many of those on the wall and drove the others away.

In other parts of the field the rest of our soldiers met with equal success. That day would have seen the walls of Troy destroyed, the city sacked, if the swift arrival of night had not restrained us. Thus we returned to the ships, rejoicing, our spirits tremendously buoyed because of the deeds of Philoctetes. To him we gave our highest praise and showed our deepest gratitude.

At daybreak, Philoctetes, accompanied by the rest of our leaders, returned to the field. And the Trojans, even with the help of their walls, could scarcely protect themselves, so great was their terror.

IV. 21.   Interim Neoptolemus apud tumulum Achillis, postquam in auctorem paternae caedis vindicatum est, initium lugendi sumit, una cum Phoenice atque omni Myrmidonum exercitu comas sepulchro deponit pernoctatque in loco. Per idem tempus filii Antimachi, de quo supra memoravimus, adiuncti Priami rebus ad Helenum veniunt eumque ut ad amicitiam cum suis redeat deprecati, ubi nihil proficiunt, ad suos remeantes Diomedi atque Aiaci alteri itineris medio occurrunt. Ab quis comprehensi perductique ad naves, quinam essent et rem ob quam venerant omnem expediunt. Tum recordati patris eorum et quae adversum legatos dixerit molitusque sit, tradi eos popularibus atque ante conspectum barbarorum produci iubent, dein lapidibus iniectis necari. Interim Alexandri funus per ‡ partem aliam portae ‡ ad Oenonem, quae ei ante Helenae raptum nupserat, necessarii sui, uti sepeliretur, perferunt. Sed fertur Oenonem viso cadavere Alexandri adeo commotam, uti amissa mente obstupefieret ac paulatim per maerorem deficiente animo concideret. Atque ita uno eodem funere cum Alexandro contegitur.

IV. 21. Meanwhile Neoptolemus, now that his father's murder was avenged, began the mourning around Achilles' mound. Along with Phoenix and the entire army of the Myrmidons, he cut off his hair and placed it on the tomb. Thus they stayed there all the night.

During the same time, the sons of Antimachus (whom we have mentioned above) came to Helenus as representatives of Priam, but he refused to do as they begged, that is, to return to his people; and so they departed. Halfway back to the city, they were encountered by Diomedes and the other Ajax, and thus were captured and brought to the ships. When they had told who they were and explained their reason for coming, we, remembering how their father had spoken and plotted against our envoys,[8] ordered the soldiers to take them and lead them out where the Trojans could see and stone them to death.

At Troy, in a different direction, the relatives of Alexander, who were seeing to his burial, were carrying his body to Oenone. They say that Oenone, she had been married to him before his abduction of Helen, was so shocked by the sight of his body that she lost all power of speech, lost her spirit and, gradually being overwhelmed with grief, fell down dead. And thus a single tomb held her and him.

---

8 See Dictys 2.23-24. In the *Iliad* (11.122-162), Agamemnon slaughs the two sons of Antimachus because their father had opposed the return of Helen and had plotted the death of Menelaus.

IV. 22.   Ceterum Troiani, ubi hostis muris infestus magis magisque saevit, neque iam resistendi moenibus spes ulterius est aut vires valent, cuncti proceres seditionem adversus Priamum extollunt atque eius regulos. Denique accito Aenea filiisque Antenoris decernunt inter se, uti Helena cum his, quae ablata erant, ad Menelaum duceretur. Quod postquam Deiphobus cognovit, traductam ad se Helenam matrimonio sibi adiungit. Ceterum ingressus consilium Priamus, ubi multa ab Aenea contumeliosa ingesta sunt, ad postremum ex consilii sententia iubet ad Graecos cum mandatis belli deponendi ire Antenorem. Qui ex muris signum ostendens legationis, ubi a nostris recessum est, ad naves venit. Ubi benigne salutatus atque exceptus summum fidei benevolentiaeque erga Graeciam testimonium capit maximeque a Nestore, quod Menelaum insidiis Troianorum appetitum consilio suo atque auxilio filiorum servaverit; pro quis Troia eversa multa praeclara polliceri hortarique, uti dignum memoria pro amicis adversum perfidos moliretur. Tunc longam exorsus orationem semper, ait, principes Troiae poenam ob male consulta divinitus consequi. Dein subiungit Laomedontis adversum Herculem famosa periuria insecutamque eius regni eversionem. Qua tempestate Priamus parvulus admodum atque expers omnium, quae gesta erant, petitu Hesionae regno impositus est. Eum male iam inde desipientem cunctos sanguine et iniuriis insectari solitum, parcum in suo atque appetentem alieni, quo exemplo veluti pessima contagione imbutos filios eius neque sacro neque profano abstinuisse.

IV. 22.   All the Trojan nobles, since they saw the enemy raging more and more fiercely around their walls and knew that their own resources were failing, felt that further resistance was hopeless. Accordingly, they plotted sedition against the princes and Priam. Having summoned Aeneas and the sons of Antenor, they were planning to return Helen to Menelaus, along with the things that had been carried off, but Deiphobus, having heard of their plans, took Helen off and married her himself.

When Priam entered the council, Aeneas heaped insults upon him. Finally the king yielded to the will of the nobles and ordered Antenor to go to the Greeks and seek an end to the war.

When Antenor signalled from the walls that the Trojans desired to negotiate, we granted permission. Thus he came to the ships, and we welcomed him gladly. Nestor, especially, told how faithful and kind he had been to the Greeks: his counsel and the aid of his sons had saved Menelaus from Trojan treachery. In return for what he had done, we promised to reward him richly when Troy was destroyed, and urged him to work with us, he knew we were friends, against those he knew to be treacherous.

Then, in a long speech, Antenor told how the gods were always punishing Trojan rulers for ill-considered acts. Laomedon, he said, had lied to Hercules, a famous story, and thus his kingdom had been destroyed. Then, through the influence of Hesione, Priam, who was still young and had had no share in all that had happened, had come to power; thereafter, becoming evil and foolish, he had been accustomed to attack everyone; he had killed and committed personal injuries, being sparing of his own property while seeking that of another. Such was the example which spread, like the worst of plagues, to his sons, who abstained from nothing either sacred or profane.

Ceterum se eadem stirpe, qua Priamum Graecis coniunctum, animo semper ab eo discerni. Hesionam quippe Danai filiam Electram genuisse, ex qua ortus Dardanus Olizonae Phinei iunctus Erichthonium dederit, eius Tros, dein ex eo Ilus, Ganymedes et Cleomestra, ex Cleomestra Assaracus atque ex eo Capys Anchisae pater. Ilum dein Tithonum et Laomedontem genuisse, ex Laomedonte Hicetaonem, Clytium, Lampum, Thymoetem, Bucolionem atque Priamum genitos rursusque ex Cleomestra et Aesyete se genitum. Ceterum Priamum cuncta iura adfinitatis proculcantem magis in suos superbiam atque odium exercuisse. Postquam finem loquendi fecit, postulat, uti, quoniam a senibus legatus pacis missus esset, darent de suo numero, cum quis super tali negotio disceptaret, electique Agamemnon, Idomeneus, Ulixes atque Diomedes, qui secreto ab aliis proditionem componunt. praeterea placet, uti Aeneae, si permanere in fide vellet, pars praedae et domus universa eius incolumis, ipsi autem Antenori dimidium bonorum Priami regnumque uni filiorum eius, quem elegisset, concederetur. Ubi satis tractatum visum est, Antenor ad civitatem dimittitur, referens ad suos composita inter se longe alia, in quis, donum Minervae parari a Graecis eosque cum gratia cupere recepta Helena acceptoque auro bellum omittere atque ad suos regredi. Ita composito negotio Antenor traditoque sibi Talthybio, quo res fidem acciperet, ad Troiam venit.

Antenor said that he himself was a very different person from Priam, in spite of the fact that they both were related to the Greeks by the same line of descent.[9] Hesione, the daughter of Danaus, was the mother of Electra, and Electra was the mother of Dardanus; Dardanus had married Olizone, the daughter of Phineus; their child was Erichthonius, who was the father of Tros; and Tros was the father of Ilus, Ganymede, and Cleomestra. Cleomestra was the mother of Assaracus, and Assaracus had begotten Capys, the father of Anchises. Ilus had begotten Tithonus and Laomedon, and Laomedon was the father of Hicetaon, Clytius, Lampus, Thymoetes, Bucolion, and finally Priam. As for himself, he was the son of Cleomestra and Aesyetes. But Priam had disregarded every bond of kinship and had acted with especial insolence and hatred toward his own relations.

When he had finished this speech, he asked us to choose representatives for the purpose of talking with him about peace; as this was the reason the Trojan elders had sent him. Accordingly, we chose Agamemnon, Idomeneus, Ulysses, and Diomedes. Thereupon these counselled together, in secret, and decided, among other things, that Aeneas, contingent upon his remaining faithful, should share the spoils, nor should his house be harmed in any way; as for Antenor, half of Priam's wealth should be given to him; and one of his sons, whomever he chose, should rule over Troy.

When they felt that their plans were complete, Antenor was sent back to Troy to make a report far different from what they had really decided. He was to say that the Greeks were preparing an offering, a gift, for Minerva, and that, providing they recovered Helen and received some gold, they were only too glad to abandon the war and return to their people. Thus Antenor went off to Troy, accompanied by Talthybius whose presence might help to produce an illusion of trust.

---

9 See Dictys 1.9 and note 8 thereto.

LIBER QUINTVS

V. 1. Antenore Talthybioque civitatem ingressis cuncti populares sociique cognita re propere concurrunt, cupientes dinoscere, quae apud Graecos actitata essent. Quis Antenor in proximum diem relata differt; atque ita dimisso conventu disceditur. Cum inter epulas Talthybius interesset, filios suos monere Antenor nihil his in vita custodiendum, quam uti antiquissimam ducerent cum Graecis amicitiam, dein singulorum probitatem, fidem atque innocentiam commemorando admiratur. Ita finito convivio tum disceditur. At lucis principio, omnibus iam in consilio expectantibus audire, si quis modus tantis malis fieret, cum Talthybio ipse venit neque multo post Aeneas, dein Priamus cum residuis regulis. Denique ubi ea, quae a Graecis audierat, dicere iussus est, hoc modo disseruit:

DICTYS V.

Book Five

V. 1.　　　When the arrival of Antenor and Talthybius was known at Troy, all the Trojans and their allies rushed to meet them, desiring to learn what had happened among the Greeks, but Antenor postponed his report until the next day, and so they dispersed and went home.

Then, at a banquet, in the presence of Talthybius, Antenor advised his sons to consider nothing so important in life as their long-standing friendship with Greece and recalled, with evident admiration, the honour, good faith, and guilelessness of individual Greeks.

After the meal, they parted company. At daybreak Antenor and Talthybius went to the meeting of the council. (The elders were already there, eager to find some end to their dreadful afflictions). Aeneas was the next to arrive, and then Priam and the rest of the princes. At last Antenor, having been ordered to tell what he had heard from the Greeks, spoke as follows:

V. 2.   *Grave, Troiani principes vosque socii, grave bellum nobis*
extitisse adversum Graeciam, gravius vero multoque durius, mulieris causa
hostes effectos quam amicissimos, qui inde iam a Pelope orti adfinitatis
etiam iure nobis coniuncti sunt. namque si praeterita mala summatim
attingere oporteat, en unquam civitas nostra depressa aerumnis ad requiem
emersit? Unquamne nobis defuere fletus aut sociis imminutae calamitates?
Quando non amici parentes propinqui filii denique in bello amissi? Et, ut
ex me reliquorum luctuum memoriam recenseam, quidnam in Glauco filio
toleravi? Cuius interitus, quamquam acerbus mihi, tamen non ita dolori
fuit, quam tempus illud, quo adiunctus Alexandro ad raptum Helenae
comitatum sui praebuit. Sed praeteritorum satias, futuris saltem
parcendum ac consulendum est. Graeci homines custodes fidei ac veritatis,
principes benevolentiae atque officiorum. testis his rebus Priamus, qui ipso
strepitu discordiarum fructum tamen misericordiae eorum tulit; neque
inferendo bellum quicquam prius temeratum ab his, quam perfidiam in ipsa
legatione insidiasque ab nostris experti sunt. In qua re, dico enim quod
sentio, Priamus eiusque filii auctores, in his etiam Antimachus, qui recens
amissis liberis iniquitatis suae poenas luit. Haec omnia in gratia Helenae
gesta, scilicet eius mulieris, quam ne Graeci quidem recipere gestiunt.
Retineatur igitur in civitate ea femina, ob quam nulla gens, nulli usquam
populi amici aut non infesti huic regno. Nonne sponte supplices, ut
recipiant eam, rogabimus? Non omni modo satisfaciemus laesis iam totiens
per nos? Non in futurum saltem reconciliabimus tales viros?

V. 2. 'It is a sad thing, Trojan princes and Trojan allies, it is a sad thing for us to be at war with the Greeks, but it is an even sadder and more painful thing that for the sake of a woman we have made enemies of the closest friends, of those who, being descendants of Pelops, are joined to us even by ties of marriage.

'If I may briefly touch on the past evils we have suffered, when has our city ever found rest, once it was lost in this quagmire of sorrows? When have we ever been without tears? When have you allies ever seen your misfortunes decrease? When have our friends, parents, relatives, and sons not been dying in battle? And, to sum up the rest of our sorrows with a personal allusion, what suffering have I not endured in the case of Glaucus, my son? His death, however, was not so painful to me as the fact that he had accompanied Alexander in the abduction of Helen.

'But enough of the past. Let us, at least, look to the future with caution and wisdom. The Greeks are faithful and true; they are rich in kindness and pious in doing their duty. Priam is a witness to this, for, in the very heat of the battle, he reaped the fruit of their pity. The Greeks were not so rash as to declare war against us until we had treated their envoys, even their envoys, with treachery and guile. It is my opinion that Priam and his sons were to blame in this matter, and also Antimachus, who has recently paid for his guilt with the loss of his sons, but the real blame for everything that has happened rests upon Helen, that woman whom not even the Greeks really want to recover. Why should we keep this woman on whose account no nation, no people, has ever been friendly or even non-hostile to us? Shall we not, rather, eagerly beg the Greeks to take her again? And shall we not offer complete compensation for all the ways we have harmed them? Shall we not be reconciled with such men at least in the future?

Ego quidem abibo hinc iam et discedam longius neque committam, ut ulterius intersim malis nostris. Fuit tempus, quo manere in hac civitate iucundum erat; socii, amici, propinquorum salus, patria denique incolumis adtinuere in hunc diem. Contra nunc quid horum non imminutum aut in totum sublatum nobis est? Non feram me cum his morari, quorum opera cuncta mihi cum patria concidere. Et eos quidem, quos in bello fortuna eripuit, utcumque iam sepelivimns concedentibus ultro veniam hostibus, sed postquam deorum arae atque delubra sanguine humano per scelus infecta sunt, hoc etiam amisimus, quippe quis maiora supplicia post mortem carissimorum, quam in amissione subeunda sunt. Quae ne accidant, nunc saltem providete. Auro atque huismodi aliis praemiis redimenda patria est. Multae in hac civitate dites domus, singuli pro facultatibus in medium consulamus, postremo offeratur pro vita hostibus, quod mox interitu nostro ipsorum futurum est. Templorum etiam, si necesse erit, ornamentis pro incolumitate patriae utendum est. solus suas opes intus custodiat Priamus, solus divitias potiores civibus suis teneat, his etiam, quae cum Helena rapta sunt, incubet, videritque, quem ad finem utendum putet patriae calamitatibus. Nos victi iam sumus malis nostris.

'For my own part, I am leaving; I am going away. I refuse to share in these injustices any longer. There was a time when it was pleasing to live in this city; until now we had allies and friends; our relatives were safe, our country unharmed. But now we have partially or totally lost all of these things. Who can deny it? I can no longer endure to remain with those whose work is all destined to ruin along with the fall of their country.

'Until now, it is true, we have found some way to bury our dead; the enemy granted this favour. But now the altars and shrines of the gods have been impiously desecrated with human blood, and thus, being unable to hold our dear ones' funerals, we will suffer even more than when they died

'At least prevent this from happening now. Our native land must be redeemed with gold and other ransom of this sort. There are many in our city who are rich; each must give whatever he can. We must offer the Greeks, in return for our lives, what they will have soon enough if they kill us. Let us give even the ornaments of our temples, if otherwise we cannot save our city.

'As for Priam, let only him keep all his wealth, let only him consider riches more important than his people, let him, the brooding miser, have even the things they carried off with Helen, and see how best to use his country's sorrows.

'Now our sins have found us out, and we are conquered'.

V. 3.   Haec atque alia cum lacrimis disserente eo cuncti simul gemitum edunt, tendentes ad caelum manus annuere, tot adversis rebus Priamum singuli vel inter se omnes finem miseriarum deprecantes, ad postremum uno ore patriam redimendam clamant. In quis Priamus dilanians caput fletu quam miserabili non solum iam se ait odio dis, verum suis hostem effectum, quippe cui non amicus antea, non propinquus, non denique civis inveniri posset, qui aerumnis suis ingemesceret. namque optasse haec non nunc demum, verum vivis Alexandro atque Hectore agi coepta. Sed quoniam praeterita revocare nulli concessum esset, praesentium habendam rationem spemque futuris adhibendam. Se namque omnium, quae haberet, ad redemptionem patriae potestatem dare. Quam rem Antenori agendam permittere. Ceterum se, quoniam odio iam suis esset, abire e conspectu consentientem his, quae inter se decernerent.

V. 3.   He was weeping as he spoke these and other things, and everyone was mourning. Stretching their hands toward heaven, they showed their agreement, praying, individually and together, that Priam, in view of their many adversities, should bring an end to their miseries; finally, with one voice, they shouted that their native land must be redeemed.

Then Priam, tearing his hair and weeping in a pitiable way, addressed them. Now, he said, he was not only hated by the gods but was even considered a public enemy by his own people. Formerly he had had friends, relatives, and fellow citizens to comfort him in his misfortunes, but now none was to be found. He had wanted to begin negotiations when Alexander and Hector were living and not wait until now. No one, however, was able to remedy the past; they must plan for the present and put their hopes in the future. He offered all that he had for the redemption of Troy, and instructed Antenor to see to the matter, but now, since they hated him so, he was leaving their presence. Whatever they decided to do was agreeable to him.

V. 4.   Tum separato rege placet, uti Antenor ad Graecos redeat exploratum voluntatem certam adiunctusque ei, uti voluerat, Aeneas. Ita composita re disceditur. Sed media ferme nocte Helena clam ad Antenorem venit suspicans tradi se Menelao et ob id iram derelictae domus metuens. itaque eum orat, uti inter cetera sui quoque apud Graecos commemorationem faceret ac pro se deprecaretur. Ceterum, ut cognitum est, post Alexandri interitum invisa ei apud Troiam fuere omnia desideratusque ad suos reditus. at lucis initio, quibus imperatum erat, ad naves veniunt, decretum civium cunctis narrant. Itaque, cum quis antea, ad confirmanda, quae tempus monebat, secedunt. Ibi cum multa de republica ac summa rerum dissererent, voluntatem quoque Helenae docent veniamque orant et ad postremum confirmant inter se proditionis pactionem. Dein ubi tempus visum est, cum Ulixe et Diomede ad Troiam veniunt cohibito Aiace ab Aenea, scilicet ne qua insidiis opprimeretur talis vir, quem solum barbari non secus quam Achillem metuebant. Igitur postquam duces Graeci in civitate conspecti sunt, cuncti cives tollunt spe animos existimantes finem belli atque discordiarum. itaque propere senatus habitus, ubi nostris praesentibus decernitur primum omnium Antimachum ex omni Phrygia exulandum, scilicet auctorem tanti mali. Dein super condicione pacis tractari coeptum.

V. 4.   When the king had left, they decided that Antenor should return to the Greeks and learn what terms they wanted exactly; and that Aeneas, as he desired, should go along too. Thus the council broke up.

About midnight, Helen came to Antenor secretly. She suspected that they were about to return her to Menelaus and feared that she would be punished for having abandoned her home. Accordingly, she begged him to mention her, when he spoke among the Greeks, and plead in her behalf. Now that Alexander was dead, she hated all Troy, as they knew, and wanted to return to her people.

At daybreak, Antenor and Aeneas came to the ships and told us all about their city's decision. Then they withdrew with those they had talked to before, to plan what action to take. It was during these discussions about Troy and their nation that they also told about Helen's desires and asked forgiveness for her; and finally they agreed on how best to betray their city.

When they were ready, they returned to Troy, accompanied by Ulysses and Diomedes. Ajax also wanted to go, but Aeneas made him remain, arguing, no doubt, that the Trojans were afraid of him no less than they had been afraid of Achilles and, therefore, might take him by treachery.

The hopes of all Trojans were raised when they saw that our leaders had come. They thought this meant that war and conflict were going to end. A meeting of the council was quickly called and there, in the presence of our men, they decided, first of all, to exile Antimachus from all of Phrygia, for he, to be sure, was the cause of their terrible troubles. Then they began to discuss the terms of peace.

V. 5.   Inter quae repente strepitus ex Pergamo, ubi regia Priamo erat, clamorque ingens editur. qua re turbati, qui in consilio erant, foras prosiliunt, credentes insidias temptatas solito ab regulis; itaque in templum Minervae propere concedunt. at paulo post ex his, qui ex arce descenderant, cognoscitur Alexandri filios, quos ex Helena susceperat, casu camerae extinctos. hique erant ‡Bunomus, Gorythus atque Idaeus. Quare consilio dilato duces nostri ad Antenorem abeunt ibique acceptis epulis pernoctant. praeterea cognoscunt ab Antenore editum quondam oraculum Troianis maximo exitio civitati fore, si Palladium, quod in templo Minervae esset, extra moenia tolleretur. namque id antiquissimum signum caelo lapsum, qua tempestate Ilus templum Minervae extruens prope summum fastigium pervenerat ibique inter opera, cum necdum tegumen superpositium esset, sedem sui occupavisse; idque signum ligno fabrefactum esse. hortantibus dein nostris, uti secum ad ea omnia eniteretur, facturum se, quae cuperent, respondit. atque his praedicit publice se in consilio super qualitate eorum, quae postulaturi essent, exertius disserturum, scilicet ne qua suspicio sui apud barbaros oriretur. ita composito negotio cum luce simul Antenor ac reliqui proceres ad Priamum vadunt, nostri ad naves redeunt.

236

V. 5. During their discussion, a huge crash and much shouting suddenly arose from Pergamum, where Priam's palace was located. Those in the council, being thrown into confusion, ran outside and, thinking that the princes, as usual, had done some treacherous deed, they rushed to the temple of Minerva. Soon afterwards, however, they learned, from those who came from the citadel, that the sons of Alexander, his children by Helen, had perished, crushed when the roof of their home had collapsed. The names of these sons were Bunomus,[1] Corythus, and Idaeus.

The business of the council was thus deferred, and our leaders went off to Antenor's, there to dine and spend the night. Moreover, they learned from Antenor about an oracle which once had informed the Trojans that Troy would fall in ruins, if the Palladium was carried outside the walls of the city. (The Palladium was an ancient statue in the temple of Minerva; it was made of wood, and had fallen from heaven and taken its place when Ilus was building the temple, and all but the roof was complete).

Antenor agreed to help our men, just as they urged, in every way; he would do whatever they wanted. Nevertheless, he warned them that, at the meeting of the Trojan council, he would speak out boldly and openly oppose the demands the Greeks were making; in order, no doubt, to give the barbarians no grounds to suspect him.

Their plans being thus completed, at daybreak Antenor went, along with the Trojan nobles, to Priam; and our leaders returned to the ships.

---

1 The spelling of this name is doubtful.

V. 6. Dein, ubi iusta pueris facta sunt, post diem tertium Idaeus supradictos duces accitum venit. quis praesentibus Panthus ceterique, quorum consilium praevalebat, multa disserere atque docere ea, quae antea gesta essent temere et inconsulta, non per se, quippe qui contempti disiectique ab regulis arbitrio alieno agerent. Ceterum quod arma adversus Graecos tulissent, non sponte factum, namque qui sub imperio alieno agerent, expectandum his atque exsequendum esse nutum eius, qui teneat. Ob quae dignum esse Graecos data venia consulere eis, qui semper auctores pacis fuerint. Ceterum a Troianis ob male consulta satis poenarum exactum. dein multo hinc atque inde habito sermone ad postremum de modo praemiorum agi coeptum. Tum Diomedes quinque milia talentorum auri ac totidem argenti optat, praeterea tritici centena milia; eaque per annos decem. Tum silentio habito a cunctis Antenor non Graecorum more agere eos adversum se ait, sed barbaro, namque quod impossibilia postularent, palam fieri praetextu pacis bellum eos instruere. Ceterum auri tantum atque argenti ne tum quidem, priusquam in auxilia conducta dilaceraretur, civitati fuisse. quod si permanere in eadem avaritia vellent, superesse Troianis, uti clausis portis incensisque intus deorum aedificiis ad postremum idem sibi cum patria exitium peterent. Contra Diomedes: *non civitatem vestram consideratum Argis venimus, verum adversum vos dimicaturi. Quocirca, sive etiam nunc bellare in animo est, parati Graeci, sive, ut ais, igni dabitis Ilium, non prohibebimus, quippe Graecis affectis iniuria ulcisci hostes suos finis est.* Tum Panthus in proximum diem veniam deliberandi orat. Ita nostri ad Antenorem abeunt atque inde in aedem Minervae.

V. 6. The sons of Alexander were buried with due ceremony. Three days later Idaeus came and summoned our leaders (those mentioned above). Panthus[2] and the other Trojans who were known for their wisdom made long speeches in which they explained that their previous actions had been rash and ill-advised. They had been constrained, they said, to act according to the will of the princes, by whom they were hated and counted as naught. They had not taken up arms against Greece willingly, for those who must follow another's command must look to his nod and try to obey it. Therefore, the Greeks should grant forgiveness and be willing to confer with those who had always been hoping for peace. Moreover, the Trojans had already suffered enough for their ill-advised acts.

After a long discussion of this point and that, finally the question of tribute was raised. Diomedes asked for five thousand talents of gold, and a like number of silver, besides one hundred thousand measures of wheat, for a period of ten years.

Then all the Trojans were silent, except for Antenor. He said that the Greeks were not acting like Greeks, but barbarians. Since they demanded what was impossible, it was evident that they were planning for war under a pretext of peace. Moreover, Troy had never had as much gold and silver as Greece was demanding, not even before she had gone to the expense of hiring auxiliaries. If the Greeks persisted in these unscrupulous demands, the Trojans must shut their gates and burn the temples of their gods, and offer themselves and their country to one and the same destruction.

Diomedes answered: 'We did not come from Argos to give special terms to Troy, but to fight you to the death. Therefore, if you are still desirous of war, the Greeks are ready, or if, as you say, you wish to burn your city, we will not prevent you. The Greeks, when treated unjustly, take vengeance. That is their way'.

Then Panthus asked for a day's reprieve during which to ponder the Greek proposal. Thus our men went home with Antenor, and from there to the temple of Minerva.

---

2 Compare Panthus' conciliatory remarks in Dictys 2.23 and 2.25.

V. 7.   Interim cognoscitur in apparatu rerum divinarum portentum ingens. Namque aris composita sacrorum consueta mox subiectus ignis non comprehendere neque consumere, uti antea, sed aspernari. Qua re turbati populares, simul uti fidem nuntii noscerent, ad aram Apollinis confluunt. Atque ibi superpositis extorum partibus ubi flamma admota est, repente cuncta, quae inerant, disturbata ad terram decidunt. Quo spectaculo perculsis atque attonitis omnibus subito avis aquila stridore magno immittit sese atque extorum partem eripit moxque supervolans ad naves Graecorum pergit, ibique raptum omittit. Id vero barbari non iam leve aut in obscuro, sed palam perniciosum credere. Interim Diomedes cum Ulixe dissimulantes, quae gerebantur, obambulare in foro circumspicientes laudantesque praeclara operum civitatis eius. At apud naves auspicio tali monitis omnium animis Calchas, uti bonum animum gererent, hortatur, brevi quippe dominos fore eorum, quae apud Troiam essent.

V. 7.   Meanwhile news of a remarkable portent was brought. It had occurred during the offering of sacrifices. Victims had been placed on the altars as usual. But the fire, having been lit, had not caught or burned in the usual way but had left the offerings untouched.

This news startled the people, and they rushed to the temple of Apollo to prove for themselves whether or not it was true. When they had placed parts of entrails on the altar and lit the fire, suddenly everything was thrown into confusion; the entrails fell to the ground. Then, while everyone was struck with astonishment, an eagle, swift and screeching, dove down and caught up a piece of the entrails and, soaring off, carried it away to the ships and there let it fall.

The Trojans received this omen as a great and very clear sign portending their doom. Diomedes and Ulysses, however, pretended not to know what had happened and walked around in the public square, like sightseers, marvelling at the wonderful buildings of Troy.

We, at the ships, were also pondering the portent's meaning. And Calchas told us to be of good cheer, for we would be masters of Troy in short order.

V. 8.   Ceterum Hecuba re cognita placatum deos egreditur ac praecipue Minervam atque Apollinem, quis cum dona multa, tum victimas opimas admovet. Sed in adolendo, quae sacra aris reddebantur, eodem modo restingui ignes ac repente interire visi. Inter quae tam sollicita Cassandra deo plena victimas ad Hectoris tumulum transferri imperat, deos quippe aspernari iam sacrificia indignatos ob commissum paulo ante scelus in Apollinem. Ita tauris, qui immolati erant, ad rogum Hectoris, sicuti imperabatur, adportatis moxque igni subiecto consumuntur cuncta. Inde, ubi iam vesperarat, domum discessum. Atque eadem nocte Antenor clam in templum Minervae venit. Ibi multis precibus vi mixtis Theano, quae ei templo sacerdos erat, persuasit, ut Palladium sibi traderet, habituram namque magna eius rei praemia. Ita perfecto negotio ad nostros venit hisque promissum offert, verum id Graeci obvolutum bene, quo ne intellegi a quoquam posset, vehiculo ad tentoria Ulixi per necessarios fidosque suos remittunt. At lucis principio postquam senatus coactus et nostri ingressi sunt, Antenor veluti iracundiam Graecorum metuens veniam eorum orare, quae adversum eos pro patria exertius disseruisset. Dein Ulixes: non se his moveri neque indignari, sed quod finis in tractando non adhiberetur, maxime cum opportunum ad navigandum tempus brevi praetervolet. tum multo invicem habito sermone ad postremum binis milibus talentorum auri atque argenti rem decidunt. Quod uti ad suos referrent, Graeci ad naves abeunt. Ibi conductis ducibus cuncta dicta gestaque exponunt. Palladium ablatum per Antenorem docent. Dein ex omnium sententia reliquus miles rem cognoscit.

V. 8.   When Hecuba learned of the portent, she went to placate the gods, especially Minerva and Apollo, with many gifts and rich sacrifices. But just as before, the fire refused to burn the victims and died out quickly.

Then Cassandra became divinely inspired and ordered the victims to be carried to Hector's tomb. She said that the gods were angry and were rejecting their sacrifices because of the crime they had recently committed against the religion of Apollo. Thus, following her orders, they slew the bulls and took them to Hector's pyre, where, when the fire was lit, the sacrifice was completely consumed. With the coming of evening, they returned to their homes.

During that night Antenor secretly went to the temple of Minerva and, threatening the priestess Theano[3] with force and promising that she would be richly rewarded, begged her to give the Palladium to him. This she did; and thus he, being true to our men, carried it off to them. And they, having wrapped it up so that no one could tell what it was, sent it away in a cart to the hut of Ulysses through close and faithful friends.

With the coming of dawn, the Trojan council met. When our envoys had entered, Antenor, as though fearing the wrath of the Greeks, begged their forgiveness for having previously spoken so boldly against them in behalf of his native land.

Ulysses replied that he was not disturbed by this so much as by the fact that negotiations were being prolonged, especially when the favourable time for sailing was quickly passing.

After a long discussion, they finally agreed on a sum of two thousand talents of gold and two thousand of silver.

Then our envoys returned to the ships to make their report to our men. When our leaders had been assembled, they told them all that had been said and done, and how Antenor had carried the Palladium off. Thereupon, since all our leaders thought best, the rest of the soldiers were given the news.

---

3 Theano is mentioned in *Iliad* 5.70 as the wife of Antenor and in *Iliad* 6.302 as the priestess of Minerva.

V. 9.   Ob quae placet universis mitti Minervae donum quam honoratissimum. Tum accitus ad eam rem Helenus cuncta, quae clam se gesta erant, ac si praesens adfuisset. Ordine exponit additque finem iam advenisse Troianarum rerum, quippe quo maxime sustentaretur summa civitatis eius, Palladium fuisse; quo ablato exitium ingruere. ceterum donum Minervae fatale Troianis esse, equum ligno fabrefactum forma ingenti, cuius magnitudine muri solvendi essent, adnitente atque administro Antenore. Dein recordatus parentem Priamum residuosque fratres fletum edit miserabilem, consternatus per dolorem atque obstupefactus ruit. Tum Pyrrhus collectum eum refectumque animi ad se deducit custodesque addit veritus, ne qua per eum hostibus, quae gesta erant, patefierent. quod ubi Helenus persensit, Pyrrhum, uti bonum animum gereret, hortatur, securum sui secretorumque; namque se cum eo etiam post patriae excidium multis tempestatibus in Graecia moraturum. Itaque ut Heleno placuerat, multa materies, quae apta huiusmodi fabricae videbatur, per Epium atque Aiacem Oilei advecta.

V. 9. In view of these developments we decided unanimously to show our gratitude to Minerva by making a splendid offering to her. Helenus was summoned to tell us how to proceed. Using his prophetic powers (he had not been informed), he was able to give a detailed account of everything that had happened so far. And he also said that Troy was doomed now that the Palladium, the safeguard of Troy, had been carried away. We must, he said, offer a wooden horse to Minerva; this gift would prove fatal to Troy. The horse must be so large that the Trojans would have to breach their walls; Antenor would urge and advise them to do this. As Helenus was speaking, the thought of his father, Priam, and of his brothers who were still living caused him to burst into tears; his grief was so strong that he lost all control of himself and collapsed.

When he had come to his senses and was able to rise, Neoptolemus took him in charge. He had him guarded for fear he might somehow inform the enemy about what had happened. However Helenus, seeing himself under guard, told Neoptolemus there was nothing to worry about, for he would prove faithful and, after Troy's fall, would live with Neoptolemus in Greece many years.

And so, following Helenus' advice, we brought in a great deal of wood for building the horse. Epeus and Ajax the son of Oileus were in charge of this work.

V. 10. Interim firmatores pactae pacis ad Troiam eunt decem lecti duces, Diomedes, Ulixes, Idomeneus, Aiax Telamonius, Nestor, Meriones, Thoas, Philocteta, Neoptolemus atque Eumelus. Quos ubi in foro animadvertere populares, laeti animos tollunt finem iam aerumnarum credentes. Itaque singuli pluresve, uti quisque occurrerat, benigne adeunt, salutant gratulantes atque exosculantur. Tum Priamus pro Heleno orare Graecos multisque adhibitis precibus commendare carissimum sibi et inter ceteros dilectum magis propter prudentiam. Dein ubi tempus visum est, convivium publice coeptum in honore ducum adscitaeque pacis Antenore deserviente Graecis atque omni modo benigne exhibente cuncta. At lucis initio senes omnes in aedem Minervae conveniunt, in quis Antenor refert missos a Graecis super condicionibus praedictae pacis decem legatos viros. Quos ubi deduci in senatum placuit et dextrae invicem datae atque acceptae sunt, statuunt inter se, uti proximo die campi medio atque in ore omnium aras statuant, in quis fidem pacis iurisiurandi religionibus firmarent. Quis perfectis Diomedes atque Ulixes iurare occipiunt permansuros se in eo, quod sibi cum Antenore convenisset, testesque in eam rem Iovem summum Terramque matrem, Solem, Lunam atque Oceanum fore. Dein excisis in partes duas hostiis, quae ad eam rem admotae erant, ita uti pars ad solem, residuum ad naves expectaret, per medium transeunt. Dein Antenor in eadem verba placitum confirmat. Ita perfecto negotio ad suos quisque abeunt. Ceterum barbari Antenorem summis efferre laudibus, advenientem singuli quasi deum venerari, solum quippe omnium credere auctorem pacis eius adscitaeque cum Graecis amicitiae. Ita sopito iam exinde bello passim, uti quisque partium voluerat, nunc Graeci cum Troianis rursusque hi apud naves amice agere. Interim ubi foedus intervenerat, cuncti barbarorum socii, qui bello residui erant, gratulantes interventu pacis ad suos discedunt ne opperientes quidem praemia tantorum discriminum atque aerumnarum, scilicet veriti, ne qua pacti fides apud barbaros dissolveretur.

DICTYS V

V. 10. Meanwhile ten leaders were chosen to go to Troy and ratify the terms of the peace: Diomedes, Ulysses, Idomeneus, Ajax the son of Telamon, Nestor, Meriones, Thoas, Philoctetes, Neoptolemus, and Eumelus.

The Trojans, seeing our men in their public square, rejoiced, believing that now their afflictions would end. Individually and in groups, whenever they met them, they greeted them warmly and embraced them like loved ones.

Priam implored our leaders on behalf of Helenus and commended him to them with many prayers. Helenus, he said, was his dearest son, dearer because of his wisdom than all of the others.

When dinnertime came, the Trojans held a public banquet in honour of the Greeks and in celebration of the peace they were making. Antenor was host and graciously served every need of our men.

At daybreak all the elders convened in the temple of Minerva, and Antenor officially announced that ten envoys had been sent by the Greeks to ratify the terms of the peace. Thereupon the envoys were escorted into the council, and they and the elders shook hands. It was decided to ratify the peace on the following day. Sacred oaths must be sworn, for the purpose of which altars must be raised in the centre of the plain where all could see.

When preparations had been made, Diomedes and Ulysses were first to swear. Calling on Highest Jupiter, Mother Earth, Sun, Moon, and Ocean to be their witnesses, they promised to abide by the agreements which they had made with Antenor. Then they walked through the centre of the portions of the sacrificial victims. (Two victims had been brought, the portions of which had been laid out, half in an easterly direction and half in the direction of our ships). Diomedes and Ulysses were followed by Antenor, who took the same oath. After ratifying the terms of the peace in this way, both sides returned to their people.

The barbarians heaped highest praises upon Antenor, reverencing him like a god whenever he approached. They believed that he alone was responsible for the treaty and peace with the Greeks.

Now everywhere, as both sides wished, war had ceased. Greeks felt free to go to Troy. Trojans came among the ships, and the Trojan allies, those who were still alive, went home, taking advantage of the treaty and feeling thankful for peace, not even waiting to be paid for their hardships and troubles, fearing, no doubt, that the barbarians would somehow break the agreements.

247

V. 11.   Interim apud naves, uti Heleno placuerat, equus tabulatis extruitur per Epium fabricatorem eius operis. cui edito in immensum ima, quae sub pedibus erant, rotis interpositis suspenderat, scilicet quo ad tractu motus facilius foret. Quem offerri donum Minervae maximum omnium ore agitabatur. Ceterum apud Troiam auri atque argenti praedictum pondus per Antenorem atque Aeneam summo studio in aedem Minervae portabatur. Et Graeci, postquam auxilia sociorum dimissa cognitum est, impensius pacem atque amicitiam agitavere nullo exinde barbarorum interfecto aut vulnerato, quo magis sine ulla discordiarum suspicione apud hostes fuere. Dein equum compactum adfabre confixumque ad muros movent praenuntiato Troianis, uti cum religione susciperent, Minervae scilicet sacrum dicatumque. Quare magna vis hominum portis egressa summa laetitia sacrificioque donum excipit attrahitque propius moenia, sed postquam magnitudine operis impediri per portas ingressum animadvertere, consilium destruendorum desuper murorum capiunt, neque quisquam secus prae tali studio decernebat. Ita inviolatum multis tempestatibus murorum opus Neptunique, ut perhibebatur, atque Apollinis maxima monumenta nullo dilectu civium manibus dissolvuntur. Sed postquam maior pars operis eius deiecta est, consulto a Graecis intercessum, confirmantibus non se passuros intra moenia induci equum, priusquam praedictum auri atque argenti pondus susceperint. Ita intermisso opere semirutisque moenibus Ulixes cunctos civitatis Troianae artifices ad reficiendas naves conducit. Composita dein universa classe, ubi cuncta navigia instructa et praemium persolutum est, iubent nostri peragere incepta. Itaque destructa murorum parte cum ioco lasciviaque induxere equum feminis inter se atque viris certatim adtrahere festinantibus.

V. 11.   During this time, at the ships, Epeus, following Helenus' advice, was directing the building of the wooden horse. It towered to an immense height. Wheels were put beneath its feet to make it easier to draw along. It was the greatest offering ever to be given to Minerva. Everyone said so.

At Troy, Antenor and Aeneas were making sure that the exact amount of gold and silver, in accordance with the terms of the peace, was carried to the temple of Minerva.

And we, having learned that the allies of the Trojans had left, were careful to keep the terms of the peace. There was no more killing and no more wounding, lest the barbarians suspect that we were breaking agreements.

When the wooden horse had been built, complete in all points, we drew it out to the walls. The Trojans were told to receive it religiously as a sacred offering to Minerva. They poured from their gates and joyously welcomed the horse. A sacrifice was made, and they drew it nearer the city. When, however, they saw that the horse was too large to pass through their gates, they decided, their enthusiasm blinding them to any objections, to tear down their walls. Thus they all joined in, and tore down their walls, those walls which had stood for centuries unharmed, and which, as tradition told, were the masterwork of Neptune and Apollo.[4]

When the work of demolition was almost complete, the Greeks purposely caused a delay. We said that the Trojans must pay the gold and silver they had promised before they could draw the horse into Troy. Thus there was an interval of time during which, the walls being half demolished, Ulysses hired all of the Trojan carpenters to help repair the ships.

When our fleet had thus been put in order, along with all of our sailing gear, and when the gold and silver had been paid, we ordered the Trojans to continue their work of destruction. As soon as a part of the walls was down, a crowd of joking men and women merrily hastened to draw the horse within their city.

---

4 See *Iliad* 7.452-453.

V. 12.   Interim Graeci, ubi cuncta navibus imposita sunt, incensis omnium tabernaculis ad Sigeum secedunt, ibique noctem opperiuntur. Fessis dein multo vino atque somno barbaris, quae utraque per laetitiam securitatemque pacis intervenerant, multo silentio ad a civitatem navigant servantes signum, quod igni elato Sinon ad eam rem clam positus sustulerat. Moxque omnes postquam intravere moenia divisis inter se civitatis locis, ubi signum datum est, magna vi caedere eos, quos fors obiecerat, atque obtruncare passim per domos atque vias, loca sacra profanaque et, si qui persenserant, priusquam armare se aut aliud pro salute capere quirent, opprimere. prorsus nulla requies stragis atque funerum, cum palam et in ore suorum liberi parentesque magno inspectantium gemitu necarentur moxque ipsi, qui spectaculo carissimorum corporum interfuerant, miserandum in modum interirent. Neque segnius per totam urbem incendiis gestum positis prius defensoribus ad domum Aeneae atque Antenoris. interim Priamus re cognita ad aram Iovis anteaedificialis confugit, multique ex eo loco ad reliqua deorum templa, in quis Cassandra in aedem Minervae. Sed postquam universos, qui in manus venerant, foede atque inultos obtruncavere, occipiente luce domum, in qua Helena erat, adgrediuntur. Ibi Menelaus Deiphobum, quem post Alexandri interitum Helenae matrimonium intercepisse supra docuimus. Exsectis primo auribus brachiisque ablatis deinde naribus ad postremum truncatum omni ex parte foedatumque summo cruciatu necat. Dein Priamum Neoptolemus sine ullo aetatis atque honoris dilectu retinentem utraque manu aram iugulat. Ceterum Cassandram Oilei Aiax e sacro Minervae captivam abstrahit.

V. 12. Meanwhile we, having stowed everything on the ships and having set fire to our huts, sailed off to Sigeum and there awaited the night.

When the Trojans, being worn out with carousing and feeling happy and secure because of the peace, had fallen asleep, we returned to the city, sailing through the dead silence, following the beacon that Sinon raised from his hidden position. Soon we had entered the walls and divided the city among us. At a given signal, we slaughtered whomever we found, in homes, on streets, in places sacred and profane. Some of the Trojans awoke, but these were cut down before they could reach for their arms or think of a way to escape. There was, in short, no end to death and slaughter. Parents and children were killed, while loved ones watched and lamented, and then the latter were killed, a pitiable sight. With equal dispatch, the buildings of the city were set on fire and destroyed; the only homes to be saved were those of Aeneas and Antenor, where guards had been posted. Priam, seeing what was happening, fled to the altar of Jupiter that stood in front of the palace. And many members of the royal family fled to other shrines of the gods; Cassandra, for instance, went to the temple of Minerva. All who fell into the hands of the enemy died cruelly, without anyone to avenge them.

At daybreak our forces came to the house where Helen was living with Deiphobus. He (as already described) had taken her to wife when Alexander had died. Now Menelaus tortured him to death, brutally cutting him to pieces, lopping off ears and arms and nose and so forth.

And Neoptolemus, with no respect for old age or the office of king, slaughtered Priam, both of whose hands were clutching the altar.

And Ajax the son of Oileus dragged off Cassandra from the temple of Minerva to be his captive.

V. 13.   Hoc modo consumptis cum civitate barbaris, deliberatio inita super his, qui ab deorum aris auxilium vitae imploraverant decretumque ab omnibus, uti per vim avulsi necarentur: tantus dolor iniuriae et ob id studium extinguendi Troiani nominis incesserat. Ita comprehensi, qui cruciatum praedictae noctis subterfugerant, trepidantes ac vice pecorum interficiuntur. Dein more belli per templa ac semiustas domos populatio rerum omnium et per dies plurimos, ne quis hostium evaderet, studium in requirendo. Interim ad coacervandum auri atque argenti materiam opportuna loca destinantur et alia ob pretiosam vestem. Igitur ubi satias Troiani sanguinis tenuit et urbs incendiis complanata est, initium solvendae per praedam militiae capiunt, primo a feminis captivis puerisque adhuc imbellibus. Itaque ex his prima omnium Helena sine sorte Menelao conceditur, dein Polyxena suadente Ulixe per Neoptolemum Achilli inferias missa, Agamemnoni Cassandra datur, postquam forma eius captus, quin palam desiderium fateretur, dissimulare nequiverat, Aethram et Clymenam Demophoon atque Acamas habuere. Reliquarum sors agi coepta atque ita Neoptolemo Andromacha adiunctis, postquam id evenerat, filiis eius in honorem tanti ducis, Ulixi Hecuba obvenere. Hactenus nobilium feminarum cessere servitia. Alii, ut quemque sors contigerat, praedam aut ex captivis, quantum pro merito distribuebatur, habuere.

V. 13.   Thus we destroyed Troy and the Trojans. But still there were those who were seeking protection at the altars of gods. We decided unanimously to pull them away and kill them; so great was our lust for vengeance and our will to destroy the power of the Trojans. Accordingly, those who had escaped the slaughter of the previous night, those trembling sheep, were slaughtered, and as is usual in war, we pillaged the temples and half-burned houses, and for many a day hunted down any of the enemy who might have escaped. Places were designated where objects of gold and of silver and costly garments were brought.

When we were sated with Trojan blood, and the city was burned to the ground, we divided the booty, in payment of our military service, beginning with the captive women and children. First of all, Helen was freely given to Menelaus; then Polyxena, at the request of Ulysses, was given to Neoptolemus, to sacrifice to Achilles; Cassandra was given to Agamemnon (he had been so moved by her beauty that, in spite of himself, he had openly said that he loved her); and Aethra and Clymene were given to Demophoon and Acamas. The other women were apportioned by lot, and thus Andromache fell to Neoptolemus (to honour whose greatness, we further allowed Andromache's sons to accompany her); and Hecuba fell to Ulysses. After enslaving the women of royal birth, we allotted booty and captives to the rest of our men in proportion as they deserved.

V. 14. Interim super Palladio ingens certamen inter se ducibus exortum Aiace Telamonis expostulante in munus sibi pro his, quae in singulos universosque virtute atque industria sua contulerat. Qua re coacti paene omnes, simul uti ne laederetur animus tanti viri, cuius praeclara facinora vigiliasque pro exercitu in animo retinebant, concedunt Aiaci renitentibus solis omnium Diomede atque Ulixe sua quippe opera insinuantibus id ablatum. Contra Aiax adfirmare non labore aut virtute eorum rem gestam, Antenorem namque contemplatione communis amicitiae abstulisse. Tum Diomedes honori eius per verecundiam concedens a certamine destitit. Igitur Ulixes cum Aiace summa vi contendere inter se atque invicem industriae meritis expostulare adnitentibus Ulixi Menelao atque Agamemnone ob servatam paulo ante opera eius Helenam. Namque post captum Ilium Aiax recordatus eorum, quae tantis tempestatibus propter mulierem experti perpessique essent, primus omnium interfici eam iusserat. Iamque adprobantibus consilium Aiacis multis bonis Menelaus amorem coniugii etiam tunc retinens singulos ambiundo orandoque ad postremum perfecerat, uti intercessu Ulixis Helena incolumis sibi traderetur. Itaque uti iudicio amborum merita expectantes, quis etiam nunc bellum in manibus atque hostiles multae nationes circumstreperent, nullo dilectu virorum fortium spretisque Aiacis egregiis facinoribus ac frumenti, quod ex Thracia advexerat, per totum exercitum distributione Ulixi Palladium tradunt.

V. 14.   Heated contention arose at this time as to which of our leaders should have the Palladium.[5] Ajax the son of Telamon demanded it in payment for the booty his courage and zeal had brought to us all. There was almost no one who was willing to offend a man of such greatness, for we vividly remembered his deeds on offence and defence. Only Diomedes and Ulysses stood in his way; they based their claims to the Palladium on the fact that they had carried it off. Ajax swore that Antenor, who had hoped thereby to win their friendship, had carried the Palladium off; and this, he said, had caused them no trouble and made no demands on their courage. Thereupon Diomedes modestly yielded to Ajax, but not so Ulysses, who contended, with all of his force, that he should have the Palladium.

Menelaus and Agamemnon favoured the cause of Ulysses, for they remembered how Helen had been saved, just a little before, by his aid. When Troy had been taken, Ajax had been the first to propose that she should be killed because of the troubles and sufferings she had caused for so long a time. Many good men had assented, but Menelaus, still loving his wife, had gone the rounds, and pleaded for her life, and finally, through the intercession of Ulysses, had won her back unharmed.

Thus we decided between Ajax and Ulysses, judging only their merits in this particular case. It made no difference which was the bravest. Yes, Ajax had performed many valourous deeds, and brought back grain from Thrace, but these were matters not pertinent here. Thus, in spite of the fact that we were surrounded by enemies and still threatened with war, the Palladium went to Ulysses.

---

5 In other accounts the armour of Achilles is the object of contention.

V. 15.   Quare cuncti duces, qui memores virtutum Aiacis nihil praeferendum ei censuerant quique secuti gratiam Ulixi impugnaverant talem virum, studio in partes discedunt. Interim Aiax indignatus et ob id victus dolore animi palam atque in ore omnium vindictam se sanguine eorum, a quis impugnatus esset, exacturum denuntiat. Itaque ex eo Ulixes, Agamemnon ac Menelaus custodiam sui augere et quo tutiores essent, summa ope invigilare. At ubi nox aderat, discedentes uno ore omnes lacerare utrumque regem neque abstinere maledictis, quippe quis magis libido desideriumque in femina quam summa militiae potiora forent. At lucis principio Aiacem in medio exanimem offendunt perquirentesque mortis genus animadvertere ferro interfectum. Inde ortus per duces atque exercitum tumultus ingens ac dein seditio brevi adulta. Cum ante iam Palamedem virum domi belloque prudentissimum nunc Aiacem, inclitum tot egregiis pugnis, atque utrosque insidiis eorum circumventos ingemescerent. Ob quae supradicti reges veriti, ne qua vis ab exercitu pararetur, intus clausi firmatique per necessarios manent. Interim Neoptolemus advecta ligni materia Aiacem cremat reliquiasque urnae aureae conditas in Rhoeteo sepeliendas procurat breviQUE tumulum extructum consecrat in honorem tanti ducis. Quae si ante captum Ilium accidere potuissent, profecto magna ex parte promotae res hostium ac dubitatum de summa rerum fuisset. Igitur Ulixes veritus vim offensi exercitus clam Ismarum aufugit atque ita Palladium apud Diomedem manet.

V. 15. This decision caused our men to split into two factions: those who, remembering the brave deeds of Ajax, thought that no one was better than he; and those who favoured Ulysses. Ajax was so angry that he lost control of himself and openly swore to kill those who had thwarted his claim. Accordingly, Ulysses, Agamemnon, and Menelaus increased their guard and kept careful watch for their personal safety. With the coming of night, as we departed, we all cursed and reviled the two kings, blaming them for letting the lust for a woman endanger the army.

At daybreak we found Ajax, out in the open, dead; upon closer investigation, we discovered that he had been killed with a sword. A great tumult arose among our leaders and men, and soon a full grown rebellion was under way. We felt that just as Palamedes, our wisest counsellor in war and peace, had been treacherously slain, so now Ajax, our most distinguished commander, had met a similar end.

Agamemnon and Menelaus stayed in their huts, guarded by trusted companions, and avoided any possible violence.

Meanwhile Neoptolemus brought wood and cremated the body of Ajax; then he gathered the remains in a golden urn and had them buried in Rhoeteum.[6] He also dedicated a monument in honour of Ajax, and this was quickly constructed.

If Ajax had died before Troy had been taken, certainly the cause of the enemy would have been greatly promoted. Who knows how the war might have ended?

Ulysses, knowing that he was hated by the army, feared personal violence, and fled across to Ismaros. He left the Palladium behind for Diomedes to have.

---

6 Rhoeteum is north of Sigeum. Strabo tells of a tomb and temple of Ajax on the shore nearby. See his *Geography* 13.1.30.

V. 16.   Ceterum post abscessum Ulixi Hecuba, quo servitium morte solveret, multa ingerere maledicta imprecarique infesta omina in exercitum. Qua re motus miles lapidus obrutam eam necat sepulchrumque apud Abydum statuitur appellatum Cynossema ob linguae protervam impudentemque petulantiam. Per idem tempus Cassandra deo repleta multa in Agamemnonem adversa praenuntiat: insidias quippe ei ex occulto caedemque domi per suos compositam; praeterea universo exercitui profectionem ad suos incommodam exitialemque. Inter quae Antenor cum suis Graecos orare, omitterent iras atque urgente navigii tempore in commune consulant. Praeterea omnes duces ad se epulatum deducit ibique singulos quam maximis donis replet. Tunc Graeci Aeneae suadent, secum uti in Graeciam naviget, ibi namque ei simile cum ceteris ducibus ius regnique eandem potestatem fore. Neoptolemus filios Hectoris Heleno concedit, praeterea reliqui duces auri atque argenti quantum singulis visum est. Dein consilio habito decernitur, uti per triduum funus Aiacis publice susciperetur. Itaque exactis his diebus cuncti reges comam tumulo eius deponunt. Atque exin contumeliis Agamemnonem fratremque agere eosque non Atrei sed Plisthenidas et ob id ignobiles appellare. Quare coacti, simul uti odium sui apud exercitum per absentiam leniretur, orant, uti sibi abire e conspectu eorum sine noxa concedant. Itaque consensu omnium primi navigant deturbati expulsique ab ducibus. Ceterum Aiacis filii, Aeantides Glauca genitus atque Eurysaces ex Tecmessa, Teucro traditi.

V. 16.   After the departure of Ulysses, Hecuba, preferring death to enslavement, called down many curses and evil omens upon us, and we, being terribly provoked, stoned her to death. Her tomb, which was raised at Abydos, was called Cynossema (The Tomb of the Bitch) because of her mad and shameless barking.

At the same time Cassandra, inspired by the god, predicted that Agamemnon would die, treacherously slaughtered by members of his household. Furthermore, she said, death and disaster awaited the rest of the Greeks, as they tried to return to their homelands.

Antenor begged us, in behalf of his people, to forget about vengeance and think of ourselves, for the time for sailing was passing. Having invited our leaders to dinner, he loaded them down with marvellous gifts.

Our leaders were urging Aeneas to sail along with us to Greece and promised to give him a kingdom as powerful as any they ruled.

Helenus was rewarded with the sons of Hector, whom Neoptolemus gave him, and with all the gold and silver which the rest of our leaders felt they should give him.

Then a meeting of the council was called, and we decided to hold a public funeral, to last for three days, in honour of Ajax. When the third day came to an end, all of our kings cut off their hair, which then they placed on the tomb.

From this time on, we began to revile Agamemnon and Menelaus, saying that they were not the sons of Atreus but of Plisthenes, and therefore ignoble. They, hoping that if they were gone our hatred would vanish, begged us to let them depart without harm. This we permitted; and so, like outcasts or exiles, they were the first to set sail.

We gave the sons of Ajax to Teucer. They were Aeantides and Eurysaces, whose mothers were Glauce and Tecmessa respectively.

V. 17. Dein Graeci veriti, ne per moram interventu hiemis, quae ingruebat, ab navigando excluderentur, deductas in mare naves remigibus reliquisque nauticis instrumentis complent. Atque ita cum his, quae singuli praeda multorum annorum quaesiverant, discedunt. Aeneas apud Troiam manet. Qui post Graecorum profectionem cunctos ex Dardano atque ex proxima paene insula adit, orat, uti secum Antenorem regno exigerent. Quae postquam praeverso de se nuntio Antenori cognita sunt, regrediens ad Troiam imperfecto negotio aditu prohibetur. Ita coactus cum omni patrimonio ab Troia navigat devenitque ad mare Hadriaticum multas interim gentes barbaras praevectus. Ibi cum his, qui secum navigaverant, civitatem condit appellatam Corcyram Melaenam. Ceterum apud Troiam postquam fama est Antenorem regno potitum, cuncti, qui bello residui nocturnam civitatis cladem evaserant, ad eum confluunt brevique ingens coalita multitudo. Tantus amor erga Antenorem atque opinio sapientiae incesserat. Fitque princeps amicitiae eius rex Cebrenorum Oenideus.

Haec ego Gnosius Dictys comes Idomenei conscripsi oratione ea, quam maxime inter tam diversa loquendi genera consequi ac comprehendere potui, litteris Punicis ab Cadmo Danaoque traditis. Neque sit mirum cuiquam, si quamvis Graeci omnes diverso tamen inter se sermone agunt, cum ne nos quidem unius eiusdemque insulae simili lingua sed varia permixtaque utamur. Igitur ea, quae in bello evenere Graecis ac barbaris, cuncta sciens perpessusque magna ex parte memoriae tradidi. De Antenore eiusque regno quae audieram retuli. Nunc reditum nostrorum narrare iuvat.

V. 17.   Winter was coming on fast and threatened to prevent us from sailing. Accordingly, we drew our ships down to the sea and fitted them out with oars and other equipment. Then we departed, each with the booty he had gained for all those years of fighting.

After our departure, Aeneas, who had been left behind at Troy, tried to drive Antenor out of the kingdom. Leaving the city, he approached all those who were inhabitants of Dardanum and the peninsula nearby, and begged them to help him. He was unsuccessful, however; and when he tried to return to Troy, Antenor, who had learned what was happening, refused him admittance. And so Aeneas was forced to set sail. Taking all of his patrimony, he departed from Troy and eventually arrived in the Adriatic Sea, after passing many barbarous peoples. Here he and those who were with him founded a city, which they called Corcyra Melaena (Black Corcyra).

When it was known at Troy that Antenor had gained control of the kingdom, all the survivors of the war, those who had escaped the slaughter of that fearful night, supported his rule. In practically no time his following had increased to immense proportions. Everyone loved him and trusted his wisdom. His closest friend was Oenideus, the king of the Cebrenians.

I, Dictys of Cnossos, the companion of Idomeneus, have written this account in the language (how many there are!) I best understand, using the Phoenician alphabet bequeathed to us by Cadmus and Danaus. No one should marvel that many different languages are spoken on this one island of mine, for such is the case all over Greece. Everything I have written about the war between the Greeks and the barbarians, in which I took a very active part, is based on firsthand knowledge. What I have told about Antenor and his kingdom was learned on inquiry from others.

Now it is time to relate the returns of our men

LIBER SEXTVS

VI. 1.   Postquam impositis cunctis, quae singuli bello quaesiverant, ascendere ipsi, solutis anchoralibus navigant. Dein a puppi secundante vento paucis diebus pervenere ad Aegaeum mare, ibi multa imbribus ventisque et ob id saeviente mari indigna experti passim, uti fors tulerat, dispalantur. In quis Locrorum classis perturbatis per tempestatem officiis nautarum et inter se implicatis ad postremum fulmine comminuta aut incensa est, et rex Locrorum Aiax postquam natando evadere naufragium enisus est aliique per noctem tabulis aut alio levamine fluitantes postquam ad Euboeam devenere, Choeradibus scopulis adpulsi pereunt. Eos namque re cognita Nauplius ultum ire cupiens Palamedis necem per noctem igni elato ad ea loca deflectere tamquam ad portum coegerat.

Book Six

VI. 1. When the Greeks had loaded the ships with all the booty they had gained, and gone aboard themselves, they weighed anchor and set sail. Blessed with a favourable wind from the stern quarter, within a few days they reached the Aegean Sea. But then, as fate would have it, a furious storm arose, a sea of troubles for all of our men, and scattered our ships.

Shattering lightning bolts, which terrified the sailors and caused them to lose all control, completely destroyed the fleet of the Locrians, commanded by Ajax. Ajax and some of the others who, having escaped the wreckage, kept afloat by clinging to boards and flotsam, were dashed to death against the Choeradian crags of Euboea. The night had kept them from seeing; and Nauplius, knowing their plight and desiring to avenge the death of his son Palamedes, had raised a torch, to lure them there, as if to a harbour.

VI. 2.   Per idem tempus Oeax Naupli filius, Palamedis frater cognito Graecos ad suos remeare Argos venit, ibi Aegialen atque Clytemestram falsis nuntiis adversum maritos armat praedicto ducere eos secum ex Troia uxores praelatas his. Praeterea addere ea, quis mobili suasu natura muliebre ingenium magis adversum suos incenderetur. Itaque Aegiale advenientem Diomedem per cives aditu prohibet. Clytemestra per Aegisthum adulterio sibi cognitum Agamemnonem insidiis capit eumque interficit. Brevique denupta adultero Erigonen ex eo edit. Interim Talthybius Orestem Agamemnonis filium manibus Aegisthi ereptum Idomeneo, qui apud Corinthum agebat, tradit. Eo Diomedes expulsus regno et Teucrus prohibitus Salamina a Telamone, scilicet quod fratrem insidiis circumventum non defendisset, conveniunt. Interim Menestheus cum Aethra Pilthei et Clymena filia eius ab Atheniensibus recipitur, Demophoon atque Acamas foris manent. Ceterum ubi plures eorum, qui mare insidiasque suorum evaserant, apud Corinthum fuere, cavent, uti iuncti inter se singula adgrederentur regna belloque aditum ad suos patefacerent. Eam rem Nestor prohibet suadens temptandos prius civium animos neque committendum, uti per seditionem Graecia omnis intestinis discordiis corrumperetur. Neque multo post cognoscit Diomedes in Aetolia ab his, qui per absentiam eius regnum infestabant, Oeneum multimodis adflictari. Ob quae profectus ad ea loca omnes, quos auctores iniuriae reppererat, interficit metuque omnibus circum locis iniecto facile ab suis receptus est. Inde per omnem Graeciam fama orta suos quisque reges accipiunt summam in his, qui apud Troiam bellaverant, virtutem neque in resistendo cuiusquam vires idoneas existimantes. Ita nos quoque cum Idomeneo rege Cretam patrium solum summa gratulatione civium remeavimus.

DICTYS VI

VI. 2. At the same time Oeax, who was the son of Nauplius and the brother of Palamedes, on learning that the Greeks were returning home, went to Argos and reported, falsely, to Clytemnestra and Aegiale that Agamemnon and Diomedes were bringing back women they preferred to their wives; and he added those things by which their womanly hearts, by nature easily persuaded, might be the more incensed against their husbands. Thus they were prompted to arm themselves against their husbands' arrivals. Accordingly, Aegiale, with the help of the citizens, prevented Diomedes from entering the city; and Clytemnestra had Aegisthus, with whom she was living in adultery, surprise Agamemnon and slay him. Soon thereafter the adulterous pair were married, and Clytemnestra gave birth to a daughter, Erigone.

Meanwhile Talthybius saved Orestes, Agamemnon's son, from the hands of Aegisthus, and brought him to Idomeneus.

Idomeneus was then a resident of Corinth; to which city Diomedes and Teucer also came when driven away from their homes. Teucer had been prohibited from landing on Salamis by Telamon, his father, because, no doubt, he had not prevented his brother Ajax' ignominious death.

Meanwhile the Athenians welcomed Menestheus along with Aethra, the daughter of Pittheus, and her daughter, Clymene. Demophoon and Acamas, however, remained outside the city.

Most of those who had escaped death from dangers at sea or plots at home came to Corinth and there made plans to recover their kingdoms. They should, they thought, combine their forces and attack their kingdoms one at a time. This action, however, was vetoed by Nestor, who said that they should try persuasion first and not tear Greece apart with civil wars.

Soon after this, Diomedes learned that his grandfather, Oeneus, was being afflicted in every way by those who had gained control of Aetolia during his absence. Accordingly, he went to that region and killed the guilty usurpers. Those who favoured his cause easily welcomed him back, for all Aetolia feared him.

When news of Diomedes' success spread, all of the Greeks reinstated their kings, thinking that no one could match the bravery or strength of those who had battled at Troy. And so we Cretans and our king Idomeneus returned to our native soil and were joyfully received by our people.

VI. 3.   Dein ubi Orestes transactis pueritiae annis officia viri exsequi coepit, orat Idomeneum, uti secum ex ea insula quam plurimos mitteret; cupere namque se Athenas navigare. Itaque collecto numero eorum, quos idoneos credebat, Athenas venit, ab his auxilium contra Aegisthum orat. Dein ad oraculum adit responsumque fert, uti matrem et cum ea Aegistum interficiat; ex quo fore, uti regnum patrium reciperet. Huiusmodi numine armatus cum praedicta manu ad Strophium venit. Is namque Phocensis, cuius filia in matrimonium Aegisthi denupserat, indignatus, quod spreto priore coniugio Clytemestram superduxerit et regem omnium Agamemnonem insidiis interfecerit, ultro ei auxilium adversum inimicissimos obtulerat. Itaque conspirato inter se cum magna manu Mycenas veniunt statimque, quod Aegisthus aberat, primo Clytemestram interficiunt multosque alios, qui resistere ausi erant. Dein cognito Aegisthum adventare insidias ponunt eumque circumveniunt. Inde per omnem Argivorum populum dissensio animorum exorta, quod diversa inter se cupientes ad postremum in partes discederent. Per idem tempus Menelaus adpulsus Cretam cuncta super Agamemnone regnoque eius cognoscit.

VI. 3. When Orestes had grown to maturity, he begged Idomeneus to give him as many men as he could and let him sail from Crete to Athens. His request being granted, having gathered a number of those he thought sufficient, he went off to Athens and there invoked the aid of the Athenians against Aegisthus.

Then, having gone to the oracle, he received the response that he was destined to kill his mother and Aegisthus, and thus to recover his father's kingdom.

Armed with this prophecy, he and his band went on to Strophius, the Phocian. Strophius willingly offered his aid, for he passionately hated Aegisthus. (Aegisthus had first married Strophius' daughter, but then had rejected her and married Clytemnestra; and he had treacherously slain Agamemnon, the great king).

Thus Orestes, having assembled a large army, marched on Mycenae. Clytemnestra was immediately slain, along with many others who dared to resist. Aegisthus was absent, but when news of his arrival was brought, he was ambushed and killed. Throughout Argos the people were forced to take sides and tried to choose where best their interest lay.

During the same time Menelaus landed on Crete and learned how Agamemnon had died and what was happening in Argos.

VI. 4. Interea per omnem insulam, postquam cognitum Helenam eo venisse, multi undique virile ac muliebre secus confluunt advenientes dinoscere, cuius gratia orbis paene omnis ad bellum conspiravisset. Ibi inter cetera Menelaus perfert Teucrum expulsum patria civitatem apud Cyprum Salamina nomine condidisse. multa etiam apud Aegyptum miranda refert et Canopi gubernatoris sui, qui ubi morsu serpentium interierat, extructum magnificum monumentum. Dein ubi tempus visum est, Mycenas navigat. Ibi multa adversum Orestem molitur. Ad postremum multitudine popularium cohibitus ab eo quod coeperat negotio restitit. Inde placet cunctis Orestem super eo facinore causam dicere apud Athenienses, ubi Ariopagitarum iudicium severissimum per omnem Graeciam memorabatur. Apud quos dicta causa iuvenis absolvitur. Erigona quae ex Aegistho edita erat, ubi fratrem absolutum intellegit, victa dolore immodico laqueo interiit. Menestheus liberatum Orestem parricidii crimine purgatumque more patrio cunctis remediis, quae ad oblivionem huiusmodi facinoris adhiberi solita erant, Mycenas remittit; ibique regnum ei concessum. Dein transacto tempore accitu Idomenei Cretam venit neque multo post Menelaus. Ibi multa in patruum severe per eum ingesta, quod sibi per dissensionem popularium multimodis periclitanti ipse etiam insidiatus esset. Ad postremum intercessu Idomenei uterque conciliatus sibi Lacedaemona discedit. Ibi Menelaus, sicuti convenerat, Hermionam in matrimonium Oresti despondit.

VI. 4.   When the Cretans heard of Helen's arrival, many men and women from all over the island came together, desiring to see her for whose sake almost all of the world had gone to war.

Menelaus told his adventures. He had learned that Teucer, who had been banished from home, had founded a city on Cyprus called Salamis. He also reported the many wonders of Egypt. The serpents there, he said, had killed his pilot, Canopus; for whom he had built a magnificent tomb.

When the time seemed right, Menelaus sailed to Mycenae. There he laid many plots against Orestes, but the people prevented him from carrying out these plans. Orestes, it was decided unanimously, should go to Athens and there stand trial before the court of the Areopagus. Thus Orestes pleaded his case, and the Areopagus acquitted him; this court was reputedly the most severe in all Greece.

This acquittal so grieved Orestes' half-sister, Erigone, who was the daughter of Aegisthus, that she hanged herself. After the verdict and after Orestes had been purified by every means, according to the ancient ritual in use for parricides, Menestheus sent him home to Mycenae.

Thereupon the people made him king.

Later Orestes and then Menelaus came to Crete at the invitation of Idomeneus. Orestes bitterly charged his uncle with plotting against him at a time when his position was already endangered by public strife. Finally, however, they were reconciled with each other by the intercession of Idomeneus and so departed to Lacedaemon, and then Menelaus, just as he had agreed to do, promised Hermione in marriage to Orestes.

VI. 5. Per idem tempus Ulixes Cretam adpulsus est duabus Phoenicum navibus mercedis pacto acceptis, namque suas cum sociis atque omnibus, quae ex Troia habuerat, per vim Telamonis amiserat scilicet infesti ob inlatam per eum filio necem, vix ipse liberatus industria sui. Percontantique Idomeneo, quibus ex causis in tantas miserias devenisset, erroris initium narrare occipit: quo pacto adpulsus Ismarum multa inde perbellum quaesita praeda navigaverit adpulsusque ad Lotophagos atque adversa usus fortuna devenerit in Siciliam, ubi per Cyclopa et Laestrygona fratres multa indigna expertus ad postremum ab eorum filiis Antiphate et Polyphemo plurimos sociorum amiserit. Dein per misericordiam Polyphemi in amicitiam receptus filiam regis Arenen, postquam Alphenoris socii eius amore deperibat, rapere conatus. ubi res cognita est, interventu parentis puella ablata per vim, exactus per Aeoli insulas devenerit ad Circen atque inde ad Calypso utramque reginam insularum, in quis morabantur, ex quibusdam inlecebris animos hospitum ad amorem sui inlicientes. Inde liberatus pervenerit ad eum locum, in quo exhibitis quibusdam sacris futura defunctorum animis dinoscerentur. Post quae adpulsus Sirenarum scopulis, ubi per industriam liberatus sit. Ad postremum inter Scyllam et Charybdim mare saevissimum et inlata sorbere solitum plurimas navium cum sociis amiserit. Ita se cum residuis in manus Phoenicum per maria praedantium incurrisse atque ab his per misericordiam reservatum. Igitur, uti voluerat, acceptis ab rege nostro duabus navibus donatusque multa praeda ad Alcinoum regem Phaeacum remittitur.

VI. 5.   During the same time Ulysses, with two ships he had hired from the Phoenicians, landed on Crete.[1] He had lost his fleet along with his comrades and all of his booty and had barely escaped with his life by using his wits. This disaster had been due to the power of Telamon, who no doubt hated Ulysses for being the cause of Ajax' death.

When Idomeneus asked Ulysses how he had met such misfortunes, he told the story of his wanderings from the beginning. First they had landed at Ismaros, where they had fought, and gained much booty.

Then they had sailed to the country of the Lotus Eaters, where they had met with a cruel fate.

Then they had gone to the island of Sicily, where the brothers Cyclops and Laestrygon had treated them with every indignity and where Polyphemus and Antiphates, who were the sons of the former, had killed many of them. Finally, however, Polyphemus, he was the king, had taken pity upon them and agreed to a truce. But then they had tried to carry off Polyphemus' daughter Arene, who had fallen desperately in love with their comrade Alphenor. Polyphemus, however, had discovered their plans.

Thus, having been forcibly deprived of the girl, they were driven away, out through the islands of Aeolus, on to the island of Circe, and then to the island of Calypso. It was well known how these queens, by using certain charms, enticed their guests to love them. Nevertheless, Ulysses escaped.

Then they had gone to that place where, having performed the requisite rites, they learned of the future from the shades of the dead. Then on past the rocks of the Sirens, whom he had cleverly eluded.

And then, finally, he had lost most of his ships and men to Scylla and Charybdis, that savage, whirling pool that sucks down everything within its reach.

Then he and the survivors had come into the hands of Phoenician pirates, and these had mercifully saved them.

Thereupon our king Idomeneus did as Ulysses wished and gave him two ships and much booty and sent him off to Alcinous, the king of the Phaeacians.

---

1 Sections 5 and 6 cover the events of the *Odyssey*.

VI. 6. Ibi ob celebritatem nominis per multos dies benigne acceptus cognoscit Penelopam ab triginta inlustribus viris diversis ex locis in matrimonium postulari; hique erant ab Zacyntho, Echinadibus, Leucata, Ithaca, ob quae multis precibus persuadet regi, uti secum ad vindicandam matrimonii iniuriam navigaret. Sed postquam devenere ad eum locum paulisper occultato Ulixe, ubi Telemachum rem, quae parabatur, edocuere, domum ad Ulixem clam veniunt; ubi multo vino atque epulis repletos iam procos ingressi interficiunt. Dein per civitatem Ulixem adventasse popularibus cognitum est, a quis benigne et cum favore exceptus cuncta, quae domi gesta erant, cognoscit; meritos donis aut suppliciis afficit. De Penelopa eiusque pudicitia praeclara fama. Neque multo post precibus atque hortatu Ulixis Alcinoi filia Nausica Telemacho denubit. Per idem tempus Idomeneus dux noster apud Gretam interiit tradito per successionem Merioni regno. Et Laerta, triennio post quam filius domum redit, finem vitae fecit. Telemacho ex Nausica natum filium Ulixes Ptoliporthum appellat.

VI. 6. There they already knew of his fame and entertained him many days. Also they told him that Penelope was being wooed by thirty handsome suitors who had come from different regions: from Zacynthus, the Echinades, Leucas, and Ithaca. Thereupon he prevailed upon Alcinous to sail with him, to avenge this insult to his marriage.

When they had come to Ithaca, Ulysses stayed concealed for a little while, until they could inform Telemachus of what they were planning. Then they proceeded to the palace and slew the suitors, who had been wined and dined to the full. When the people knew that Ulysses had come, they welcomed him back and showed that they favoured his cause; and from them he learned everything that had happened at home. Ulysses repaid the faithful with gifts, the unfaithful with punishments. As for Penelope, her reputation for virtue is famous.

Soon afterwards, in answer to Ulysses' hopes and prayers, Nausicaa, the daughter of Alcinous, was married to Telemachus. This was also the time when our leader Idomeneus died in Crete, and according to the right of succession, the kingdom passed to Meriones. Laertes, three years after his son had returned, ended his life. Nausicaa and Telemachus had a son, to whom Ulysses gave the name Ptoliporthus (Sacker of Cities).

VI. 7.   Dum haec apud Ithacam aguntur, Neoptolemus apud Molossos naves quassatas tempestatibus reficit. Atque inde, postquam cognitum ab Acasto expulsum regno Pelea, ultum ire iniurias avi cupiens primo exploratum duos quam fidissimos et incognitos illis locis Chrysippum et Aratum Thessaliam mittit hique cuncta, quae gerebantur, insidiasque ei paratas per Acastum ab Assandro non alieno Pelei cognoscunt. Is namque Assandrus iniquitatem tyranni evitans, Peleo consenserat notusque adeo eius domus, uti inter cetera originem etiam nuptiarum Pelei cum Thetide Chironis filia Chrysippo atque Arato narraverit. Qua tempestate multi undique reges acciti domum Chironis inter ipsas epulas novam nuptam magnis laudibus veluti deam celebraverant, parentem eius Chirona appellantes Nerea ipsamque Nereidam; et ut quisque eorum regum, qui convivio interfuerant, choro modulisque carminum praevaluerat, ita Apollinem Liberumque, ex feminis plurimas Musas cognominaverant. Unde ad id tempus convivium illud deorum appellatum.

VI. 7.   While these things were happening on Ithaca, Neoptolemus was among the Molossians repairing his ships, which had been wrecked in a storm. There he had learned that Acastus had driven Peleus out of his kingdom in Thessaly. Accordingly, as he desired to avenge this wrong to his grandfather, he sent Chrysippus and Aratus to explore the situation; they were very reliable men, and no one in Thessaly knew them.

These learned from Assandrus, a follower of Peleus, everything that had happened and how Acastus had treacherously attacked Peleus. This Assandrus had eluded the tyranny of Acastus and sided with Peleus, with whom he had become so intimate that he was able to tell, among other things, about Peleus' marriage with Thetis, Chiron's daughter.

At that time many kings had been invited from everywhere to the wedding, which was at Chiron's home. During the banquet they had praised the bride and offered her toasts as if to a goddess, saying that she was a Nereid and that Chiron was Nereus. In the same way they had called any of their number who excelled in dancing or singing Apollo or Bacchus, and had given the names of Muses to many of the women. Accordingly, from that time on, this banquet was known as 'a banquet of the gods'.

VI. 8.   Itaque ubi cuncta, quae voluerant, cognovere, ad regem redeunt, ei singula per ordinem narrant. Ob quae coactus Neoptolemus adverso mari et multis regionis eius prohibentibus classem exornat ascenditque ipse. Dein saevitia hiemis multum mari fatigatus adpulsusque ad Sepiadum litus, quod propter saxorum difficultatem nomen eiusmodi quaesiverat, omnes fere naves amittit vix ipse cum his, qui in eodem navigio fuerant, liberatus. Ibi Pelea avum repperit occultatum spelunca abdita et tenebrosa, ubi senex vim atque insidias Acasti evitans assidue nepotis desiderio navigantes et si forte eo adpulsi essent speculari consuerat. Dein ubi cuncta domus fortunarumque edoctus est, consilium adgrediendi hostes inire occipit, cum forte cognoscit filios Acasti Menalippum et Plisthenem venatum profectos devenisse ad ea loca. Itaque mutata veste Iolcium simulans iuvenibus offert sese eisque cupitum sui interitum refert. Ob quae iunctus his in venando, ubi seorsum ab ceteris Menalippum videt, eumque et paulo post fratrem eius insecutus interficit. In quorum inquisitionem servus quidam Cinyras nomine perquam fidus profectus in manus iuvenis devenit comprehensusque Acastum adfore nuntiat atque ita occiditur.

VI. 8.   When Chrysippus and Aratus had learned what they wanted to know, they returned to Neoptolemus and made a full report.

Thereupon Neoptolemus, though the sea was rough and there were reasons enough to stay where he was, equipped his fleet and set sail. Having been much harassed on sea by a savage storm and having been driven to the shore of the Sepiades (so called because of their dangerous rocks), he lost almost all of his ships; he himself and those who were sailing with him barely escaped. There he found his grandfather, Peleus, who was hiding in a dark, secluded cave. The old man, while avoiding the treacherous plots of Acastus, was keeping a lookout for all who happened to sail there, hoping his grandson would come.

When Peleus had told Neoptolemus all that had befallen his house, the latter was beginning to decide on a plan of attack when by chance he learned that the sons of Acastus, Menalippus and Plisthenes, were coming to hunt near Peleus' cave. Accordingly, he changed into the clothes of that region; and then, pretending to be an Iolchian, he presented himself to the sons of Acastus and asked permission to join in their sport. This being granted, soon afterwards he came upon Menalippus and Plisthenes, they were close together but separated some distance from the rest of their party, and slew them. Then he captured and slew their faithful slave, Cinyras, who had come in search of his masters; but not before he had learned that Acastus also was coming.

VI. 9.   Itaque Neoptolemus mutata Phrygia veste tamquam filius Priami Mestor, qui captivus cum Pyrrho ad ea loca navigaverat, Acasto obvius venit eique, quinam esset, et Neoptolemum in spelunca fatigatum navigio somnoque iacere. Ob quae anxius Acastus opprimere quam inimicissimum cupiens ad speluncam pergit atque in ipso aditu a Thetide, quae ad ea loca inquisitum Pelea venerat, re cognita reprimitur. Dein cunctis, quae adversum domum Achillis inique et adversum fas gesserat, enumeratis increpatisque ad postremum intercessu suo manibus iuvenis liberat persuadens nepoti, ut ne sanguine ulterius ulcisci cuperet ea, quae antecesserant. Itaque Acastus ubi se praeter spem liberatum animadvertit, sponte et in loco cuncta regni Neoptolemo tradit. Inde iuvenis cum avo ac Thetide reliquisque, qui secum navigaverant, summam regni adeptus in civitatem venit. Ibi a cunctis popularibus quique iuxta inhabitantes sub imperio eius agebant benigne et cum gratulatione exceptus amorem sui brevi confirmat.

278

DICTYS VI

VI. 9.   Thereupon Neoptolemus changed into Phrygian clothes, so as to look like Mestor, the son of Priam, whom he had brought along as a captive.[2] When, dressed in this guise, he met with Acastus, he claimed to be Mestor and said that Neoptolemus was wearied from sailing and was sleeping there in the cave.

Since Acastus desired to trap this most hated of enemies, he went straight to the cave, but Thetis was there and kept him from entering. (She, having learned what was happening, had come to be with Peleus). She roundly berated Acastus for his crimes against the house of Achilles and against the laws of the gods. Then she used her influence to save him from Neoptolemus' power, for she urged her grandson to refrain from further vengeance and slaughter.

Acastus, being grateful for his unexpected escape, willingly, right then and there, gave Neoptolemus complete control of the kingdom.

Then Neoptolemus, having gained control of the kingdom, went to the city with his grandfather, Peleus, and his grandmother, Thetis, and those of his men who had survived the voyage. All the citizens and all the people round about who were under his power welcomed him joyously and with a devotion which, as he was soon to prove, was not misplaced.

---

2 According to Dictys 2.43 (end), Mestor was slain at Troy.

VI. 10. Haec ego cuncta ab Neoptolemo cognita mihi memoriae mandavi accitus ab eo, qua tempestate Hermionam Menelai in matrimonium susceperat. Ab eo etiam de reliquiis Memnonis cognitum mihi, uti tradita ossa eius apud Paphum his, qui cum Pallante duce Memnonis mari ad Troiam profecti ductore interfecto ablataque praeda ibidem morabantur, utque Himera, quam nonnulli materno nomine Hemeram appellabant, soror Memnonis, ad investigandum cadaver fratris eo profecta, postquam reliquias repperit et de intercepta praeda Memnonis palam ei factum est, utrumque recipere cupiens intercessu Phoenicum, qui in eo exercitu plurimi fuerant, optionem rerum omnium ac seorsum fratris acceperit, praelataque sanguinis affectione recepta urna Phoenicem navigaverit. Delata dein ad regionem eius Phalliotim nomine sepultisque fratris reliquiis nusquam repente comparuerit. Cuius opinio exorta triplex, seu quod post occasum solis cum matre Himera ex conspectu hominis excesserit, sive super modum dolore affecta fraternae mortis ultro praeceps ierit, vel ab his, qui incolebant, ob eripienda, quae secum habuerat, circumventa interierit. Haec de Memnone eiusque sorore comperta mihi per Neoptolemum.

VI. 10. Neoptolemus told me everything which I have written about him, when I attended his marriage to Hermione, the daughter of Menelaus. I also learned from him about the burial of Memnon's remains.

Memnon's bones came into the hands of those of his men who had stayed on Paphos. They had slain Pallas,[3] under whose leadership they were sailing to Troy, and had taken the booty for themselves.

Then his sister Himera, or Hemera as some call her after her mother,[4] came to Paphos, looking for the body of her brother. When she found the remains and learned what had happened to the booty, she wanted to recover both. Thereupon, through the influence of the Phoenicians, who composed a majority of Memnon's soldiers there, she was given a choice: she could have either the booty or the bones, but not both. Accordingly, yielding to sisterly affection, she chose the latter; she took the urn and, setting sail, carried it off to Phoenicia.

When she had come to the part of this country called Phalliotis, she buried the urn. Then she suddenly vanished from sight. There were three explanations for her disappearance: either she had vanished at sunset along with her mother, Himera; or she had killed herself, overwhelmed with grieving over her brother; or the inhabitants of Phalliotis had killed her, desiring to steal whatever she had.

Neoptolemus is my source for what I have told about Memnon and his sister.

---

3 Compare Dictys 4.4, where Memnon's forces slay their leader Phalas (not Pallas) and choose to stay on Rhodes (not Paphos).

4 Aurora (Dawn) is the mother of Himera (Longing) - Hemera (Day).

VI. 11.   Post quae profectus Cretam anno post nomine publico cum duobus aliis ad oraculum Apollinis remedium petitum venio. Namque nulla certa causa ex improviso tanta vis lucustarum insulam eam invaserat, uti cuncta fructuum, quae in agris erant, corrumperentur. Itaque multis precibus suppliciisque responso editur, divina ope animalia interitura insulamque provectu frugum brevi redundaturam. Dein navigare cupientes ab his, qui apud Delphos erant, prohibemur: importunum namque et perniciosum tempus esse. Lycophron et Ixaeus, qui una ad oraculum venerant, contemptui habentes escendunt navem medioque fere spatio fulmine icti intereunt. Interim, uti praedictum divinitus erat, eodem ictu fulminum sedata vis mali inmersaque mari et regio omnis repleta frugibus.

VI. 12.   Per idem tempus Neoptolemus confirmato iam cum Hermiona matrimonio Delphos ad Apollinem gratulatum, quod in auctorem paternae caedis Alexandrum vindicatum esset, proficiscitur relicta in domo Andromacha eiusque filio Laodamante, qui reliquis iam filiorum Hectoris superfuerat. Sed Hermiona post abscessum viri victa dolore animi neque pelicatum captivae patiens parentem suum Menelaum accitum mittit; cui multa conquesta super iniuria praelatae sibi a viro captivae mulieris persuadet, uti filium Hectoris necet. Ceterum Andromacha re cognita instantis periculi vim subterfugit auxilio popularium liberata; qui miserati fortunas eius ultro Menelaum contumeliis prosecuti vix a pernicie viri retenti sunt.

VI. 11. The year after I returned to Crete, I went to the oracle of Apollo as a public representative, along with two others, in order to seek relief from a plague. For no apparent reason and all unexpectedly, a great horde of locusts had attacked our island and was destroying all of the crops in the fields. The response of the oracle, in answer to our many prayers and supplications, was that living creatures must die, divinely slain, before the crops of our island would grow and abound.

The people at Delphi prohibited us from sailing home at this time; the weather, they said, was unfavourable and dangerous. Nevertheless, Lycophron and Ixaeus, they were the two who had come along with me, refused to obey this injunction. Thus they sailed. When, however, they were half way to Crete, a bolt of lightning struck them dead, and then, just as the god had predicted, with the same bolt of lightning, the locusts departed, swallowed up by the sea, and the crops of our island began to increase.

VI. 12. During the same time Neoptolemus, having consummated his marriage with Hermione, went to Delphi. He wanted to give thanks to Apollo for the fact that Alexander, who had murdered his father, had paid for his impiety. Andromache was left behind at home, along with Laodamas, her only surviving son by Hector.[5]

Now Hermione, after the departure of her husband, was tortured by the thought of her captive rival, and summoned her father, Menelaus. Then, bitterly complaining about her poor treatment, how Neoptolemus preferred a captive woman to her, she urged Menelaus to kill Hector's son. Andromache, however, having learned of this plot, saved her son and escaped with the aid of the people, who pitied her fate; furthermore, these heaped abuses upon Menelaus, and were barely prevented from killing him.

---

5 Compare Dictys 5.16, where Neoptolemus gives the sons of Hector to Helenus.

VI. 13.   Interim Orestes adveniens rem cunctam cognoscit, hortatur
Menelaum, ut incepta perageret, ipse dolens praereptum sibi a Neoptolemo
Hermionae matrimonium insidias advenienti parare occipit. Itaque primo
ex his, quos secum habebat quam fidissimos, speculatum de adventu
Neoptolemi Delphos mittit. Quis cognitis Menelaus vitare huiuscemodi
facinus cupiens Spartam concedit. Sed illi, qui praemissi erant, regressi
Neoptolemum Delphis esse negant. Quare coactus Orestes ipse ad
inquisitionem viri profectus alio quam ierat die remeat, ut sermo hominum
ferebatur, negotio perfecto. Dein post paucos dies fama perfertur interisse
Neoptolemum eumque sermone omnium circumventum insidiis Orestis per
populum disseminatur. Ita iuvenis, ubi de Pyrrho palam est, recepta
Hermiona, quae sibi antea desponsa erat, Mycenas discedit. Interim Peleus
cum Thetide cognito nepotis interitu ad investigationem eius profecti
cognoscunt iuvenem Delphis sepultum. Ibi, ut mos erat, iusta persolvunt
cognoscuntque in his locis interisse, ubi visus Orestes negabatur. Ea res per
populum haud credita, adeo praesumpta ante iam opinio de Orestis insidiis
cunctorum animis inhaeserat. Ceterum Thetis ubi Hermionam Oresti
iunctam videt, Andromacham partu gravidam ex Neoptolemo Molossos
mittit dolum Orestis eiusque coniugis de interimendo fetu evitans.

VI. 13.   Meanwhile Orestes arrived and learned all that was happening. Thereupon he urged Menelaus to carry out the plot, for he himself was planning to kill Neoptolemus when he returned. He hated Neoptolemus for having married Hermione; she had been promised to him. Accordingly, the first thing he did was to send some trusted scouts to Delphi to find out when Neoptolemus would come.

Menelaus, being thus apprised of Orestes' plans, returned to Sparta, for he wanted no part in such a crime.

Then the scouts who had been sent to Delphi reported that Neoptolemus was not to be found in that place, and thus Orestes was forced to set out in search of his man.

When he returned, but not on the same day he had left, everyone believed that he had accomplished his purpose. Within a short time the popular story was that Neoptolemus was dead and that Orestes had treacherously slain him.

Then Orestes returned to Mycenae, taking Hermione with him. She had been promised to him.

Meanwhile Peleus and Thetis, having heard of their grandson's death, set out to learn for themselves exactly how he had died. They discovered that he had been buried at Delphi (where then they performed his funeral rites according to custom), but that he had died in a place where Orestes had never been seen. This, however, the people refused to believe, so strong was their presumption of Orestes' treachery.

Furthermore, Thetis, seeing that Hermione and Orestes were married, sent Andromache off to the Molossians. Andromache was pregnant by Neoptolemus, and Thetis feared that Orestes and Hermione might try to kill the baby.

VI. 14.   Per idem tempus Ulixes territus crebris auguriis somniisque adversis omnes undique regionis eius interpretandi somnia peritissimos conducit. Hisque refert inter cetera visum sibi saepius simulacrum quoddam inter humanum divinumque vultum formae perlaudabilis ex eodem loco repente edi. Quod complecti summo desiderio cupienti sibi porrigentique manus responsum ab eo humana voce sceleratam huiusmodi coniunctionem quippe eiusdem sanguinis atque originis; namque ex eo alterum alterius opera interiturum. Dein versanti sibi vehementius cupientique causam eius rei perdiscere signum quoddam mari editum intervenire visum. Idque secundum imperium eius in se iactum, utrumque diiunxisse. Quam rem cuncti qui aderant uno ore exitialem ei pronuntiant adduntque, caveret ab insidiis filii. Ita suspectus parentis animo Telemachus agris, qui in Cephalenia erant, relegatur additis ei quam fidissimis custodibus. Praeterea Ulixes secedens in alia loca abdita remotaque quantum poterat somniorum vim evitare nitebatur.

VI. 14.   During the same time Ulysses had been frightened by frequent omens and nightmares. Accordingly, he summoned all those in his area who were skilled in interpreting dreams, and told them everything, but especially this dream he frequently had:[6]

A form, half human and half divine,[7] and beautiful to behold, suddenly arose from the same place. As he passionately reached out his arms and tried to embrace it, he received a rebuke, in a human voice: such a union was wicked, a union between those of the same flesh and blood, one of whom was destined to die at the hands of the other; and while he pondered and wondered how this could be, a shaft, hurled by the apparition's command, appeared to arise from the sea and, coming between them, caused them to part.

Everyone who was there interpreted this vision as fatal to him; and, furthermore, they begged him to beware of the treacherous acts of his son. Accordingly, Telemachus, because of his father's suspicions, was sent to the island of Cephalenia, there to farm where trusted guards could watch him. Furthermore, Ulysses, by withdrawing into a region that was hidden and remote, strove to avoid what his dream had foretold.

---

6 Compare the prophecy of Tiresias in *Odyssey* 11.134-137: "Death will come to you out of the sea...."

7 Telegonus is the son of the mortal Ulysses and the immortal Circe.

VI. 15.   Per idem tempus Telegonus, quem Circe editum ex Ulixe apud Aeaeam insulam educaverat, ubi adolevit, ad inquisitionem patris profectus Ithacam venit gerens manibus quoddam hastile, cui summitas marinae turturis osse armabatur, scilicet insigne insulae eius in qua genitus erat. Dein edoctus, ubi Ulixes ageret, ad eum venit. Ibi per custodes agri patrio aditu prohibitus, ubi vehementius perstat et e diverso repellitur, clamare occipit indignum facinus prohiberi se a parentis complexu. Ita credito Telemachum ad inferendam vim regi adventare acrius resistitur, nulli quippe compertum esse alterum etiam Ulixi filium. Dein iuvenis ubi se vehementius et per vim repelli videt, dolore elatus multos custodum interficit aut graviter vulneratos debilitat. Quae postquam Ulixi cognita sunt, existimans iuvenem a Telemacho inmissum egressus lanceam, quam ob tutelam sui gerere consueverat, adversum Telegonum iaculatur. Sed postquam huiusmodi ictum iuvenis casu quodam intercipit, ipse in parentem insigne iaculum emittit infelicissimum casum vulneri contemplatus. At ubi ictu eo Ulixes concidit, gratulari cum fortuna confiterique optime secum actum, quod per vim externi hominis interemptus parricidii scelere Telemachum carissimum sibi liberavisset. Dein reliquum adhuc retentans spiritum iuvenem percontari quisnam et ex quo ortus loco se domi belloque inclitum Ulixem Laertae filium interficere ausus esset. Tunc Telegonus cognito parentem esse utraque manu dilanians caput fletum edit quam miserabilem maxime discruciatus ob inlatam per se patri necem. Itaque Ulixi, uti voluerat, nomen suum atque matris, insulam, in qua ortus erat et ad postremum insigne iaculi ostendit. Ita Ulixes ubi vim ingruentium somniorum praedictumque ab interpretibus vitae exitum animo recordatus est, vulneratus ab eo, quem minime crediderat, triduo post mortem obiit senior iam provectae aetatis neque tamen invalidus virium.

DICTYS VI

VI. 15. Meanwhile, however, Telegonus, whom Circe had borne to Ulysses and raised on the island of Aeaea, having grown to manhood, came to Ithaca in search of his father. He was carrying a spear, whose point was the bone of a sea bird, the turtledove, which was the symbol of Aeaea, where he was born. When he learned where Ulysses was living off in the country, he went to that place; but the guards there prohibited him entry. Persisting but always being resisted, he began to shout that this was disgraceful, a crime, to prevent a son from embracing his father. But the guards, not knowing that Ulysses had fathered a second son and believing that this was Telemachus who had come to murder the king, resisted ever more fiercely. And thus Telegonus, becoming more and more angry because of this increasingly vehement opposition, ended by killing or wounding many of the guards.

Ulysses, having learned what was happening, thought that this was a young man whom Telemachus had sent to harm him. Accordingly, he entered the fray and let fly with his spear, which he always carried for protection. Telegonus, however, parried the blow, and then, aiming to make a mortal wound and letting fly with his own remarkable weapon, he hit his father.

Ulysses, as he fell, was thankful for this sort of fate. It was all for the best, he thought; by dying at the hands of a foreigner he would prevent Telemachus, whom he dearly loved, from being guilty of parricide. Still breathing, he asked the young man who he was and where he was from and how he had dared to kill Ulysses, the son of Laertes, a man famous for virtues in war and peace.

And then Telegonus realized that this was his father whom he had slain. He wept in a very pitiable way and pulled his hair with both his hands, being terribly tortured because he had caused his father's death. Then, as Ulysses had asked, he told him his name and the name of his mother and the name of the island where he was born; and he showed him the point of the spear.

And so Ulysses knew that his recurring dream had been correctly interpreted; he had been fatally struck by one whom he had never suspected. And thus, within three days, he died, a man advanced in years, whose strength, however, was as yet unimpaired.

DARETIS PHRYGII DE EXCIDIO TROIAE HISTORIA.

Cornelius Nepos Sallustio Crispo suo salutem.

Cum multa ago Athenis curiose, inveni historiam Daretis Phrygii ipsius manu scriptam, ut titulus indicat, quam de Graecis et Troianis memoriae mandavit. Quam ego summo amore conplexus continuo transtuli. cui nihil adiciendum vel diminuendum rei reforniandae causa putavi, alioquin mea posset videri. Optimum ergo duxi ita ut fuit vere et simpliciter perscripta, sic eam ad verbum in latinitatem transvertere, ut legentes cognoscere possent, quomodo res gestae essent: utrum verum magis esse existiment, quod Dares Phrygius memoriae commendavit, qui per id ipsum tempus vixit et militavit, cum Graeci Troianos obpugnarent, anne Homero credendum, qui post multos annos natus est, quam bellum hoc gestum est.

De qua re Athenis iudicium fuit, cum pro insano haberetur, quod deos cum hominibus belligerasse scripserit. Sed hactenus ista: nunc ad pollicitum revertamur.

THE
FALL OF TROY:
A HISTORY

by

Dares the Phrygian

[Letter][1]

Cornelius Nepos sends greetings to his Sallustius Crispus.

While I was busily engaged in study at Athens, I found the history which Dares the Phrygian wrote about the Greeks and the Trojans. As its title indicates, this history was written in Dares' own hand. I was very delighted to obtain it and immediately made an exact translation into Latin, neither adding nor omitting anything, nor giving any personal touch. Following the straightforward and simple style of the Greek original, I translated word for word.

Thus my readers can know exactly what happened according to this account and judge for themselves whether Dares the Phrygian or Homer wrote the more truthfully; Dares, who lived and fought at the time the Greeks stormed Troy, or Homer, who was born long after the War was over. When the Athenians judged this matter, they found Homer insane for describing gods battling with mortals. But so much for this. Let us now turn to what I have promised.

---

1 The brackets indicate that the heading has been supplied, without any manuscript support, for the purpose of easy reference. For a discussion of problems concerning the letter, see Introduction.

D. I.   Pelias rex [in Peloponneso] Aesonem fratrem habuit. Aesonis filius erat Iason virtute praestans, et qui sub regno eius erant, omnes hospites habebat et ab eis validissime amabatur. Pelias rex ut vidit Iasonem tam acceptum esse omni homini, veritus est, ne sibi iniurias faceret et se regno eiceret. Dicit Iasoni Colchis pellem inauratam arietis esse dignam eius virtute: ut eam inde auferret, omnia se ei daturum pollicetur. Iason ubi audivit, ut erat animi fortissimi et qui loca omnia nosse volebat et quod clariorem se existimabat futurum, si pellem inauratam Colchis abstulisset, dicit Peliae regi se eo velle ire, si vires sociique non deessent. Pelias rex Argum architectum vocari iussit et ei imperavit, ut navim aedificaret quam pulcherrimam ad voluntatem Iasonis. Per totam Graeciam rumor cucurrit navim aedificari, in qua Colchos eat Iason pellem auream petitum. Amici et hospites ad Iasonem venerunt et pollicentur se una ituros. Iason illis gratias egit et rogavit, ut parati essent cum tempus supervenisset: interea navis aedificatur et cum tempus anni supervenisset, Iason litteras ad eos misit, qui erant polliciti sese una ituros et ilico convenerunt ad navem, cuius nomen erat Argo. Pelias rex quae opus erant in navim inponi iussit et hortatus est Iasonem et qui cum eo profecturi erant, ut animo forti ad perficiendum irent, quod conati essent. ea res claritatem Graeciae et ipsis factura videbatur. Demonstrare eos qui cum is Iasone profecti sunt non videtur nostrum esse: sed qui volunt eos cognoscere, Argonautas legant.

DARES

D. 1. King Pelias, who ruled in the Peloponnese,[2] was the brother of Aeson, and Aeson was the father of Jason.

Jason was known for his courage and goodness. He treated everyone in the realm as his personal friend, and therefore everyone loved him.

When King Pelias saw that Jason was popular with everyone, he feared that he might do him some harm or drive him out of the kingdom. Accordingly, he told Jason that there was something worthy of his prowess at Colchis: the golden fleece of a ram. If Jason would bring it back, he would give him complete control of the kingdom.

On hearing this, Jason, who was the bravest of men, since he desired to see the world and hoped to add to his glory by bringing the golden fleece from Colchis, told the king he wanted to go. He needed, however, supplies and companions.

King Pelias ordered the architect-craftsman Argus to come and build the most beautiful ship he could, according to Jason's specifications. Thus the rumour went throughout Greece that they were building a ship and that Jason was going to Colchis to fetch the golden fleece. Friends and acquaintances came and promised to go along with him. Jason was grateful to them and urged them to prepare to sail. When the ship was finished and the time for sailing had come, he sent them notice by letter. Immediately those who had promised to go along with him assembled at the ship, to which the name Argo was given.

King Pelias, after ordering the necessary supplies to be stowed, exhorted Jason and those who were about to set forth with him to show their courage. They must, he said, accomplish their mission, for this was a voyage which surely would glorify Greece and themselves.

(It is not our business to tell about those who set forth with Jason. If anyone wishes to know about them, he should read the *Argonautica*).[3]

---

2 But Pelias ruled in Thessaly, not in the Peloponnese.

3 There is an *Argonautica* attributed to Orpheus which, however, is dependent upon Apollonius Rhodius. Orpheus was one of the Argonauts.

D. II.   Iason ubi ad Phrygiam venit, navim admovit ad portum Simoenta: deinde omnes de navi exierunt in terram. Laomedonti regi nuntiatum est mirandam navim in portum Simoenta intrasse et in ea multos iuvenes de Graecia venisse. Ubi audivit Laomedon rex, commotus est: consideravit commune periculum esse, si consuescerent Graeci ad sua litora adventare navibus. Mittit ad portum, qui dicant, ut Graeci de finibus excedant, si non dicto obaudissent, sese armis eos de finibus eiecturum. Iason et qui cum eo venerant graviter tulerunt crudelitatem Laomedontis sic se ab eo tractari, cum nulla ab eis iniuria facta esset. Simul timebant multitudinem barbarorum, si contra imperium conarentur permanere, ne obprimerentur, cum ipsi non essent parati ad proeliandum: navim conscenderunt et a terra recesserunt, Colchos profecti sunt, pellem abstulerunt, domum reversi sunt.

D. 2.   When Jason came to Phrygia, he docked at the port of the Simois River, and everyone went ashore.

Soon news was brought to King Laomedon that a strange ship unexpectedly had entered the port of the Simois, and that many young men had come in it from Greece. On hearing this, the king was disturbed. Thinking that it would endanger the public welfare if Greeks began landing on his shores, he sent word to the port for the Greeks to depart from his boundaries. If they refused to obey, he would drive them out forcibly.

Jason and those who had come with him were deeply upset at the barbarous way Laomedon was treating them; they had done him no harm. Nevertheless, they were afraid to oppose him. They were not ready for battle and would certainly be crushed by the greater forces of the barbarians.

Thus, reembarking, they departed from Phrygia.

And set out for Colchis.

And stole the fleece.

And returned to their homeland.

D. III.   Hercules graviter tulit a rege Laomedonte contumeliose se tractatum et eos qui una profecti erant Colchos cum Iasone, Spartam ad Castorem et Pollucem venit, agit cum his, ut secum suas iniurias defendant, ne Laomedon inpune ferat, quod illos a terra et portu prohibuisset: multos adiutores futuros, si se accommodassent. Castor et Pollux omnia promiserunt se facturos quae Hercules vellet. Ab his Salaminam profectus ad Telamonem venit: rogat eum, ut secum ad Troiam eat, ut suas suorumque iniurias defendat. Telamon promisit omnibus se paratum esse, quae Hercules facere vellet. inde ad Phthiam profectus est ad Peleum rogatque eum, ut secum eat ad Troiam. Pollicitusque est ei Peleus se iturum. Inde Pylum ad Nestorem profectus est rogatque eum Nestor, quid venerit. Hercules dicit quod dolore commotus sit, velle se exercitum in Phrygiam ducere. Nestor Herculem conlaudavit operamque suam ei pollicitus est. Hercules, ubi omnium voluntates intellexit, naves paravit, milites elegit. Ubi tempus datum est proficiscendi, litteras ad eos, quos rogaverat, misit ut venirent cum suis omnibus: cum venissent, profecti sunt in Phrygiam: ad Sigeum noctu accesserunt inde Hercules Telamon et Peleus exercitum eduxerunt: navibus qui praesidio essent Castorem et Pollucem et Nestorem reliquerunt. quod ubi Laomedonti regi nuntiatum est classem Graecorum ad Sigeum accessisse, et ipse cum equestri copia ad mare venit et coepit proeliari. Hercules ad Ilium ierat et inprudentes qui erant in oppido urgere coepit. Quod ubi Laomedonti nuntiatum est urgeri ab hostibus Ilium, ilico revertitur et in itinere obvius Graecis factus ab Hercule occiditur. Telamon primus Ilium oppidum introiit, cui Hercules virtutis causa Hesionam Laomedontis regis filiam dono dedit.

Ceteri uero qui cum Laomedonte ierant occiduntur. Priamus in Phrygia erat, ubi eum Laomedon eius pater exercitui praefecerat. Hercules et qui cum eo venerant praedam magnam fecerunt et ad naves deportaverunt. Inde domum proficisci decreverunt, Telamon Hesionam secum convexit.

D. 3. Hercules was deeply upset at the insulting way Laomedon had treated him and those who had gone with Jason to Colchis. He went to Sparta and urged Castor and Pollux to help him take vengeance against Laomedon, saying that if only they promised their aid, many others would follow. Castor and Pollux promised to do whatever he wanted.

He departed from them and went on to Salamis. There he visited Telamon and asked him to join the expedition against Troy, to avenge the ill treatment he and his people had suffered. Telamon promised that he was ready for anything Hercules wanted to do.

He set out from Salamis and went on to Phthia. There he asked Peleus to join the expedition against Troy. Peleus promised to go.

Next he went to Pylos to visit Nestor. When Nestor asked why he had come, Hercules answered that he was stirred to seek vengeance and that he was leading an army against Phrygia. Nestor praised him and promised his aid.

Hercules, knowing that he had everyone's support, readied his ships and gathered an army. When the time for sailing was right, he sent letters to those he had asked and told them to come in full force. On their arrival, they all set sail for Phrygia.

They came to Sigeum at night. Hercules, Telamon, and Peleus led the army into the country, leaving Castor, Pollux, and Nestor behind to guard the ships.

When news was brought to King Laomedon that the Greek fleet had landed at Sigeum, he took command of the cavalry himself and went to the shore and opened hostilities.

But Hercules, having gone on to Troy, was beginning to besiege the unsuspecting inhabitants of the city. When Laomedon learned what was happening at home, he tried to return immediately. But the Greeks stood in his way, and Hercules slew him.

Telamon proved his prowess by being the first to enter Troy. Therefore, Hercules gave him the prize of King Laomedon's daughter Hesione.

Needless to say, all those who had gone with Laomedon were killed.

At this time Priam was in Phrygia, where Laomedon, his father, had put him in charge of the army.[4]

Hercules and those who had come with him plundered the country and carried much booty off to their ships. Then they decided to set out for home. Telamon took Hesione with him.

---

4 Perhaps this army was fighting the Amazons. See *Iliad* 3.182-190.

D. IV. Hoc ubi Priamo nuntiatum est patrem occisum, cives direptos, praedam devectam, Hesionam sororem dono datam, graviter tulit tam contumeliose Phrygiam tractatam esse a Grais, Ilium petit cum uxore Hecuba et liberis Hectore Alexandro Deiphobo Heleno Troilo Andromacha Cassandra Polyxena. Nam erant ei etiam alii filii ex concubinis nati, sed nemo ex regio genere dixit esse nisi eos qui essent ex legitimis uxoribus. Priamus ut Ilium venit, ampliora moenia extruxit, civitatem munitissimam reddidit. Et militum multitudinem ibi esse fecit, ne per ignorantiam opprimeretur, ita ut Laomedon pater eius oppressus est. Regiam quoque aedificavit et ibi aram Iovi statuamque consecravit. Hectorem in Paeoniam misit, Ilio portas fecit, quarum nomina sunt haec: Antenorea Dardania Ilia Scaea Thymbraea Troiana et postquam Ilium stabilitum vidit, tempus expectavit. Ut visum est ei iniurias patris ulcisci, Antenorem vocari iubet dicitque ei velle se eum legatum in Graeciam mittere: graves sibi iniurias ab his qui cum exercitu venerant factas in Laomedontis patris nece et abductione Hesionae: quae omnia tamen aequo se animo passurum, si Hesiona ei reddatur.

D. 4. When news was brought to Priam that his father had been killed, his fellow citizens decimated, his country plundered, and his sister Hesione carried off as a prize of war, he was deeply upset to think that the Greeks had treated Phrygia with such contempt. He returned to Troy, along with his wife, Hecuba, and his children, Hector, Alexander, Deiphobus, Helenus, Troilus, Andromache, Cassandra, and Polyxena. (He had other sons by concubines, but only those by lawfully wedded wives could claim a truly royal lineage). Arriving in Troy, he saw to the maximum fortification of the city, built stronger walls, and stationed a greater number of soldiers nearby. Troy must not fall again, as it had under his father, Laomedon, through lack of preparedness.

He also constructed a palace, in which he consecrated an altar and statue to Jupiter; sent Hector into Paeonia; and built the gates of Troy, the Antenorean, the Dardanian, the Ilian, the Scaean, the Thymbraean, and the Trojan.

When he saw that Troy was secure, he waited until the time seemed right to avenge the wrongs his father had suffered. Then he summoned Antenor and told him he wished him to go as an envoy to Greece. The Greek army, he said, had done him grave wrongs by killing his father, Laomedon, and by carrying off Hesione. Nevertheless, if only Hesione were returned, he would cease to complain.

D. V.   Antenor, ut Priamus imperavit, navim conscendit et profectus venit Magnesiam ad Peleum: quem Peleus hospitio triduo recepit, die quarto rogat eum, quid venerit. Antenor dicit quae a Priamo mandata erant, ut Graios postularet, ut Hesiona redderetur. Haec ubi Peleus audivit, graviter tulit et quod haec ad se pertinere videbat, iubet eum de finibus suis discedere. Antenor nihil moratus navim ascendit, secundum Boeotiam iter fecit, Salaminam advectus est ad Telamonem, rogare eum coepit, ut Priamo Hesionam sororem redderet: non enim esse aequum in servitute habere regii generis puellam. Telamon Antenori respondit nihil a se Priamo factum, sed quod virtutis causa sibi donatum sit se nemini daturum: ob hoc Antenorem de insula discedere iubet. Antenor navim conscendit et in Achaiam pervenit. inde ad Castorem et Pollucem delatus coepit ab his is postulare, ut Priamo satisfacerent et ei Hesionam sororem redderent. Castor et Pollux negaverunt iniuriam Priamo factam esse, Antenorem discedere iubent. Inde Pylum ad Nestorem venit, dixit Nestori qua de causa venisset. Qui ut audivit coepit Antenorem obiurgare, cur ausus sit in Graeciam venire, cum a Phrygibus priores Graeci laesi fuissent. Antenor ubi uidit nihil se impetrasse et contumeliose [Priamum] tractari, navim conscendit, domum reversus est. Priamo regi demonstrat, quid unusquisque responderit et quomodo ab illis tractatus sit simulque hortatur Priamum, ut eos bello persequatur.

D. 5. In obedience to Priam's command, Antenor boarded a ship and sailed to Magnesia to visit Peleus. For three days Peleus entertained him hospitably, and on the fourth asked why he had come. Antenor, following Priam's instructions, said that he had come to demand that the Greeks return Hesione. On hearing this, Peleus was deeply upset, and since he saw that this was a matter which touched his interests[5] he ordered Antenor to depart from his boundaries.

Antenor, without any delay whatsoever, boarded his ship and, sailing along past Boeotia, came to the island of Salamis. There he tried to persuade Telamon to return to Priam his sister Hesione. It was not right, he said, to hold a girl of royal rank in servitude. Telamon answered that he had committed no wrong against Priam. He refused to return her whom he had received as a prize of war and ordered Antenor to depart from his island.

Antenor, having boarded his ship, went on to Achaea. There he was taken to Castor and Pollux and tried to persuade them to make reparation to Priam by returning his sister Hesione. Castor and Pollux denied that Priam had suffered any injury and ordered Antenor to depart.

Then he went to Pylos and told Nestor the purpose of his mission. When Nestor knew why he had come, he began to scold him. How, he asked, had he dared to undertake this mission? The Phrygians had been the first to offend.

When Antenor saw that he was accomplishing nothing, but that he was being treated with scorn, he boarded his ship and returned to his homeland. Reporting to Priam, he told what each one had said and how each one had treated him; and he urged the king to make war.

---

5 Peleus was Telamon's brother.

D. VI. Continuo Priamus filios vocari iubet et omnes amicos suos Antenorem Anchisen Aenean Ucalegonta Bucolionem Panthum Lamponem et omnes filios, qui ex concubinis nati erant. Qui ut convenerunt, dixit eis se Antenorem legatum in Graeciam misisse, ut hi sibi satisfacerent quod patrem suum necassent, Hesionam sibi redderent: illos contumeliose tractasse Antenorem et Antenorem ab eis nihil impetrasse. Verum quoniam suam voluntatem facere noluissent, videri sibi exercitum in Graeciam mitti qui poenas repeterent ab eis, ne barbaros Graeci inrisui haberent. Hortatusque est Priamus liberos suos, ut eius rei principes forent, maxime Hectorem, erat enim maior natu. Qui coepit dicere se voluntatem patris vindicaturum et Laomedontis avi sui necem et quascumque iniurias Graeci Troianis fecissent, executurum, ne inpunitum id Grais foret, sed vereri, ne perficere non possent quod conati essent: multos adiutores Graeciae futuros, Europam bellicosos homines habere, Asiam semper in desidia vitam exercuisse et ob id classem non habere.

D. 6.   Immediately Priam summoned his sons and all of his friends: Antenor, Anchises, Aeneas, Ucalegon, Bucolion, Panthus, and Lampus, and all of the sons he had fathered by concubines. When they had come, he told them about Antenor's unsuccessful mission, how he had gone to Greece and demanded as satisfaction for Laomedon's death the return of Hesione; and how the Greeks had treated him scornfully and sent him home empty handed. Now, Priam concluded, since the Greeks refused to do as he wished, he would send an army to make them pay for their injuries, lest they think barbarians worthy of scorn. He urged his sons, especially Hector since he was the oldest, to take command of the forces.

Hector responded by saying that he would carry out his father's wishes and avenge the death of his grandfather, Laomedon, and the other injustices the Greeks had done to the Trojans. The Greeks, he said, must pay for their depredations. He feared, however, that the Trojan expedition would fail, for Europe had bred many warlike men who would come to Greece's aid, while they themselves, who lived in Asia, had spent their time in idleness and built no ships.

D. VII. Alexander cohortari coepit, ut classis praepararetur et in Graeciam mitteretur: se eius rei principem futurum, si pater velit: in deorum benignitate se confidere, victis hostibus laude adepta de Graecia domum rediturum esse. Nam sibi in Ida silva, cum venatum abisset, in somnis Mercurium adduxisse Iunonem Venerem et Minervam, ut inter eas de specie iudicaret: et tunc sibi Venerem pollicitam esse, si suam speciosam faciem iudicaret, daturam se ei uxorem, quae in Graecia speciosissima forma videretur: ubi ita audisset, optimam facie Venerem iudicasse. Unde sperare coepit Priamus Venerem adiutricem Alexandro futuram. Deiphobus placere sibi dixit Alexandri consilium et sperare Graecos Hesionam reddituros et satisfacturos, si, ut dispositum esset, classis in Graeciam mitteretur. Helenus vaticinari coepit Graios venturos, Ilium eversuros, parentes et fratres hostili manu interituros, si Alexander sibi uxorem de Graecia adduxisset. Troilus minimus natu non minus fortis quam Hector bellum geri suadebat et non debere terreri metu verborum Heleni. ob quod omnibus placuit classem conparare et in Graeciam proficisci.

D. 7.   Then Alexander began to exhort them. They must build a fleet and go against Greece. If his father wished, he would take charge of this venture; he would conquer the enemy and return from Greece with great renown. There was reason to believe that the gods would aid him, for, while hunting in the woods on Mount Ida, he had fallen asleep and dreamt as follows:

Mercury brought Juno, Venus, and Minerva to him to judge of their beauty. Then Venus promised, if he judged her most beautiful, to give him in marriage whoever was deemed the loveliest woman in Greece. Thus, finally, on hearing Venus' promise, he judged her most beautiful.

This dream inspired Priam with the hope that Venus would aid Alexander. And Deiphobus approved of what Alexander had said. He believed that the Greeks would return Hesione and make reparations if, as had been proposed, they would send a fleet against Greece.

Helenus, however, began to predict that if Alexander brought home a Greek wife, the Greeks would pursue, and overpower Troy and slay – oh cruel might – his parents and brothers.

But Troilus, who, though youngest of Priam's sons, equalled Hector in bravery, urged them to war and told them not to be frightened by Helenus' fearful words.

And so they unanimously decided to ready a fleet and set out for Greece.

D. VIII. Priamus Alexandrum et Deiphobum in Paeoniam misit, ut milites legerent. Ad concionem populum venire iubet, commonefacit filios, ut maiores natu minoribus imperarent, monstravit quas iniurias Graeci Troianis fecissent: ob hoc Antenorem legatum in Graeciam misisse, ut sibi Hesionam sororem redderent et satis Troianis facerent: Antenorem a Grais contumeliose tractatum neque ab his quicquam impetrare potuisse: placere sibi Alexandrum in Graeciam mitti cum classe qui avi sui mortem et Troianorum iniurias ulciscatur. Antenorem dicere iussit, quomodo in Graecia tractatus esset. Antenor hortatus est Troianos, ne horrescerent, ad debellandam Graeciam suos alacriores fecit, paucis demonstravit quae in Graecia gesserat. Priamus dixit, si cui displiceret bellum geri, suam voluntatem ediceret. Panthus Priamo et propinquis prodit ea, quae a patre suo Euphorbo audierat, dicere coepit si Alexander uxorem de Graecia adduxisset, Troianis extremum exitium futurum, sed pulchrius esse in btio vitam degere, quam in tumultu libertatem amittere [et periculum inire]. populus auctoritatem Panthi contempsit, regem dicere iusserunt quid vellet fieri. Priamus dixit naves praeparandas esse, ut eatur in Graeciam, utensilia quoque populo non deesse. Populus conclamavit per se moram non esse, quo minus regis praeceptis pareatur. Priamus illis magnas gratias egit, concionemque dimisit. Ac mox in Idam silvam misit, qui materiem succiderent, naves aedificarent, Hectorem in superiorem Phrygiam misit, ut exercitum pararet [et ita paratus est]. Cassandra postquam audivit patris consilium, dicere coepit quae Troianis ratura essent, si Priamus perseveraret classem in Graeciam mittere.

D. 8.   Priam sent Alexander and Deiphobus into Paeonia to raise an army.

Then he called the people to assembly. Having arranged a line of command beginning with his older and ending with his younger sons, he told how the Greeks had wronged the Trojans. He had sent Antenor as an envoy to Greece to regain his sister Hesione and obtain reparation for the Trojans, but the Greeks had treated Antenor scornfully and sent him home empty handed. For this reason he had decided to send Alexander with a fleet against Greece. Thus Alexander would avenge the death of his grandfather and the other wrongs that the Trojans had suffered.

Then Priam ordered Antenor to tell how he had been treated in Greece. Antenor briefly described his mission and, urging the Trojans to have no fear, made them more eager for war against Greece.

Then Priam asked for other opinions: Would anyone like to speak against war?

Thereupon Panthus, addressing himself to the king and his party, told what he had heard from his father, Euphorbus: if Alexander brought home a wife from Greece, Troy would utterly fall. It was much better, he said, to spend one's life in peace than to risk the loss of liberty in war.

Panthus' speech won the contempt of the people, and they asked the king what had to be done. When he told them that they must build ships to go against Greece and gather supplies for the army, they cried out that they were ready to obey any order he gave them. For this he thanked them profusely, and then dismissed the assembly.

Soon afterwards he ordered men to go to the forests of Ida and there cut wood for building the ships; and he sent Hector into Upper Phrygia to levy an army.

When Cassandra heard of her father's intentions, she told what the Trojans were going to suffer if Priam should send a fleet into Greece.

D. IX.   Interea tempus supervenit: naves aedificatae sunt, milites supervenerunt, quos Alexander et Deiphobus in Paeonia elegerant. Et ubi visum est navigari posse, Priamus exercitum alloquitur, Alexandrum imperatorem exercitui praeficit, mittit cum eo Deiphobum Aenean Polydamantem imperatque Alexandro, ut primum Spartam accedat, Castorem et Pollucem conveniat et ab his petat, ut Hesiona soror reddatur et satis Troianis fiat: quod si negassent, continuo ad se nuntium mittat, ut exercitum possit in Graeciam mittere. post haec Alexander in Graeciam navigavit adducto secum duce eo, qui cum Antenore iam navigaverat. Non multos ante dies quam Alexander in Graeciam navigavit, et antequam insulam Cytheream accederet, Menelaus ad Nestorem Pylum proficiscens Alexandro in itinere occurrit et mirabatur classem regiam quo tenderet. Utrique occurrentes aspexerunt se invicem inscii quo quisque iret. Castor et Pollux ad Clytemestram ierant secum Hermionam neptem suam Helenae filiam adduxerant Argis Iunonis dies festus erat his diebus, quibus Alexander in insulam Cytheream venit, ubi fanum Veneris erat: Dianae sacrificavit. Hi qui in insula erant, mirabantur classem regiam, interrogabant ab illis, qui cum Alexandro venerant, qui essent, quid venissent. Responderunt illi a Priamo rege Alexandrum legatum missum ad Castorem et Pollucem, ut eos conveniret.

D. 9.   Soon preparations were made. The ships were built, and the army which Alexander and Deiphobus had raised in Paeonia had come. When the time seemed right for sailing, Priam addressed the troops. He appointed Alexander as commander-in-chief, and made Deiphobus, Aeneas, and Polydamas officers. First, he said, Alexander must go to Sparta and ask Castor and Pollux to return his sister Hesione, and to make reparations to the Trojans. Then, if Castor and Pollux refused, Alexander must send home word immediately. Thus he, Priam, would feel able to order the army to go against Greece.

Accordingly, Alexander sailed for Greece, piloted by the same man who had gone with Antenor. Several days before they reached Greece, before they came to the island of Cythera, they passed Menelaus, who was on his way to visit Nestor at Pylos. Menelaus marvelled at the royal fleet and wondered where it was heading. In fact, each party, surprised at seeing the other, wondered where the other was going.

Castor and Pollux had gone to visit Clytemnestra at Argos, where the festival of Juno was being held; and they had taken along their niece Hermione, the daughter of Helen.

It was at this time that Alexander arrived on Cythera and sacrificed to Diana at a place where the temple of Venus was.[6] The inhabitants of the island marvelled at the royal fleet and asked the sailors who they were and why they had come. They answered that King Priam was sending Alexander to confer with Castor and Pollux.

---

6 The compiler, who is here basing his work upon Dracontius, has substituted 'Diana' for 'Dione', which is the reading of Dracontius *Romulea* 8.435. Dione, of who the compiler appears to agnore, was according to *Iliad* 5.370, the mother of Venus. See Schissel von Fleschenberg, pp. 154-156.

D. X.   At Helena vero Menelai uxor, cum Alexander in insula Cytherea esset, placuit ei eo ire. Qua de causa ad litus processit. Oppidum ad mare est Helaea, ubi Dianae et Apollinis fanum est. Ibi rem divinam Helena facere disposuerat. Quod ubi Alexandro nuntiatum est Helenam ad mare venisse, conscius formae suae in conspectu eius ambulare coepit cupiens eam videre. Helenae nuntiatum est Alexandrum Priami regis filium ad Helaeam oppidum, ubi ipsa erat, venisse. Quem etiam ipsa videre cupiebat. Et cum se utrique respexissent, ambo forma sua incensi tempus dederunt, ut gratiam referrent. Alexander imperat, ut omnes in navibus sint parati, nocte classem solvant, de fano Helenam eripiant, secum eam auferant. Signo dato fanum invaserunt, Helenam non invitam eripiunt, in navim deferunt et cum ea mulieres aliquas depraedantur. Quod cum Helenam abreptam oppidani vidissent, diu pugnaverunt cum Alexandro, ne Helenam eripere posset: quos Alexander fretus sociorum multitudine superavit, fanum expoliavit, homines secum quam plurimos captivos abduxit, in naves inposuit, classem solvit, domum reverti disposuit, in portum Tenedon pervenit, ubi Helenam maestam alloquio mitigat, patri rei gestae nuntium mittit Menejao postquam nuntiatum est Pylum, cum Nestore Spartam profectus est, ad Agamemnonem fratrem misit Argos rogans, ut ad se veniat.

DARES

D. 10. While Alexander was on Cythera, Helen, the wife of Menelaus, decided to go there. Thus she went to the shore, to the seaport town of Helaea,[7] intending to worship in the temple of Diana and Apollo.[8] Alexander, on hearing that she had arrived, wanted to see her. Confident in his own good looks, he began to walk within sight of her. When Helen learned that the Alexander who was the son of King Priam had come to Helaea, she also wanted to see him. Thus they met and spent some time just staring, struck by each other's beauty.

Alexander ordered his men to be ready to sail that night. They would seize Helen in the temple and take her home with them.

Thus at a given signal they invaded the temple and carried her off, she was not unwilling, along with some other women they captured. The inhabitants of the town, having learned about the abduction of Helen, tried to prevent Alexander from carrying her off. They fought long and hard, but Alexander's superior forces defeated them. After despoiling the temple and taking as many captives as his ships would hold, he set sail for home.

On the island of Tenedos, where they landed, he tried to comfort Helen, who was having regrets; and he sent news to his father of his success.

Menelaus, having learned what had happened, left Pylos accompanied by Nestor, and returned to Sparta whither he summoned his brother Agamemnon from Argos.[9]

---

7 This name does not appear in Dracontius, who is the source for this passage. Accordingly, 'Helaea', which is probably to be derived from 'Helen', must have been added later either by the compiler or someone else. See Schissel von Fleschenberg, p. 156.

8 The compiler, having already substituted Diana for Dione, now adds Diana's brother, Apollo. See note 6 above.

9 Schissel von Fleschenberg (pp. 147 ff.) thinks that this sentence begins the translation of the original Dares somewhere in the middle of its introduction, a large part of which has been replaced by the material in sections 1 through 10.

311

D. XI.   Interea Alexander ad patrem suum cum magna praeda pervenit et rei gestae ordinem refert. Priamus gavisus est sperans Graecos ob causam recuperationis Helenae sororem Hesionam reddituros et ea quae inde a Troianis abstulerunt. Helenam maestam consolatus est et eam Alexandro coniugem dedit. Quam ut aspexit Cassandra, vaticinari coepit memorans ea quae ante praedixerat. Quam Priamus abstrahi et includi iussit. Agamemnon postquam Spartam venit, fratrem consolatus est et placuit, ut per totam Graeciam conquisituri mitterentur ad convocandos Graecos et Troianis bellum indicendum. Convenerunt autem hi: Achilles cum Patroclo Euryalus Tlepolemus Diomedes. Postquam Spartam accesserunt, decreverunt iniurias Troianorum persequi, exercitum et classem conparare: Agamemnonem imperatorem et ducem praeficiunt. Hi legatos mittunt, ut tota Graecia conveniant cum classibus et exercitibus ornati paratique ad Atheniensem portum, ut inde pariter ad Troiam proficiscantur ad defendendas suas iniurias. Castor et Pollux in recenti, postquam audierunt Helenam suam sororem raptam, navem conscenderunt et secuti sunt. Cum in litore Lesbio navem solverent, maxima tempestate exorta nusquam eos conparuisse creditum est, postea dictum est eos inmortales factos, itaque Lesbios navibus eos usque ad Troiam quaesitum isse neque eorum usquam vestigium inventum domum renuntiasse.

D. 11. Meanwhile Alexander arrived home with his booty and gave his father an exact description of everything he had done. Priam was delighted. He hoped that the Greeks would seek to recover Helen, and thus would return his sister Hesione,[10] and the things they had taken from Troy. He consoled Helen, who was having regrets, and gave her to Alexander to marry. When Cassandra saw Helen, she began to prophesy, repeating what she had already said, until Priam ordered her carried away and locked up.

Agamemnon, upon his arrival in Sparta, consoled his brother. They decided to send men throughout Greece to gather an army for war against Troy. Among those who assembled at Sparta were Achilles, who came with Patroclus; and Euryalus, Tlepolemus, and Diomedes. They swore to avenge the wrongs the Trojans had done and to ready an army and fleet for this purpose. Agamemnon was chosen commander-in-chief, and messengers were sent to summon all the Greeks to the Athenian port with their ships and armies. From there they would set out for Troy together to avenge the wrongs they had suffered.

Castor and Pollux, immediately upon learning of their sister Helen's abduction, had set sail in pursuit.[11] When, however, they landed on the island of Lesbos, a great storm arose and, lo and behold, they were nowhere in sight. That was the story. Later, people thought that they had been made immortal. The Lesbians, taking to the sea and searching even to Troy, had returned to report that they had found no trace of Castor or Pollux.

---

10 Sections 1 through 10 give the capture of Hesione, and the failure of Antenor's mission to seek her return, as the cause of the War, whereas the original Dares, as shown in sections 11 through 43, cite the cause as Helen's abduction. Accordingly, references to Hesione and to Antenor's mission in sections 11 through 43 are probably additions of the translator-compiler for the purpose of harmonising his different sources. See Schissel von Fleschenberg, p. 147.

11 Schissel von Fleschenberg (pp. 9-12, and 147) thinks that references to Castor and Pollux in sections 11 and 12 are additions of the translator-compiler for the purpose of connecting his Dares translation with the earlier sections, in which Castor and Pollux play important roles.

D. XII.   Dares Phrygius, qui hanc historiam scripsit, ait se miUtasse usque dum Troia capta est, hos se vidisse, cum indutiae essent, partim proelio interfuisse, a Dardanis autem audisse qua facie et natura fuissent Castor et Pollux. Fuerunt autem alter alteri similis capillo flavo oculis magnis facie pura bene figurati corpore deducto. Helenam similem illis formosam animi simplicis blandam cruribus optimis notam inter duo supercilia habentem ore pusillo. Priamum Troianorum regem vultu pulchro magnum voce suavi aquilino corpore. Hectorem blaesum candidum crispum strabum pernicibus membris vultu venerabili barbatum decentem bellicosum animo magno in civibus clementem dignum amore aptum. Deiphobum et Helenum similes patri dissimili natura, Deiphobum fortem Helenum clementem doctum vatem. Troilum magnum pulcherrimum pro aetate valentem fortem cupidum virtutis. Alexandrum candidum longum fortem oculis pulcherrimis capillo molli et flavo ore venusto voce suavi velocem cupidum imperii. Aeneam rufum quadratum facundum affabilem fortem cum consilio pium venustum oculis hilaribus et nigris. Antenorem longum gracilem velocibus membris versutum cautum. Hecubam magnam aquilino corpore pulchram mente virili piam iustam. Andromacham oculis claris candidam longam formosam modestam sapientem pudicam blandam. Cassandram mediocri statura ore rotundo rufam oculis micantibus futurorum praesciam.

D. 12. Dares the Phrygian, who wrote this history, says that he did military service until the capture of Troy and saw the people listed below either during times of truce or while he was fighting.[12] As for Castor and Pollux, he learned from the Trojans what they were like and how they looked: they were twins, blond haired, large eyed, fair complexioned, and well built with trim bodies.[13]

Helen resembled Castor and Pollux.[14] She was beautiful, ingenuous, and charming. Her legs were the best; her mouth the cutest. There was a beauty mark between her eyebrows.

Priam, the king of the Trojans, had a handsome face and a pleasant voice. He was large and swarthy.

Hector spoke with a slight lisp. His complexion was fair, his hair curly. His eyes would blink attractively. His movements were swift. His face, with its beard, was noble. He was handsome, fierce, and high spirited, merciful to the citizens, and deserving of love.

Deiphobus and Helenus both looked like their father, but their characters were not alike. Deiphobus was the man of forceful action; Helenus was the gentle, learned prophet.

Troilus, a large and handsome boy, was strong for his age, brave, and eager for glory.

Alexander was fair, tall, and brave. His eyes were very beautiful, his hair soft and blond, his mouth charming, and his voice pleasant. He was swift, and eager to take command.

Aeneas was auburn haired, stocky, eloquent, courteous, prudent, pious, and charming. His eyes were black and twinkling.

Antenor was tall, graceful, swift, crafty, and cautious.

Hecuba was beautiful, her figure large, her complexion dark. She thought like a man and was pious and just.

Andromache was bright eyed and fair, with a tall and beautiful body. She was modest, wise, chaste, and charming.

Cassandra was of moderate stature, round mouthed, and auburn haired. Her eyes flashed. She knew the future.

Polyxena was fair, tall, and beautiful. Her neck was slender, her eyes lovely, her hair blond and long, her body well proportioned, her fingers tapering, her legs straight, and her feet the best. Surpassing all the others in beauty, she remained a completely ingenuous and kindhearted woman.

---

12 According to Schissel von Fleschenberg, this sentence probably belongs to an original Greek Preface. See Introduction.

13 See note 11 above.

14 Helen, as well as her brothers, is perhaps out of place here. See note 11 above.

D. XIII.   Agamemnonem albo corpore magnum membris valentibus facundum prudentem nobilem divitem. Menelaum mediocri statura rufum formosum acceptum.gratum. Achillem pectorosum ore venusto membris valentibus et magnis iubatum bene crispatum clementem in armis acerrimum vultu hilari largum dapsilem capillo myrteo. Patroclum pulchro corpore oculis coesiis viribus magnis verecundum certum prudentem dapsilem. Aiacem Oileum quadratum valentibus membris aquilino corpore iocundum fortem. Aiacem Telamonium valentem voce clara capillis nigris coma crispa simplici animo in hostem atrocem. Ulixem firmum dolosum ore hilari statura media eloquentem sapientem. Diomedem fortem quadratum corpore honesto vultu austero in bello acerrimum clamosum cerebro calido inpatientem audacem. Nestorem magnum naso obunco longo latum candidum consiliarium prudentem. Protesilaum corpore candido vultu honesto velocem confidentem temerarium. Neoptolemum magnum viriosum stomachosum blaesum vultu bonum aduncum oculis rotnndis superciliosum. Palamedem gracilem longum sapientem animo magnum blandum. Podalirium crassum valentem superbum tristem. Machaonem fortem magnum certum prudentem patientem misericordem. Merionem rufum mediocri statura corpore rotundo viriosum pertinacem crudelem inpatientem. Briseidam formosam non alta statura candidam capillo flavo et molli superciliis iunctis oculis venustis corpore aequali blandam affabilem verecundam animo simplici piam.

D. 13.   Agamemnon was blond, large, and powerful. He was eloquent, wise, and noble, a man richly endowed.

Menelaus was of moderate stature, auburn haired, and handsome. He had a pleasing personality.

Achilles had a large chest, a fine mouth, and powerfully formed arms and legs. His head was covered with long wavy chestnut coloured hair. Though mild in manner, he was very fierce in battle. His face showed the joy of a man richly endowed.

Patroclus was handsome and powerfully built. His eyes were grey. He was modest, dependable, wise, a man richly endowed.

Ajax, the son of Oileus, was stocky, powerfully built, swarthy a pleasant person, and brave.

Ajax, the son of Telamon, was powerful. His voice was clear, his hair black and curly. He was perfectly singleminded and unrelenting in the onslaught of battle.

Ulysses was tough, crafty, cheerful, of medium height, eloquent, and wise.

Diomedes was stocky, brave, dignified, and austere. No one was fiercer in battle. He was loud at the war cry, hot tempered, impatient, and daring.

Nestor was large, broad, and fair. His nose was long and hooked. He was the wise adviser.

Protesilaus was fair skinned, and dignified. He was swift, self confident, even rash.

Neoptolemus was large, robust, and easily irritated. He lisped slightly, and was good looking, with hooked nose, round eyes, and shaggy eyebrows.

Palamedes was tall and slender, wise, magnanimous, and charming.

Podalirius was sturdy, strong, haughty, and moody.

Machaon was large and brave, dependable, prudent, patient, and merciful.

Meriones was auburn haired, of moderate height, with a well proportioned body. He was robust, swift, unmerciful, and easily angered.

Briseis was beautiful. She was small and blond, with soft yellow hair. Her eyebrows were joined above her lovely eyes. Her body was well proportioned. She was charming, friendly, modest, ingenuous, and pious.

D. XIV.   Deinde ornati cum classe Graeci Athenas convenerunt: Agamemnon ex Mycenis cum navibus numero C, Menelaus ex Sparta cum navibus numero LX, Arcesilaus et Prothoenor ex Boeotia cum navibus numero L, Ascalaphus et Ialmenus ex Orchomeno cum navibus numero XXX, Epistrophus et Schedius ex Phocide cum navibus numero XL, Aiax Telamonius ex Salamina adduxit secum Teucrum fratrem, ex Buprasione Amphimachum Diorem Thalpium Polyxenum cum navibus numero XL, Nestor ex Pylo cum navibus numero LXXX, Thoas ex Aetolia cum navibus numero XL, Nireus ex Syme cum navibus numero LIII, Aiax Oileus ex Locris cum navibus numero XXXVII, Antiphus et Phidippus ex Calydna cum navibus numero XXX, Idomeneus et Meriones ex Creta cum navibus numero LXXX, Ulixes ex Ithaca cum navibus numero XII, Eumelus ex Pheris cum navibus numero X, Protesilaus et Podarces ex Phylaca cum navibus numero XL, Podalirius et Machaon Aesculapii filii ex Tricca cum navibus numero XXXII, Achilles cum Patroclo et Myrmidonibus ex Phthia cum navibus numero L, Tlepolemus ex Rhodo cum navibus numero IX, Eurypylus ex Ormenio navibus numero XL, Antiphus et Amphimachus ex Elide navibus numero XI, Polypoetes et Leonteus ex Argisa, navibus numero XL, Diomedes Euryalus Sthenelus ex Argis navibus numero LXXX, Philoctetes ex Melibea navibus numero VII, Guneus ex Cypho navibus numero XXI, Prothous ex Magnesia navibus numero XL, Agapenor ex Arcadia navibus numero XL, Menestheus ex Athenis navibus numero L. Hi fuerunt duces Graecorum numero XLVIIII, qui adduxerunt naves numero mille CXXX.

D. 14. The following is a list of Greek leaders and the ships they brought to Athens.[15] Agamemnon came from Mycenae with 100 ships; Menelaus from Sparta with 60; Arcesilaus and Prothoenor from Boeotia with 50; Ascalaphus and Ialmenus from Orchomenus with 30; Epistrophus and Schedius from Phocis with 40; Ajax the son of Telamon brought along Teucer, his brother, from Salamis, and also Amphimachus, Diores, Thalpius, and Polyxenus from Buprasion, with 40 ships; Nestor came from Pylos with 80; Thoas from Aetolia with 40; Nireus from Syme with 53; Ajax the son of Oileus from Locris with 37; Antiphus and Phidippus from Calydna with 30; Idomeneus and Meriones from Crete with 80; Ulysses from Ithaca with 12; Eumelus from Pherae with 10; Protesilaus and Podarces from Phylaca with 40; Podalirius and Machaon, the sons of Aesculapius, from Tricca with 32; Achilles, accompanied by Patroclus and the Myrmidons, from Phthia with 50; Tlepolemus from Rhodes with 9; Eurypylus from Ormenion with 40; Antiphus and Amphimachus from Elis with 11; Polypoetes and Leonteus from Argisa with 40; Diomedes, Euryalus, and Sthenelus from Argos with 80; Philoctetes from Meliboea with 7; Guneus from Cyphos with 21; Prothous from Magnesia with 40; Agapenor from Arcadia with 40; and Menestheus from Athens with 50. There were 49 Greek leaders, and they brought a total of 1,130 ships.

---

15 This list is for the most part based on Homer's catalogue of ships in *Iliad* 2.494-759.

D. XV. Postquam Athenas venerunt, Agamemnon duces in consilium vocat, conlaudat hortatur, ut quam primum iniurias suas defendant. Rogat, si cui quid placeat suadetque, ut, antequam proficiscerentur, Delphos ad Apollinem consulendum mitterent: cui omnes adsentiunt. Cui rei praeficitur Achilles, hic cum Patroclo proficiscitur. Priamus interea, ut audivit quia hostes parati sunt, mittit per totam Phrygiam qui finitimos exercitus adducant, domique milites magno animo comparat. Achilles cum Delphos venisset, ad oraculum pergit: et ex adyto respondetur Graecos victuros, decimoque anno Troiam capturos. Achilles res divinas, sicut imperatum est, fecit. et eo tempore venerat Calchas Thestore natus divinus. dona pro Phrygibus a suo populo missus Apollini portabat, simul consuluit de regno rebusque suis. Huic ex adyto respondetur, ut cum Argivorum classe militum contra Troianos proficiscatur eosque sua intellegentia iuvet, neve inde prius discedant, quam Troia capta sit postquam in fanum ventum est, inter se Achilles et Calchas responsa contulerunt, gaudentes hospitio amicitiam confirmant, una Athenas proficiscuntur, perveniunt eo. Achilles eadem, in consilio refert, Argivi gaudent, Calchantem secum recipiunt, classem solvunt. Cum eos ibi tempestates retinerent, Calchas ex augurio respondet, uti revertantur et in Aulidem proficiscantur. profecti perveniunt. Agamemnon Dianam placat dicitque sociis suis, ut classem solvant, ad Troiam iter faciant. Utuntur duce Philocteta, qui cum Argonautis ad Troiam fuerat. Deinde applicant classem ad oppidum quod sub imperio Priami regis erat, et id expugnant, praedaque facta proficiscuntur. Veniunt Tenedum, ubi omnes occidunt. Agamemnon praedam divisit, consilium convocavit.

D. 15.   When they had arrived at Athens, Agamemnon called the leaders to council. He praised them and urged them to avenge the wrongs they had suffered as quickly as possible. Let each one, he said, tell how he felt. Then he advised that, before setting sail, they should consult the oracle of Apollo at Delphi. The council agreed unanimously and appointed Achilles to be in charge of this mission; and thus he, along with Patroclus, set out to Delphi. Meanwhile Priam, having learned that the Greeks were preparing for war, sent men throughout Phrygia to enlist the support of the neighbouring armies. He himself zealously readied his forces at home.

When Achilles had come to Delphi, he went to the oracle. The response, which issued from the holiest of holies, said that the Greeks would conquer and capture Troy in the tenth year. Then Achilles performed his religious duties as ordered.

At the same time the seer Calchas, the son of Thestor, had arrived, sent by his people, the Phrygians, to bring gifts to Apollo. When he inquiring in behalf of his kingdom and of himself consulted the oracle, the response which issued from the holiest of holies said that the Greeks would sail against Troy and would continue their siege until they had captured it, and that he would go with them and give them advice.

Thus Achilles and Calchas met in the temple and, after comparing responses, rejoiced in each other's friendship and set out for Athens together.

At Athens Achilles made his report to the council. The Greeks were delighted. And they accepted Calchas as one of their own.

Then they set sail. But a storm arose and prevented their progress. Thereupon Calchas, interpreting the omens, said that they must return and go up to Aulis.

On arriving at Aulis, Agamemnon appeased the goddess Diana. Then he commanded his followers to sail onwards to Troy. Philoctetes, who had gone with the Argonauts to Troy, acted as pilot.[16]

Then they landed at a city which was ruled by King Priam. They took it by storm and carried off much booty.

On coming to the island of Tenedos, they killed all the people, and Agamemnon divided the booty.

---

16 Compare Dictys 2.10 and note.

D. XVI. Inde legatos ad Priamum mittit, si velit Helenam reddere et praedam quam Alexander fecit restituere. Legati eleguntur Diomedes et Ulixes, hi ad Priamum proficiscuntur. Dum legati mandatis parent, mittuntur Achilles et Telephus ad praedandam Mysiam. Ad Teuthrantem regem veniunt praedamque faciunt. Teuthras cum exercitu superveniunt. Quem Achilles fugato exercitu vulnerat: quem iacentem Telephus clipeo protexit, ne ab Achille interficeretur. Commemorant inter se hospitium, quod Telephus cum adhuc puer erat, a patre Hercule progenitus, a Teuthrante rege hospitio receptus est. Diomedem regem ferunt eo tempore venantem cum equis potentibus et feris ab Hercule interfectum Teuthranti regnum totum tradidisse: ob hoc eius filium Telephum ei subpetias venisse. Quod cum Teuthras intellegeret se eodem vulnere mortem effugere non posse, regnum suum Mysiam vivus Telepho tradidit et eum regem ordinavit. Tum regem Teuthrantem Telephus magnifice sepelivit. Suadet ei Achilles, ut novum regnum conservet: ait plus multo eum exercitum adiuvaturum, si commeatum frumenti exercitui praepararet, quam si ad Troiam iret. Itaque Telephus remanet. Achilles cum magno praedae commercio ad exercitum Tenedum revertitur, Agamemnoni rem gestam narrat, Agamemnon adprobat conlaudat.

D. 16.   Then, having called a meeting of the council, he sent envoys to Priam to ask for the return of Helen and the booty Alexander had taken; Diomedes and Ulysses were chosen to go on this mission. At the same time Achilles and Telephus were sent to plunder Mysia, the region ruled by King Teuthras.[17]

They had come to this region and had begun to despoil the country when Teuthras arrived with his army. Thereupon Achilles put the enemy to flight, and also wounded the king. He would have finished him off if Telephus had not stood in his way. Telephus came to Teuthras' aid and protected him under his shield, for he remembered their friendship, the time in his boyhood when Teuthras had been his generous host: Teuthras had felt indebted to Telephus' father, Hercules, for Hercules, so they said, had slain Diomedes, the previous king of Mysia, from whom Teuthras had inherited the kingdom. (Diomedes had met his death while hunting with his wild and powerful horses). Nevertheless, now Teuthras realized that he was unable to live much longer, and so he appointed Telephus heir to the throne and king of Mysia.

Telephus held a magnificent funeral for Teuthras. Then Achilles urged him to stay behind and take care of his newly gained kingdom. Telephus, he said, would aid the Greeks much more by sending supplies than by going to Troy. Thus Telephus stayed behind in his kingdom, and Achilles, carrying much booty, returned to the army on Tenedos. His report of what had been done won Agamemnon's approval and praise.

---

17 Compare this section with Dictys 2.1-6 and note.

D. XVII.   Interea legati missi ad Priamum veniunt. Ulixes mandata Agamemnonis refert, postulat, ut Helena et praeda reddatur satisque Graecis fiat, ut pacifice discedant. Priamus iniurias Argonautarum commemorat, patris interitum, Troiae expugnationem et Hesionae sororis servitutem, denique Antenorem legatum cum miserit, quam contumeliose ab eis tractatus sit, pacem repudiat, bellum indicit, Graecorum legatos de finibus repelli iubet. Legati in castra Tenedum revertuntur renuntiantes responsum. res consulto geritur.

D. XVIII.   Aderant vero ad auxilium Priamo adversus Graecos ducatores hi cum exercitibus suis, quorum nomina et provincias insinuandas esse duximus: de Zelia Pandarus Amphius Adrastus, de Colophonia Mopsus, de Phrygia Asius, de Caria Amphimachus Nastes, de Lycia Sarpedon Glaucus, de Larisa Hippothous et Cupesus, de Ciconia Euphemus, de Thracia Pirus et Acamas, de Paeonia Pyraechmes et Asteropaeus, de Phrygia Ascanius et Phorcys, de Maeonia Antiphus et Mesthles, de Paphlagonia Pylaemenes, de Aethiopia Perses et Memnon, de Thracia Rhesus et Archilochus, de Adiestia Adrastus et Amphius, de Alizonia Epistrophus et Odius. His ductoribus et exercitibus qui paruerunt praefecit Priamus principem et ductorem Hectorem, dein Deiphobum Alexandrum Troilum Aenean Memnonem. Dum Agamemnon consulit de tota re, ex Cormo advenit Naupli filius Palamedes cum navibus XXX. Ille excusavit se morbo adfectum Athenas venire non potuisse: quod venerit, cum primum potuerit, gratias agunt rogantque eum in consilio esse.

D. 17. Meanwhile the envoys had come to Priam, and Ulysses stated Agamemnon's demands. If Helen and the booty, he said, were returned and proper reparations were made, the Greeks would depart in peace.

Priam answered by reviewing the wrongs the Argonauts had done:[18] the death of his father, the sack of Troy, and the capture of his sister Hesione. He ended by describing how contemptuously the Greeks had treated Antenor when sent as his envoy. He therefore repudiated peace. He declared war and commanded that the envoys of the Greeks be expelled from his boundaries.

Thus the envoys returned to their camp on Tenedos and reported what Priam had answered. And the council discussed what to do.

D. 18. This seems to be a good place to list the leaders who brought armies to aid King Priam against the Greeks and to tell the countries from which they came.[19] Pandarus, Amphius, and Adrastus came from Zelia; Mopsus from Colophon; Asius from Phrygia; Amphimachus and Nastes from Caria; Sarpedon and Glaucus from Lycia; Hippothous and Cupesus from Larissa; Euphemus from Ciconia; Pirus and Acamas from Thrace; Pyraechmes and Asteropaeus from Paeonia; Ascanius and Phorcys from Phrygia; Antiphus and Mesthles from Maeonia; Pylaemenes from Paphlagonia; Perses and Memnon from Ethiopia; Rhesus and Archilochus from Thrace; Adrastus and Amphius from Adrestia; and Epistrophus and Odius from Alizonia. Priam made Hector commander-in-chief of these leaders and their armies. Second-in-command were Deiphobus, Alexander, Troilus, Aeneas, and Memnon. While Agamemnon was making his plans complete, Palamedes, the son of Nauplius, arrived with thirty ships from Cormos.[20] He had been incapacitated by sickness from coming to Athens and begged their pardon. They thanked him for coming when he was able and asked him to share in their counsels.

---

18 According to Schissel von Fleschenberg, most of this speech is probably the work of the translator-compiler. See note 10 above.

19 This catalogue of Trojan allies is based for the most part on *Iliad* 2.824-877.

20 Schissel von Fleschenberg (p. 162) points out that the non-Homeric hero Palamedes (with his ships) is not listed in section 14 along with the other Greek leaders (and their ships) but is given a special place here after the listing of the Trojan leaders.

D. XIX. Deinde cum Argivis non constaret exeundum ad Troiam clam noctu an interdiu foret, Palamedes suadet et rationem reddit luce in Troiam escensionem fieri oportere et manum hostium deduci. Itaque omnes ei adsentiunt. Consulte Agamemnonem praeficiunt. Legatos ad Mysiam ceterisque locis mittunt, ut exercitui commeatus subportandos curent, Thesidas Demophoontem et Acamantem et Anium: deinde exercitum ad concionem convocat conlaudat imperat hortatur monet diligenter, ut dicto obaudientes sint. Signo dato naves solvunt, tota classis ad latitudinem accedit ad Troiae litora. Troiani fortiter defendunt. Protesilaus in terram excursionem facit fugat caedit. Cui Hector obviam venit et eum interfecit, ceteros perturbat. Unde Hector recedebat, ibi Troiani fugabantur. Postquam magna caedes utrimque facta est, advenit Achilles. Is totum exercitum in fugam vertit, redegit in Troiam. Nox proelium dirimit. Agamemnon exercitum totum in terram educit, castra facit. Postera die Hector exercitum ex urbe educit et instruit. Agamemnon contra clamore magno occurrit. Proelium acre iracundumque fit, fortissimus quisque in primis cadit. Hector Patroclum occidit et spoliare parat. Meriones eum ex acie, ne expoliaretur, eripuit. Hector Merionem persequitur et occidit. Quem cum similiter spoliare vellet, advenit subpetias Menestheus, Hectori femur sauciat, saucius quoque multa milia occidit et perseverasset Achivos in fugam mittere, nisi obvius illi Aiax Telamonius fuisset. Cum quo cum congrederetur, cognovit eum esse de sanguine suo, erat enim de Hesiona sorore Priami natus. Quo pacto Hector a navibus ignem removeri iussit et utrique se invicem remuneraverunt, et amici discesserunt.

D. 19. The Greeks debated whether they should make their attack against Troy secretly at night or during the day. Palamedes urged them to land by day, for thus they would draw the enemy forces out of the city. His advice was accepted unanimously. Then they decided to give Agamemnon command; and three envoys were appointed to gather supplies in Mysia and other places: Anius[21] and the two sons of Theseus, Demophoon and Acamas.

Then Agamemnon, having called the soldiers to assembly, praised them and demanded their immediate and total allegiance.

When the signal was given, the ships set sail and landed at Troy, with the whole fleet widely deployed. The Trojans bravely defended their country. Hector met and slew Protesilaus and caused great confusion among the rest of the Greeks.[22] (Protesilaus had gone inland, wreaking slaughter and putting the Trojans to flight.) But wherever Hector withdrew, the Trojans fled. The losses on both sides were heavy until the arrival of Achilles caused all the Trojans to flee back to Troy. When night brought an end to the battle, Agamemnon led forth all of his army onto the land and set up camp.

On the next day Hector led forth his army out of the city ready for battle. Agamemnon's forces moved opposite, shouting their war cry. The battle that arose was fierce and raging; the bravest of those who fought in the vanguard fell. Hector slew Patroclus; he was trying to strip off his armour when Meriones snatched the body out of the action. Then Hector pursued and cut down Meriones. This time, however, while trying to despoil the body, he was wounded in the leg by Menestheus, who had come to the aid of his comrade. Hector, though wounded, slew a great number of the enemy and would have successfully turned the Greek forces to flight had Ajax the son of Telamon not stood in his way. Immediately upon meeting Ajax, Hector remembered that they were related: Ajax' mother was Priam's sister Hesione. Therefore, he commanded the Trojans to stop setting fire to the ships. And then the two men gave gifts to each other and departed in friendship.[23]

---

21 For Anius, compare Dictys 1.23 (end) and note thereto.

22 According to Dictys (2.11), Aeneas slew Protestilaus.

23 Compare *Iliad* 7, where Hector and Ajax, after their duel, exchange gifts and part in friendship.

D. XX.   Postera die Graiugenae indutias petunt. Achilles Patroclum plangit, Graiugenae suos. Agamemnon Protesilaum magnifico funere effert ceterosque sepeliendos curat. Achilles Patroclo ludos funebres facit. Dum indutiae sunt, Palamedes non cessat seditionem facere: indignum regem Agamemnonem esse, qui exercitui imperaret. Ipse coram exercitu multa sua studia ostendit: primum suam excursionem castrorum munitionem vigiliarum circuitionem signi dationem librarum ponderumque dimensionem exercitusque instructionem. Haec cum a se orta essent, non aequum esse, cum a paucis imperium Agamemnoni datum sit, eum omnibus qui postea convenissent imperare, praesertim cum omnes ingenium virtutemque exspectassent in ducibus suis. Dum Achivi de imperio inter se vicissim certant, proelium post biennium repetitum est. Agamemnon Achilles Diomedes Menelaus exercitum educunt. Contra Hector Troilus Aeneas occurrunt. Fit magna caedes, ex utraque parte fortissimi cadunt: Hector Boetem Arcesilaum Prothoenorem occidit. Nox proelium dirimit. Agamemnon noctu in consilium omnes duces convocat suadet hortatur, ut omnes in aciem prodeant et maxime Hectorem persequantur, quia de his aliquos duces fortissimos occidit.

D. 20.   On the next day the Greeks obtained a truce.[24] Achilles mourned for Patroclus, and the Greeks for their dead. Agamemnon held a magnificent funeral for Protesilaus and saw to the proper burial of the others. And Achilles celebrated funeral games in honour of Patroclus.

During this truce Palamedes continuously pressed for sedition. King Agamemnon, he said, ill deserved the command of the army. Palamedes openly boasted of his own numerous accomplishments, particularly his tactics on offence, his fortifications of the camp, his regulation of guard duty, his invention of signals and scales, and his training of the army for battle. These things were due to him, and it was therefore not right, he said, for Agamemnon, whom only a few had chosen as leader, to command all those who had joined the campaign later. All of them had a right to expect a man who was brilliant and brave in this position.

After two years, during which time the Greeks debated who should command them, the war was resumed. Agamemnon, Achilles, Diomedes, and Menelaus led forth their army. The forces of Hector, Troilus, and Aeneas moved opposite. A great slaughter arose, and many very brave men fell on both sides. Hector slew Boetes, Arcesilaus, and Prothoenor. When night brought an end to the battle, Agamemnon called all the leaders to council and urged them to enter the fray and try to kill Hector especially, for Hector had slain some of their bravest commanders.

---

24 There are eleven truces reported in Dares, lasting, all told, more than seven and a half years.

D. XXI. Mane facto Hector Aeneas Alexander exercitum educunt. Omnes duces Achivorum prodeunt. Fit magna caedes. Multa milia invicem Orco dimittuntur. Menelaus Alexandrum persequi coepit: quem respiciens Alexander sagitta Menelai femur transfigit. Ille dolore commotus pariter cum Aiace Locro non cessant eum persequi. Quos ut vidit Hector instanter fratrem suum persequi, subpetias cum Aenea ei venit. Quem Aeneas clipeo protexit, et de proelio ad civitatem secum adduxit. Nox proelium dirimit. Achilles postera die cum Diomede exercitum educit. Contra Hector et Aeneas. Fit magna caedes: Hector Orcomeneum Ialmenum Epistrophum Schedium Elephenorem Dioren. Polyxenum duces occidit, Aeneas Amphimachum et Nireum, Achilles Euphemum Hippothoum Pylaeum Asteropaeam, Diomedes Antiphum Mesthlen. Agamemnon ut vidit duces fortissimos cecidisse, pugnam revocavit. laeti Troiani in castra revertuntur. Agamemnon sollicitus duces in consilium vocavit, hortatur, ut fortiter pugnarent neque desisterent, quoniam maior pars ex suis superata sit, sperare se exercitum ex Mysia cotidie superventurum.

D. 21. With the coming of morning, Hector, Aeneas, and Alexander led forth their army. And all the Greek leaders advanced with their forces. A great slaughter arose, and on both sides countless numbers were sent down to Orcus.[25] Menelaus began to pursue Alexander who, turning around, pierced him in the leg with an arrow. Nevertheless, though pained by his wound, Menelaus continued to pursue, and Locrian Ajax accompanied him. Hector saw what was happening, and immediately he and Aeneas came to the aid of their brother. While Aeneas, using his shield, provided protection, Hector led Alexander out of the fighting and into the city.[26] Night brought an end to the battle.

On the next day Achilles and Diomedes led forth their army. The forces of Hector and Aeneas came opposite. A great slaughter arose. Hector slew the leaders Orcomeneus, Ialmenus, Epistrophus, Schedius, Elephenor, Diores, and Polyxenus. Aeneas slew Amphimachus and Nireus. Achilles slew Euphemus, Hippothous, Pylaeus, and Asteropaeus. And Diomedes slew Antiphus and Mesthles. When Agamemnon saw that his bravest leaders had fallen, he called back his forces; and the Trojans returned to their city, rejoicing. Agamemnon was worried. Calling the leaders to council, he urged them to fight on bravely and not to give way. More than half of their forces had fallen, but any day now an army was coming from Mysia.

---

25 Compare *Iliad* 1.1-4, in which the Wrath of Achilles hurls many brave souls of heroes to Hades.

26 Compare the duel between Alexander and Menelaus in *Iliad* 3, where Venus rescues Alexander out of the battle; and in Dictys 2.40, where the barbarians rescue him. Notice that Dares has Alexander (and not Pandarus, as in Homer and Dictys) wound Menelaus with an arrow.

331

D. XXII. Postera die Agamemnon totum exercitum et omnes duces in pugnam prodire coegit. Contra Troiani. Fit magna caedes, acriter ex utraque parte pugnatur, multa milia hinc et inde cadunt nec differebatur pugna, ita ut continuis LXXX diebus animose pugnatum sit. Agamemnon ut vidit multa milia cotidie occidi neque sufficere mortuos sine intermissione funerari, misit legatos Ulixen et Diomedem ad Priamum, ut indutias in triennium peterent, ut suos funerarent, vulneratos curarent, naves reficerent, exercitum compararent, commeatum conueherent. Ulixes et Diomedes noctu ad Priamum vadunt [legati]. Occurrit illis ex Troianis Dolon. qui cum interrogaret, quid ita armati noctu ad oppidum venissent, dixerunt se ab Agamemnone legatos ad Priamum missos. Quos ut audivit Priamus venisse et desiderium suum exposuisse, in consilium omnes duces convocat, quibus refert legatos venisse ab Agamemnone, ut indutias in triennium peterent. Hectori suspectum videtur quod tam longum tempus postulassent. Priamus dicere imperat, quid cuique videatur. Omnibus placitum est indutias in triennium dare. Interim Troiani moenia renovant, suos quisque saucios curant, mortuos cum ingenti honore sepeliunt.

D. 22.   On the next day Agamemnon ordered the whole army, with all of the leaders, to go forth to battle. The Trojans came opposite. A great slaughter arose, with both sides battling fiercely and losing countless numbers of men, there being no break in the fighting, which raged for eighty consecutive days. Agamemnon, seeing the steadily mounting casualties, felt that time was needed for burying the dead. Therefore, he sent Ulysses and Diomedes as envoys to Priam to seek a truce of three years. During this time the Greeks would also be able to heal their wounded, repair the ships, reinforce the army, and gather supplies.

Ulysses and Diomedes, while on their way to Priam by dark, met a Trojan named Dolon. When he asked why they were coming to the city, in arms and at night, they told him that they were envoys from Agamemnon to Priam.[27]

When Priam heard of their coming and knew what they wanted, he called all of his leaders to council. Then he announced that these were envoys Agamemnon had sent to seek a truce of three years. Hector suspected something was wrong. They wanted, he said, a truce for too long a time. Nevertheless, when Priam ordered the members of the council to give their opinions, they voted to grant a truce of three years.

During the truce the Trojans repaired their walls, healed their wounded, and buried their dead with great honour.

---

27 Compare Dictys 2.3 (end) and Dares 39 (beginning).

D. XXIII.   Tempus pugnae post triennium supervenit. Hector et Troilus exercitum educunt. Agamemnon Menelaus Achilles et Diomedes etiam ipsi exercitum educunt. Fit magna caedes. Hector in prima acie Phidippum et Antiphum duces interficit, Achilles Lycaonem et Phorcyn occidit et ex cetera plebe multa milia ex utraque parte cadunt. Acriter pugnatur diebus continuis XXX. Priamus ut vidit multos de suo exercitu cecidisse, mittit legatos ad Agamemnonem, ut indutias peterent mensibus VI et ex consilii sententia Agamemnon concedit indutias. tempus pugnae supervenit. Acriter per duodecim dies pugnatur. Multi duces fortissimi hinc et inde cadunt, plures vulnerantur, plurimi in curatione moriuntur. Agamemnon mittit ad Priamum legatos et triginta dierum indutias postulat, ut funerare mortuos suos possit. Priamus consulte fecit.

D. 23.   After three years, the war was resumed. Hector and
Troilus led forth their army. Agamemnon, Menelaus, Achilles, and
Diomedes commanded the Greeks. A great slaughter arose, with
Hector killing the leaders of the first rank, Phidippus and
Antiphus, and Achilles slaying Lycaon and Phorcys. Countless
numbers of others fell on both sides, as the battle raged for thirty
consecutive days. Priam, seeing that many of his men were
falling, sent envoys to seek a truce of six months. This
Agamemnon, following the will of his council, conceded.

With the resumption of hostilities, the battle raged for twelve
days. On both sides many of the bravest leaders fell; and even
more were wounded, a majority of whom died during treatment.
Therefore, Agamemnon sent envoys to Priam to seek a thirty-day
truce for burying the dead. Priam, after consulting his council,
agreed.

D. XXIV. At ubi tempus pugnae supervenit, Andromacha uxor Hectoris in somnis vidit Hectorem non debere in pugnam procedere: et cum ad eum visum referret, Hector muliebria verba abicit. Andromacha maesta misit ad Priamum, ut ille prohiberet, ne ea die pugnaret. Priamus Alexandrum Helenum Troilum et Aenean in pugnam misit. Hector ut ista audivit, multa increpans Andromacham arma ut proferret poposcit nec retineri ullo modo potuit. Maesta Andromacha summissis capillis Astyanactem filium protendens ante pedes Hectoris eum revocare non potuit tunc planctu femineo oppidum concitat, ad Priamum in regiam currit, refert quae in somnis viderit velle Hectorem ueloci saltu in pugnam ire, proiectoque ad genua Astyanacte filio suo eum revocare mandat. Priamus omnes in pugnam prodire iussit, Hectorem retinuit. Agamemnon Achilles Diomedes Aiax Locrus ut viderunt Hectorem in pugna non esse, acriter pugnaverunt multosque duces de Troianorum numero occiderunt. Hector ut audivit tumultum Troianosque in bello saeve laborare, prosiluit in pugnam. statimque Idomeneum obtruncavit, Iphinoum sauciavit, Leonteum occidit, Stheneli femur iaculo figit. Achilles ut respexit multos duces eius dextera cecidisse, animum in eum dirigebat, ut illi obvius fieret. Considerabat enim Achilles nisi Hectorem occideret plures de Graecorum numero eius dextera perituros. Proelium interea conliditur. Hector Polypoetem ducem fortissimum occidit dumque eum spoliare coepit.

Achilles supervenit. Fit pugna maior, clamor ab oppido et a toto exercitu surgit. Hector Achillis femur sauciavit. Achilles dolore accepto magis eum persequi coepit nec destitit, nisi eum occideret. Quo interempto Troianos in fugam vertit et maxima caede laesos usque ad portas persequitur: cui tamen Memnon restitit. Et inter se acriter pugnaverunt, laesi utrique discesserunt. Nox proelium dirimit. Achilles saucius de bello rediit. Noctu Troiani Hectorem lamentantur, Graiugenae suos.

D. 24.   When time for fighting returned, Andromache, Hector's wife, had a dream which forbade Hector to enter the fray. He, however, dismissed this vision as due to her wifely concern. She, being deeply upset, sent word to Priam to keep her husband out of the battle that day. Priam, therefore, divided the command of his forces between Alexander, Helenus, Troilus, and Aeneas. Hector, on learning of this, bitterly blamed Andromache and told her to bring forth his armour; nothing, he said, could keep him from battle. She tried in vain to make him relent, falling at his feet, like a woman in mourning, her hair let down, holding the baby, their son Astyanax, out in her hands. Then, rushing to the palace, her wailing rousing the city as she went, she told King Priam how she had dreamt that Hector would eagerly leap into battle; and, holding Astyanax, she knelt before him and begged him not to allow this. Accordingly, Priam sent all the others to battle, but kept Hector back.

When Agamemnon, Achilles, Diomedes, and the Locrian Ajax saw that Hector was not on the field, they fought the more fiercely, slaying many leaders of the Trojans. But Hector, hearing the tumult and knowing that the Trojans were being hard pressed, leaped into battle. Immediately he slew Idomeneus, wounded Iphinous, cut down Leonteus, and thrust a spear into Sthenelus' leg. Achilles, seeing these leaders fall and wanting to prevent other Greeks from meeting a similar fate, determined to go against Hector and slay him. But by the time he caught up with Hector, the battle continuing to rage, the latter had already killed Polypoetes, the bravest of leaders, and was trying to strip off the armour. The fight that arose was terrific, as was the clamour from city and armies. Hector wounded Achilles' leg. But Achilles, though pained, pressed on all the harder and kept pressing on until he had won. Hector's death caused the Trojans to turn and flee for their gates, their numbers greatly depleted. Only Memnon resisted. He and Achilles fought fiercely, and neither got off without injuries. When night brought an end to the battle, the wounded Achilles returned to camp. The Trojans lamented for Hector, and the Greeks for their dead.

D. XXV.   Postera die Memnon Troianos educit contra Graecorum exercitum. Agamemnon exercitum consulit suadetque indutias duum mensium postulari, ut suos quisque sepelire possit. Legati ad Priamum Troiam proficiscuntur, venientes desiderium prosecuti sunt, duum mensium indutias accipiunt. Priamus Hectorem suorum more ante portas sepelivit ludosque funebres fecit. Dum indutiae sunt, Palamedes iterum non cessat de imperio conqueri. Itaque Agamemnon seditioni cessit et dixit se de ea re libenter laturum, ut quem vellent imperatorem praeficerent. postera die populum ad concionem vocat, negat se umquam cupidum imperii fuisse, animo aequo se accipere, si cui vellent dare: se libenter cedere: satis sibi esse, dum hostes ulciscantur et parvi facere cuius id opera fiat. Se tamen regnum Mycenis habere, iubet dicere, si cui quid placeat. Palamedes prodit, suum ingenium ostendit. Itaque Argivi libenter ei imperium tradunt. Palamedes Argivis agit gratias, imperium accipit administrat. Achilles vituperat imperii commutationem.

D. 25.   On the next day Memnon led forth the Trojans against the Greeks. Agamemnon, having called the army to assembly, urged a truce of two months for burying the dead. Thus envoys set out for Troy, and there, having told what they wanted to Priam, received a truce of two months.

Then Priam, following the custom of his people, buried Hector in front of the gates and held funeral games in his honour.

During the truce, Palamedes continued to complain about the Greek leadership, and so Agamemnon yielded to sedition. He said that the Greeks might choose as their general whomever they wished, so far as he cared.

On the next day he called the people to assembly and denied he had ever wanted to command them. He was ready to accept whomever they chose. He willingly yielded. All he desired was to punish the enemy, and it mattered little how this was done. Nevertheless, as he was still king of Mycenae, he commanded them to speak as they wished.

Then Palamedes came forward and, showing his qualifications, won the acclaim of the Greeks. They made him commander-in-chief, a position he gratefully accepted and began to administer. Achilles, however, disparaged the change.

D. XXVI. Interea indutiae exeunt. Palamedes ornatum paratumque exercitum educit instruit hortatur: contra Deiphobus. Pugnatur acriter a Troianis. Sarpedon Lycius cum suis inpressionem in Argivos facit caedit prosternit. Obvius ei fit Tlepolemus Rhodius, sed diu stando pugnandoque male vulneratus cadit. Succedit Pheres Admeti filius proelium restituit diuque cum Sarpedone comminus pugnando occiditur. Sarpedon quoque vulneratus de proelio recedit. Itaque per aliquot dies proelia fiunt, ex utraque parte multi ductores occiduntur sed plures a Priamo. Troiani mittunt legatos, indutias postulant, ut mortuos sepeliant, saucios curent. Palamedes indutias facit in annum, mortuos utrique sepeliunt, saucios curant. Fide data ultro citroque in oppidum et castra Argivorum commeant. Palamedes Agamemnonem legatum mittit ad Thesidas Acamantem et Demoiphoontem, quos legatos Agamemnon praefecerat, ut commeatus compararent et frumentum de Mysia a Telepho acceptum subportarent. Ut eo venit, seditionem Palamedis narrat. Illi moleste ferunt, Agamemnon ait se moleste non ferre, sua voluntate esse factum. Interea naves onerandas curat Palamedes, castra munit, turribusque circumdat. Troiani exercitum exercent, murum diligenter instaurant, fossam et vallum addunt, cetera diligenter conparant.

D. 26. When the truce was over, Palamedes, arranging his forces and urging them on, led forth the army ready for battle. Deiphobus commanded the Trojans, who offered fierce opposition. The Lycian Sarpedon, leading his men, attacked and caused great slaughter and havoc. The Rhodian Tlepolemus met and resisted Sarpedon, but finally fell badly wounded. Then Pheres, the son of Admetus, came up and, after a long hand-to-hand fight with Sarpedon, was killed, but Sarpedon also was wounded and forced from the battle. Thus for several days there was fighting, and many leaders died on both sides. The Trojan casualties, however, were greater. When they sent envoys to seek a respite for burying their dead and healing their wounded, Palamedes granted a truce of one year.

Both sides buried their dead and cared for their wounded. Their agreement allowed them to go to each other's areas; the Trojans went to the camp, the Greeks to the city.

Palamedes sent Agamemnon to Mysia to Acamas and Demophoon, Theseus' sons, whom Agamemnon had put in charge of bringing supplies and grain from Telephus. Upon his arrival in Mysia, Agamemnon told them about Palamedes' sedition. When, however, he saw that they were displeased, he admitted that he had agreed to the change.

Meanwhile Palamedes was readying the ships and fortifying the camp with walls and towers. The Trojans were training their army, repairing their walls, adding a rampart and ditch, and diligently getting everything ready.

D. XXVII. Postquam anni dies venit, quo Hector sepultus est, Priamus et Hecuba et Polyxena ceterique Troiani ad Hectoris sepulchrum profecti sunt. Quibus obvius fit Achilles: Polyxenam contemplatur, figit animum, amare vehementer eam coepit. Tunc ardore conpulsus odiosam in amore vitam consumit et aegre ferebat ademptum imperium Agamemnoni sibique Palamedem praepositum. Cogente amore Phrygio servo fidelissimo mandata dat ferenda ad Hecubam et ab ea sibi uxorem Polyxenam poscit: si dederit, se cum suis Myrmidonibus domum rediturum, quod cum ipse fecerit, ceteros porro ductores idem facturos. Servus proficiscitur ad Hecubam convenit mandata dicit. Hecuba respondit velle se, si Priamo placeat viro suo: dum ipsa cum Priamo agat, servum reverti iubet. Servus Achilli quid egerit nuntiat. Agamemnon cum magno comitatu ad castra revertitur. Hecuba cum Priamo de condicione Achillis conloquitur. Priamus respondet fieri non posse, non ideo, quod eum indignum adfinitate existimet, sed si ei dederit et ipse discesserit ceteros non discessuros et iniquum esse filiam suam hosti coniungere. Quapropter si id fieri velit, pax perpetua fiat, et exercitus discedat, foedus iure sanciatur: si id factum sit, se illi filiam libenter daturum. Itaque Achilles ut constitutum erat servum ad Hecubam mittit, ut sciat quid cum Priamo egerit. Hecuba omnia quae cum Priamo egerat mandat servo. is Achilli refert. Achilles queritur in vulgus, unius mulieris Helenae causa totam Graeciam et Europam convocatam esse, tanto tempore tot milia hominum perisse, libertatem in ancipiti esse, unde oportere pacem fieri, exercitum reducere.

D. 27.   On the first anniversary of Hector's funeral, Priam, Hecuba, Polyxena, and other Trojans went to the tomb. There they happened to meet Achilles, who, being struck by Polyxena's beauty, fell madly in love. The burning power of his love took all the joy out of life. (His soul was also rankled by the fact that the Greeks had deposed Agamemnon and made Palamedes commander-in-chief instead of himself). Accordingly, urged by his love, he sent a trusted Phrygian slave to make this proposal to Hecuba: if she would give him Polyxena to marry, he would go home with his Myrmidons, and thus would set an example which the other leaders would follow. When the slave went to Hecuba and made this proposal, she answered that she would be willing, if Priam agreed, but that she must talk with him first. Then the slave, as Hecuba ordered, returned to Achilles and told him her answer.

Agamemnon, coming from Mysia with a large group of followers, arrived in camp at this time.

When Hecuba talked to Priam about Achilles' proposal, Priam refused to agree. Granted that Achilles would make a good relative, it was not right to marry one's daughter to an enemy; and even if Achilles himself went home, the other Greeks would not follow. Therefore, if Achilles wanted this marriage, he must promise a lasting peace, a treaty with sacred oaths; and the Greeks must depart. On these conditions, Priam would willingly give him his daughter in marriage.

The slave of Achilles, according to his understanding with Hecuba, returned to her and learned what Priam had said. Then he reported all he had heard back to his master. Thereupon Achilles complained, to any and everyone, that for the sake of one woman, that is, Helen, all Europe and Greece were in arms, and now, for a very long time, thousands of men had been dying. Their very liberty, he said, was at stake, and this was the reason they ought to make peace and take their army back home.

D. XXVIII. Annus circumactus est. Palamedes exercitum educit instruit, Deiphobus contra. Achilles iratus in proelium non prodit. Palamedes occasionem nactus inpressionem in Deiphobum facit eumque obtruncat. Proelium acre insurgit, acriter ab utrisque pugnatur, multa milia hominum cadunt. Palamedes in prima acie versatur hortaturque, proelium ut fortiter gerant. Contra eum Sarpedon Lycius occurrit eumque Palamedes interficit. Eo facto laetus in acie versatur. Cui exultanti et glorianti Alexander Paris sagitta collum transfigit. Phryges animadvertunt, tela coniciunt atque ita Palamedes occiditur. Rege occiso cuncti hostes inpressionem faciunt Argivi cedunt, in castra confugiunt: Troiani persecuntur, castra obpugnant, naves incendunt. Achilli nuntiatum est, dissimulat. Aiax Telamonius fortiter defendit. Nox proelium dirimit. Argivi in castris Palamedis scientiam aequitatem clementiam bonitatem lamentantur. Troiani Sarpedonem et Deiphobum deflent.

D. 28. When the year was over, Palamedes led forth the army and drew it up. And the Trojans came opposite commanded by Deiphobus. (Achilles, however, refused to take part because of his anger). Palamedes seized an opportunity to attack Deiphobus and slaughtered him.

A fierce battle arose, fiercely fought on both sides; there were countless numbers of casualties. Palamedes, active in the first ranks, urging his men to fight bravely, encountered and slew the Lycian Sarpedon, but as he continued to prowl in the vanguard, spurred on by success, exulting, and vaunting his prowess, Alexander (Paris) pierced his neck with an arrow; and then the Phrygians, seeing their chance, hurled their spears and finished him off. King Palamedes was dead. Accordingly, all the Trojans attacked. They pursued the Greeks, and the Greeks retreated and fled to the camp. The camp was besieged, the ships set on fire.

Achilles, though told what was happening, chose to pretend that things were all right.

Ajax the son of Telamon bravely led the defence until night brought an end to the battle. Then the Greeks lamented the loss of Palamedes' wisdom, justice, mercy, and goodness; and the Trojans bewailed the deaths of Sarpedon and Deiphobus.

D. XXIX. Nestor qui maior natu erat noctu ductores in consilium vocat suadet hortatur, ut imperatorem praeficiant et si eis videatur eundem Agamemnonem minima cum discordia fieri posse. Item commemorat, dum ille imperator fuit, res prospere cessisse, felicem fuisse exercitum: si cui quid aliud videatur dicere suadet. Omnes adsentiunt, Agamemnonem summum imperatorem praeficiunt. Postera die Troiani alacres in aciem prodeunt. Agamemnon exercitum contra educit. Proelio commisso uterque exercitus inter se pugnat. Postquam maior pars diei transiit, prodit in primo Troilus, caedit devastat, Argivos in castra fugat. Postera die exercitum Troiani educunt: contra Agamemnon. Fit maxima caedes, uterque exercitus inter se pugnat acriter. Multos duces Argivorum Troilus interficit. Pugnatur continuis diebus VII. Agamemnon indutias petit in duos menses. Palameden magnifico funere effert ceterosque duces ac milites utrique sepeliendos curant.

D. 29.   Also during this night Nestor, since he was the eldest, called the Greek leaders to council and, speaking with tact, urged them to choose a new general. He felt that, if they thought best, Agamemnon's reappointment would cause the least discord. He reminded them that while Agamemnon was general things had gone well and the army had prospered. If, however, anyone had a better idea, he urged him to speak. But all, agreeing with him, made Agamemnon commander-in-chief.

On the next day the Trojans quickly came forth. And Agamemnon led the Greeks opposite. The battle was joined, and the two forces clashed. Towards evening Troilus advanced to the front and, wreaking slaughter and havoc, sent the Greeks flying back to their camp.

On the next day the Trojans led forth their army. And the forces of Agamemnon came opposite. A horrible slaughter arose. Both armies fought fiercely; Troilus slaughtered many Greek leaders, as the battle lasted seven days.

Then Agamemnon, having obtained a truce of two months, held a magnificent funeral in Palamedes' honour. Both sides saw to the burial of all the leaders and soldiers who had died.

D. XXX. Agamemnon dum indutiae sunt mittit ad Achillem Ulixen Nestorem et Diomeden, ut rogent eum in bellum prodire. Abnegat Achilles maestus, quod iam destinaverat in bellum non prodire ob id quod promiserat Hecubae, aut certe se minus pugnaturum eo quod Polyxenam valde amabat: coepit male eos accipere qui ad eum venerant, dicens debere perpetuam pacem fieri, tanta pericula unius mulieris causa fieri, libertatem periclitari, tanto tempore desidere: pacem expostulat, pugnare negat. Agamemnoni renuntiatur quid cum Achille actum sit, illum pertinaciter negare. Agamemnon omnes duces in consilium vocat, exercitum quid fieri debeat consulit, imperat dicere quid cuique videatur. Menelaus hortari coepit fratrem suum, ut exercitum in pugnam produceret, nec debere terreri, si Achilles se excusaverit, se tamen persuasurum ei, ut in bellum prodeat, nec vereri, si noluerit. Commemorare coepit Troianos non habere alium virum tam fortem sicut Hector fuit. Diomedes et Ulixes dicere coeperunt Troilum non minus quam Hectorem virum fortissimum esse. Diomedi et Ulixi Menelaus resistens bellum geri suadebat. Calchas ex augurio respondit debere pugnare nec vereri quod modo superiores Troiani fuerint.

D. 30.   During the truce, Agamemnon sent Ulysses, Nestor, and Diomedes to Achilles to ask him to reenter the fighting. But Achilles, still moody, refused to budge from his decision to stay out of battle. He told about his promise to Hecuba and said that he would certainly fight rather poorly because of his passionate love for Polyxena. They whom Agamemnon had sent were not welcome. A lasting peace, that was the need. For the sake of one woman, he said, the Greeks were risking their lives, endangering their freedom, and wasting a great deal of time. Thus Achilles demanded peace, and refused to reenter the fighting.

When Agamemnon learned of Achilles' stubborn refusal, he summoned all the leaders to council and asked them to tell what they thought should be done.

Menelaus urged Agamemnon to lead the army to battle and not to worry about the withdrawal of Achilles. He himself would try to win over Achilles, but if he should fail, he would not be dejected. Furthermore, he said, the Trojans now had no one to take Hector's place, no one so brave.

Diomedes and Ulysses answered that Troilus was the bravest of men and the equal of Hector.

But Menelaus denied this and urged the council to continue the war.

Calchas, taking the omens, informed them that they ought to do battle and not be frightened by the Trojans' recent successes.

D. XXXI. Tempus pugnae supervenit. Agamemnon Menelaus Diomedes Aiax exercitum educunt. Contra Troiani. Fit magna caedes, pugnatur acriter, uterque exercitus inter se saeviunt. Troilus Menelaum sauciat, multos interficit, ceteros paulatim persequitur. Nox proelium dirimit. Postera die Troilus cum Alexandro exercitum educit, contra omnes Argivi prodeunt, acriter pugnatur. Troilus Diomeden sauciat, in Agamemnonem inpressionem facit nec non et ipsum sauciat, Argivos caedit. Per aliquot dies pugnatur acriter, multa milia hominum ex utraque parte trucidantur. Agamemnon ut vidit maiorem partem exercitus se cotidie amittere nec sufficere posse, petit indutias in sex menses. Priamus consilium cogit, indicat Argivorum desideria. Troilus negat debere dari tam longo tempore indutias, sed potius inpressionem fieri, naves incendi. Priamus quid cuique videatur dicere imperat. Omnibus placitum est debere fieri quod Argivi petunt. Priamus itaque in sex menses indutias dedit. Agamemnon honorifice suos sepeliendos curat, Diomeden Menelaum sauciatos curat. Troiani suos aeque sepeliunt. Dum indutiae sunt, ex consilii sententia Agamemnon ad Achillem proficiscitur, ut eum ad pugnam provocaret. Achilles tristis negare coepit se proditurum, sed pacem peti oportere, conqueri coepit, quod Agamemnoni nihil negare possit: tamen cum tempus pugnae supervenisset, se milites suos missurum, ipsum excusatum haberet. Agamemnon ei gratias egit.

D. 31.   When the time for fighting returned, Agamemnon, Menelaus, and Ajax led forth the army. The Trojans came opposite. A great slaughter arose, a fierce and raging battle on both sides. Troilus, having wounded Menelaus, pressed on, killing many of the enemy and harrying the others. Night brought an end to the battle.

On the next day Troilus and Alexander led forth the Trojans. And all the Greeks came opposite. The battle was fierce. Troilus wounded Diomedes and, in the course of his slaughter, attacked and wounded Agamemnon himself.

For several days the battle raged on. Countless numbers fell on both sides. Then Agamemnon, seeing that he was losing more of his forces each day, and knowing that they were unable to last, sought a truce of six months.

Priam, having called a meeting of his council, reported the desires of the Greeks. Troilus felt that they were asking for too long a time; he urged the Trojans to continue fighting, and fire the ships. When, however, Priam ordered the members of the council to give their opinions, the vote was unanimous in favour of the Greek petition, and thus they granted a truce of six months.

Agamemnon buried his dead with honours and saw to the care of the wounded, such as Diomedes and Menelaus. The Trojans also buried their dead.

During the truce Agamemnon, following the advice of his council, went to rouse Achilles to battle, but Achilles, still gloomy, refused to go forth; he felt that the king should be suing for peace. Nevertheless, after complaining that it was impossible to refuse Agamemnon, he said that he would send forth his forces when war was resumed, though he himself would stay back. For this Agamemnon gave him his thanks.

D. XXXII. Tempus pugnae supervenit. Troiani exercitum educunt. Contra Argivi prodeunt. Achilles primo Myrmidones instruit, ad Agamemnonem paratos mittit. Fit pugna maior, acriter saevitur. Troilus in prima acie Argivos caedit, Myrmidones fugat, inpressionem usque in castra facit, multos occidit, plurimos sauciat. Aiax Telamonius obstitit. Troiani victores in oppidum revertuntur. Postera die Agamemnon exercitum educit, omnes duces et Myrmidones prodeunt: contra Troiani in aciem laeti exeunt. Proelio commisso uterque exercitus inter se dimicat, acriter per aliquot dies pugnatur, multa milia hominum ex utraque parte cadunt. Troilus Myrmidones persequitur sternit fugat. Agamemnon ut vidit ex sua parte multos occisos, indutias in dies triginta petit, ut suos funerare possit. Priamus indutias dedit. suos quisque sepeliendos curat.

D. 32. When the time for war returned, the Trojans led forth their army. And the forces of the Greeks came opposite. Achilles, having drawn up his Myrmidons, sent them to Agamemnon ready for combat. A great battle arose, fierce and raging. Troilus, fighting in the first ranks, slaughtered the Greeks and put the Myrmidons to flight. He pressed his attack even into the camp, killing many and wounding most who stood in his way until Ajax the son of Telamon stopped him. The Trojans returned to the city victorious.

On the next day Agamemnon led forth his army along with the Myrmidons and all of his leaders. And the Trojans came opposite, eager to fight. The battle was joined. For several days both sides fought fiercely, and countless numbers were lost. Troilus, attacking the Myrmidons and breaking their order, put them to flight.

When Agamemnon saw that many of his men had been killed, he sought a thirty-day truce for holding their funerals. This was granted by Priam, and thus the Greeks and Trojans buried their dead.

D. XXXIII. Tempus pugnae supervenit. Troiani exercitum educunt. Contra Agamemnon omnes duces in pugnam cogit. Proelio commisso fit magna caedes, acriter saevitur. postquam primum diei tempus transiit, prodit in primo Troilus caedit prosternit: Argivi fugam cum clamore fecerunt. Achilles ut animadvertit Troilum iracunde saevire et Argivis insultare simulque sine intermissione Myrmidones prosternere, procedit in bellum. Quem Troilus continuo excipit et sauciat. Achilles de proelio saucius redit. Pugnatur continuis diebus sex. Die septimo dum utrique exercitus proelio facto inter se pugnant, Achilles, qui aliquot dies vexatus in pugnam non prodierat, Myrmidones instruit: alloquitur hortatur, ut fortiter inpressionem in Troilum faciant. Postquam maior pars diei transiit, prodit Troilus ex equo laetus. Argivi maximo clamore fugam faciunt, Myrmidones supervenerunt, inpressionem in Troilum faciunt, de quorum numero multi a Troilo occiduntur: dum acriter proeliantur, equus vulneratus corruit, Troilum inplicitum excutit. Eum cito Achilles adveniens occidit, ex proelio trahere coepit, quod Achilles interventu Memnonis complere non potuit. Adveniens enim Memnon et Troili corpus eripuit et Achillem vulnere sauciavit. Achilles de proelio saucius rediit. Memnon insequi eum cum multis coepit, quem Achilles ut respexit, substitit: curato vulnere et aliquamdiu proeliatus Memnonem multis plagis occiclit et ipse vulneratus ab eo ex proelio recessit. Postquam Persarum ductor occisus est, reliqui in oppidum confugerunt, portas clauserunt. Nox proelium dirimit. Postera die a Priamo legati ad Agamemnonem missi sunt qui dierum XX indutias peterent, quod continuo Agamemnon concedit. Priamus igitur Troilum Memnonemque magnifico funere effert: ceterosque milites utrique sepeliendos curant.

354

D. 33. When the time for war returned, the Trojans led forth their army and Agamemnon came opposite with all of his leaders. The battle was joined. A great slaughter, fierce and raging, arose. When the morning had passed, Troilus advanced to the front, slaying the Greeks and making them flee with loud cries in general confusion. It was then that Achilles, seeing this mad and savage advance, the Greeks being crushed and the Myrmidons being relentlessly slaughtered, reentered the battle; but almost immediately he had to withdraw, wounded by Troilus. The others continued to fight for six days.

On the seventh, the battle still raging, Achilles (who until then had stayed out of action because of his wound) drew up his Myrmidons and urged them bravely to make an attack against Troilus. Toward the end of the day Troilus advanced on horseback, exulting, and caused the Greeks to flee with loud cries. The Myrmidons, however, came to their rescue and made an attack against Troilus. Troilus slew many men, but, in the midst of the terrible fighting, his horse was wounded and fell, entangling and throwing him off; and swiftly Achilles was there to dispatch him.

Then Achilles tried to drag off the body. But Memnon maintained a successful defence, wounding Achilles and making him yield. When, however, Memnon and his followers began to pursue Achilles, the latter, merely by turning around, brought them to halt.

After Achilles' wound had been dressed and he had fought for some time, he slew Memnon, dealing him many a blow, and then, having been wounded himself, yielded from combat again. The rest of the Trojan forces, knowing that the king of the Persians was dead, fled to the city and bolted the gates. Night brought an end to the battle.

On the next day Priam sent envoys to Agamemnon to seek a twenty-day truce. This Agamemnon immediately granted. Accordingly, Priam held a magnificent funeral in honour of Troilus and Memnon and both sides buried their dead.

D. XXXIV. Hecuba maesta, quod duo filii eius fortissimi Hector et Troilus ab Achille interfecti essent, consilium muliebre temerarium iniit ad ulciscendum dolorem. Alexandrum filium arcessit orat hortatur, ut se et fratres suos vindicaret, insidias Achilli faceret et eum nec opinantem occidat, quoniam ad se miserit et rogaverit, ut sibi Polyxenam daret in matrimonium: se ad eum missuram Priami verbis, pacem inter se foedusque firment constituant in fano Apollinis Thymbraei, quod est ante portam: eo Achillem venturum, conlocuturum ibique se illi insidias collocare, satis sibi victum esse, si eum occideret. quod temptaturum se Alexander promisit. Noctu de exercitu eliguntur fortissimi et in fano Apollinis collocantur, signum accipiunt. Hecuba ad Achillem, sicuti condixerat, nuntium mittit. Achilles laetus Polyxenam amans postera die ad fanum se venturum constituit. Interea Achilles sequenti die cum Antilocho Nestoris filio ad constitutum veniunt simulque fanum Apollinis ingrediuntur, undique ex insidiis occurrunt, tela coniciunt: Paris hortatur. Achilles cum Antilocho brachio sinistro chlamyde involuto enses dextra tenentes impetum faciunt. Exinde Achilles multos occidit. Alexander Antilochum interimit ipsumque Achillem multis plagis confodit. Ita Achilles animam ex insidiis nequiquam fortiter faciens amisit. Quem Alexander feris et volucribus proici iubet. Hoc ne faciat Helenus rogat, tunc eos de fano eici iubet et suis tradi: quorum corpora accepta Argivi in castra ferunt. Agamemnon eos magnifico funere effert Achillique sepulchrum ut faciat a Priamo indutias petit ibique ludos funebres facit.

D. 34. Hecuba, bewailing the loss of Hector and Troilus, her two bravest sons, both slain by Achilles, devised, like the woman she was, a treacherous vengeance. Summoning her son Alexander, she urgently begged him to kill Achilles, and thus to uphold the honour of himself and his brothers. This he could do in an ambush, catching his victim off guard. She would summon Achilles, in Priam's name, to come to the temple of the Thymbraean Apollo in front of the gate, to settle an agreement according to which she would give him Polyxena to marry. When Achilles came to this meeting, Alexander could treacherously kill him. Achilles' death would be victory sufficient for her.

Alexander promised to do as she asked. During that night he chose the bravest of the Trojans and stationed them in the temple with instructions to wait for his signal. Hecuba, as she had promised, sent word to Achilles and Achilles, because of his love for Polyxena, gladly agreed to come to the temple that morning.

Accordingly, on the next day Achilles, along with Antilochus, Nestor's son, came for the meeting. Upon entering the temple, he was treacherously attacked. Spears were hurled from all sides, as Alexander exhorted his men. Achilles and Antilochus counterattacked, with their left arms wrapped in their cloaks for protection, their right hands wielding their swords; and Achilles slew many, but finally Alexander cut down Antilochus and then slaughtered Achilles, dealing him many a blow. Such was the death of this hero, a treacherous death and one ill suiting his prowess.

Alexander's order to throw the bodies to the dogs and birds was countermanded by that of Helenus to take them out of the temple and hand them over to the Greeks. Thus the Greeks received their dead and carried them back to the camp. Agamemnon gave them magnificent funerals. He obtained a truce from Priam for the purpose of burying Achilles,[28] and then held funeral games in his honour.

---

28 Compare Dictys 4.15, where Ajax sees to the building of a tomb for Achilles.

D. XXXV.   Deinde consilium convocat, Argivos alloquitur. Placet omnibus, ut ea quae Achillis essent Aiaci propinquo eius commendarentur atque ita Aiax ait: cum filius Neoptolemus ei supersit, neminem aequius super Myrmidones principatum habere quam eum, oportere eum ad pugnam accersiri eique universa quae patris erant restitui. Consilium idem placuit Agamemnoni et omnibus, datur negotium Menelao. hic Scyrum proficiscitur ad Lycomedem avum eius, imperat, ut nepotem suum mittat. Quod Argivis Lycomedes libenter concedit. Postquam indutiae exierunt, Agamemnon exercitum educit instruit hortatur. Contra Troiani ex urbe prodeunt. Proelium committitur, in prima acie Aiax nudus versatur. Clamore magno orto multi ex utroque exercitu pereunt. Alexander arcum tetendit, multos interfecit, Aiacis latus nudum figit. Aiax saucius Alexandrum persequitur, nec destitit, nisi eum occideret. Aiax fessus vulnere in castra refertur, sagitta exempta moritur. Alexandri corpus ad urbem refertur. Diomedes virili animo in hostes inpressionem facit. Phryges fessi in urbem confugiunt, quos Diomedes usque in urbem persequitur. Agamemnon exercitum circa oppidum ducit et tota nocte circa murum obsedit, curat, ut alterna vice vigilias agant. Postera die Priamus Alexandrum in oppido sepelit, quem magno ululatu Helena prosecuta est, quoniam ab eo honorifice tractata est. Quam Priamus et Hecuba ut filiam aspexerunt et diligenter curaverunt, quod numquam Troianos despexisset Argivosque non desiderasset.

D. 35. Then he called a meeting of the Greek council, at which he gave an address. It was unanimously decided that Achilles' command should be given to Ajax, who was Achilles' cousin, but Ajax objected that Neoptolemus, Achilles' son, was still living, and thus had first claim; therefore, they should bring Neoptolemus to Troy and give him command of the Myrmidons and all of his father's prerogatives.

Agamemnon and the rest of the council agreed and chose Menelaus to go on this mission.

When Menelaus had come to the island of Scyros, he urged King Lycomedes (Neoptolemus' grandfather) to send Neoptolemus to battle. The king gladly granted the Greeks this request.

The truce having come to an end, Agamemnon drew up his forces and, urging them on, led them to war. The Trojans came opposite out of the city. The battle was joined, with Ajax fighting up front, but wearing no armour. Great was the clamour that arose, and many died on both sides. Alexander, using his bow with frequent success, pierced the unarmed Ajax' body; Ajax, however, though wounded, pursued and finally killed his assailant. Then, as the wound had exhausted his strength, he was carried back to the camp; and there, though they drew out the arrow, he died.[29]

The Trojans, having rescued Alexander's body, fled back to the city, exhausted, before Diomedes' fierce onslaught. Diomedes pursued right up to the walls. Then Agamemnon, having ordered his forces to encircle the city, spent the whole night ready for battle, his guards always alert.

On the next day, in the city, Priam buried Alexander. Helen took part in the funeral with loud lamentations. Alexander, she said, had treated her kindly; and thus she had become like a daughter to Priam and Hecuba, who always made her welcome at Troy and never let her remember her homeland.

---

29 Compare the different account in Dictys 5.15

D. XXXVI. Postera die Agamemnon coepit exercitum ante portas instruere et Dardanos ad proelium provocare. Priamus subsistere, urbem munire et quiescere, usque dum Penthesilea cum Amazonibus superveniret. Penthesilea postea supervenit, exercitum contra Agamemnonem educit. Fit proelium ingens, per aliquot dies pugnatur. Argivi fugantur in castra, obprimuntur. Cui vix Diomedes obsistit, alioquin naves incendisset et Argivorum universum exercitum devastasset. Proelio dirempto Agamemnon se in castris continuit. Penthesilea vero cotidie prodit Argivos devastat et in bellum provocat. Agamemnon ex consilio castra munit tueturque et in bellum non prodit, usque dum Menelaus veniat. Menelaus ad Scyrum venit, arma Achillis Neoptolemo filio eius tradit, quae cum sumpsisset, venit et in Argivorum castris vehementer circa patris tumulum lamentatus est. Penthesilea ex consuetudine aciem instruit et usque ad Argivorum castra prodit. Neoptolemus Myrmidonum princeps contra aciem ducit, Agamemnon exercitum instruit. Pariter ambo concurrunt. Neoptolemus stragem facit. Occurrit Penthesilea et fortiter in proelio versatur, utrique per aliquot dies acriter pugnaverunt, multosque occiderunt. Penthesilea Neoptolemum sauciat: ille dolore accepto Amazonidum ductricem Penthesileam obtruncat. Eo facto totum exercitum Troianorum in fugam convertit, in urbem victi refugiunt, Argivi cum exercitu murum circumdant, ut foras Troiani exire non possent.

D. 36. On the next day Agamemnon drew up his army in front of the gates and challenged the Trojans to come out and fight, but Priam stayed in the city, increasing his fortifications and waiting for Penthesilea to come with her Amazons.

When Penthesilea arrived, she led forth her army against Agamemnon. A huge battle arose. It raged several days, and then the Greeks, being overwhelmed, fled for their camp. Diomedes could hardly prevent Penthesilea from firing the ships and destroying all the Greek forces.

After this battle, Agamemnon kept his forces in camp. Penthesilea, to be sure, came forth each day and, slaughtering the Greeks, tried to provoke him to fight, but he, following the advice of his council, fortified the camp, strengthened the guard, and refused to go out to battle until Menelaus arrived.

When, on Scyros, Menelaus had given Neoptolemus the arms of his father, Achilles, he brought him to join the Greeks at Troy, and here Neoptolemus wept and lamented above the tomb of his father.

Penthesilea, according to her custom, drew up her army and advanced as far as the camp of the Greeks. Neoptolemus, in command of the Myrmidons, led forth his forces and Agamemnon drew up his army. Greeks and Trojans clashed head-on. Neoptolemus wreaked great slaughter. Penthesilea, having entered the fray, proved her prowess again and again.

For several days they fought fiercely, and many were killed.

Finally Penthesilea wounded Neoptolemus, and then fell at his hands; in spite of his wound, he cut her down.[30] The death of Penthesilea, the queen of the Amazons, caused all the Trojans to turn and flee in defeat for their city, and then the Greeks surrounded the walls with their forces and prevented anyone's leaving.

---

30 Compare the different account in Dictys 4.3.

XXXVII.   Hoc postquam Troiani viderunt, Antenor Polydamas Aeneas ad Priamum veniunt, agunt cum eo, ut consilium convocet et deliberet quid de fortunis suis futurum sit. Priamus consilium convocat. Qui postulaverunt sibi loquendi facultatem dari, iubet eis dicere, quid desiderent. Antenor memorat principes defensores Troiae Hectorem ceterosque natos eius cum advenis ductoribus interfectos esse, Argivis remanere fortissimos Agamemnonem Menelaum Neoptolemum non minus fortem quam pater eius fuit, Diomeden Aiacem Locrum ceterosque conplures summaeque prudentiae Nestorem Ulixen, contra Troianos clausos et metu contritos esse. suadet potius esse, ut Helena his reddatur et ea quae Alexander cum sociis abstulerat et pax fiat. Postquam multis verbis de pace concilianda egerunt, surgit Amphimachus filius Priami adulescens fortissimus, malis verbis Antenorem adortus est et eos qui consenserant, increpare facta eorum, suadere is potius educendum exercitum, inruptionem in castra faciendam, usque dum vincant aut victi pro patria occumbant. Postquam is finem fecit, Aeneas exurgit, lenibus mitibusque dictis Amphimacho repugnat, ab Argivis pacem petendam magnopere suadet: Polydamas eadem suadet.

D. 37.   When the Trojans saw their predicament, Antenor, Polydamas, and Aeneas went to Priam and asked him to call a meeting of the council to discuss the future of Troy and the Trojans.

Priam agreed, and so the meeting was called. Antenor spoke first, he and the other two having obtained permission to give their advice. The Trojans, he said, had lost their foremost defenders, Hector and the other sons of the king, along with the leaders from other places, but the Greeks still had their bravest commanders, Agamemnon, Menelaus, Neoptolemus, who was no less brave than his father, Diomedes, the Locrian Ajax, and many others besides, like Nestor and Ulysses, who were very shrewd men. Furthermore, the Trojans were surrounded and worn out with fear. Therefore, he urged the return of Helen and the things Alexander and his men had carried off with her. They must make peace.

After they had discussed making peace at some length, Amphimachus, Priam's son, a very brave youth, arose and, calling down curses upon Antenor and his associates, blamed them for the way they were acting.[31] He felt that the Trojans should lead forth their army and make an attack on the camp and never give up until they had either conquered or died fighting in behalf of their country.

After Amphimachus had spoken, Aeneas arose and tried to refute him. Speaking calmly and gently, but with persistence, he urged the Trojans to sue for peace with the Greeks.

Then Polydamas urged the same course as Aeneas.

---

31 Apparently Dares has created the character of Amphimachus after that of Antimachus in the traditional account. Compare Dictys 2.23-24 and 4.21.

D. XXXVIII. Postquam dicendi finis factus est, Priamus magno animo surgit, ingerit multa mala Antenori et Aeneae. Eos belli appetendi auctores fuisse, ut legati in Graeciam mitterentur, Antenorem quidem obiurgat, quia pacem suadeat, cum ipse quoque legatus ierit et renuntiaverit se contumeliose tractatum esse et ipse bellum suaserit, deinde Aeneam qui cum Alexandro Helenam et praedam eripuerit: quapropter certum sibi esse pacem non fieri. Imperatque, uti omnes parati sint, ut cum signum dederit, e portis inruptionem faciant, aut vincere aut mori sibi certum esse. Haec postquam multis verbis dixit hortatusque est eos, consilium dimittit, Amphimachum secum in regiam ducit dicitque ei vereri se ab his qui pacem suaserunt, ne oppidum prodant, eos habere de plebe multos qui una sentiant, opus esse eos interfici. Quod si hoc factum sit, se esse patriam defensurum et Argivos superaturum. Simulque rogat, ut sibi fidelis et obaudiens paratusque cum armatis sit, id sine suspitione posse fieri, postera die se in arce ita uti solet rem divinam facturum eosque ad cenam vocaturum, tunc Amphimachus cum armatis inruptionem faciat eosque interimat. Amphimachus consilium eius approbat seque hoc facturum promittit. Atque ita ab eo discedit.

D. 38. After this speech Priam arose with great eagerness and hurled many curses at Antenor and Aeneas. They had been the means, he said, by which war had arisen, for they were the envoys who had been sent to Greece; Antenor, who now urged peace, had then urged war when, on returning from Greece, he had told how scornfully he had been treated; and Aeneas had helped Alexander carry off Helen and the booty. In view of these facts, he, Priam, had made up his mind. There would be no peace.[32]

He commanded everyone to be prepared. When the signal was given, they must rush from the gates and either conquer or die. He had made up his mind.

After exhorting them thus at some length, Priam dismissed them. Then, taking Amphimachus along to the palace, he told him that those who urged peace must be killed. He feared that they would betray the city. Also, they had won much support for their views among the people. Once they were killed, he, Priam, would see to his country's defence and the Greeks' defeat.

Begging Amphimachus to be faithful and true, he told him to gather a band of armed men. This could be done without any suspicion. As for his part, tomorrow after going to the citadel to worship as usual, he would invite those men to dine with him. Then Amphimachus, along with his band, must rush in and kill them.

Amphimachus agreed to this plan and promised to carry it out. And then he departed from Priam.

---

32 According to Schissel von Fleschenberg, Priam's speech is, up to this point, probably the work of the translator-compiler. See note 9 above.

D. XXXIX. Eodemque die clam conveniunt Antenor Polydamas Ucalegon Dolon, dicunt se mirari regis pertinaciam, qui inclusus cum patria et comitibus perire malit quam pacem facere. Antenor ait se invenisse quod sibi et illis in commune proficiat, quod quo pacto fieri possit dicturum, si sibi fides servaretur. Omnes se in fidem Antenori obstringunt. Antenor ut vidit se obstrictum, mittit ad Aenean, dicit patriam prodendam esse et sibi et suis esse cavendum, ad Agamemnonem de his rebus aliquem esse mittendum, qui id sine suspitione curet, maturandum esse, animadvertisse se Priamum iratum de consilio surrexisse, quia ei pacem suaserit, vereri se, ne quid novi consilii ineat. Itaque omnes promittunt, statim Polydamantem qui ex his minime invidiosus erat ad Agamemnonem clam mittunt. Polydamas in castra Argivorum pervenit, Agamemnonem convenit, dicit ei quae suis placuerint.

D. 39. During the same day, Antenor, Polydamas, Ucalegon, and Dolon met in secret. They were amazed at the stubbornness of the king, who, when surrounded by the enemy, preferred to die rather than sue for peace, thus causing the destruction of his country and people. Antenor had a plan for solving their problems, and if the others would swear their allegiance, he would reveal it.

When all had sworn as he wished, he first sent word to Aeneas, and then told them his plan. They must, he said, betray their country, and in such a way that they might safeguard themselves and their families. Someone must go, someone that no one could suspect, and tell Agamemnon. They must act quickly. He had noticed that Priam, when leaving the council, was enraged because he had urged him to sue for peace; and he feared that the king was devising some treachery.

All promised their aid and immediately chose Polydamas, he would arouse least suspicion, to go in secret and see Agamemnon.

Thus Polydamas, having gone to the camp of the Greeks, saw Agamemnon and told him the plan.

D. XL.   Agamemnon clam noctu omnes duces in consilium convocat eadem refert, quid cuique videatur dicere imperat. Omnibus placitum est, ut fides proditoribus servaretur. Ulixes et Nestor dixerunt se vereri hanc rem subire, Neoptolemus hos refutat, dum inter se certant, placitum est signum a Polydamante exigi et id ipsum propter Sinonem ad Aenean et Anchisen et Antenorem mitti. Sinon ad Troiam proficiscitur et quia nondum claves portae Amphimachus custodibus tradiderat, signo dato Sinon vocem Aeneae et Anchisae et Antenoris audiendo confirmatus Agamemnoni renuntiat. Tunc placitum est omnibus, ut fides daretur iureiurando confirmaretur, ut si oppidum proxima nocte tradidissent Antenori Ucalegonti Polydamanti Aeneae Doloni suisque omnibus parentibus fides servaretur nec non liberis coniugibus consanguineis amicis propinquis, qui una consenserant suaque omnia incolumia sibi habere liceat. Hoc pacto confirmato et iureiurando adstricto suadet Polydamas noctu exercitum ad portam Scaeam adducant, ubi extrinsecus caput equi sculptum est, ibi praesidia habere noctu Antenorem et Anchisen, exercitui Argivorum portam reseraturos eisque lumen prolaturos, id signum eruptionis fore.

D. 40. That night Agamemnon called all the leaders to a secret meeting of the council, and gave them the news, and asked their advice. The council decided unanimously to trust the traitors. As for the plan, Ulysses and Nestor said that they were afraid to carry it out, but Neoptolemus spoke in its favour; and thus a disagreement arose, which it was decided to settle by obtaining a password from Polydamas that Sinon might test with Aeneas, Anchises, and Antenor.

Thus Sinon went to Troy and tested the password (Amphimachus had not yet stationed his guards at the gate), and returned and told Agamemnon that Aeneas, Anchises, and Antenor had given the correct countersign. Then the members of the council, binding themselves on oath, promised that if Troy were betrayed the next night, no harm would come to Antenor, Ucalegon, Polydamas, Aeneas, and Dolon, or to any of their parents, or indeed to their children, wives, relatives, friends, and associates, or to any of their property.

When they had sworn to this promise, Polydamas gave them instructions. At night, he said, they must lead the army to the Scaean gate, the one whose exterior was carved with a horse's head.[33] Antenor and Aeneas would be in charge of the guard at this point, and they would open the bolt and raise a torch as the sign for attack.

---

33 Thus Dares explains the wooden horse away

D. XLI. Postquam pacta dicta demonstrata sunt, Polydamas in oppidum redit, rem peractam nuntiat dicitque Antenori et Aeneae ceterisque quibus placitum erat, uti suos omnes in eam partem adducant, noctu Scaeam portam aperiant, lumen ostendant, exercitum inducant. Antenor et Aeneas noctu ad portam praesto fuerunt, Neoptolemum susceperunt, exercitui portam reseraverunt, lumen ostenderunt, fugam praesidio sibi suisque ut sit providerunt. Neoptolemus praesidium dat, Antenor eum in regiam ducit, ubi Troianis positum praesidium erat. Neoptolemus in regiam inruptionem facit, Troianos caedit, Priamum persequitur, quem ante aram Iovis obtruncat. Hecuba dum fugit cum Polyxena, Aeneas occurrit: Polyxena tradit se ei, quam Aeneas ad patrem Anchisen abscondit. Andromacha et Cassandra se in aede Minervae occultant. Tota nocte non cessant Argivi devastare praedasque facere.

D. 41.   Their agreement being complete in every detail, Polydamas returned to the city and reported the success of his mission. Antenor, Aeneas, and all their associates, he said, must go by night to the Scaean gate and open the bolt, and raise a torch, and thus welcome the Greeks.

That night Antenor and Aeneas were ready at the gate and let Neoptolemus in. After opening the bolt and raising the torch, they looked to a means of escape for themselves and their people.

Antenor, with Neoptolemus providing protection, led the way to the palace, to the point where the Trojans had posted a guard. Then Neoptolemus, breaking into the palace and slaughtering the Trojans, pursued and cut down Priam at the altar of Jupiter.

Hecuba, fleeing with Polyxena, met with Aeneas and entrusted her daughter to him. He had her concealed at the home of his father, Anchises.

Andromache and Cassandra hid in the temple of Minerva.

During the whole night the Greeks did not cease wreaking slaughter and carrying off plunder.

D. XLII. Postquam dies inluxit, Agamemnon universos duces in arce convocat, diis gratias agit, exercitum conlaudat, omnem praedam iubet in medio reponendam, quam cum omnibus partitus est simulque consulit exercitum, an placeat Antenori et Aeneae et his qui una patriam prodiderint, fidem servari. Exercitus totus conclamat placere sibi. itaque convocatis omnibus sua omnia reddit. Antenor rogat Agamemnonem, ut sibi loqui liceat: Agamemnon dicere iubet. principio omnibus Graiugenis gratias agit simulque commemorat Helenum et Cassandram pacem semper patri suasisse, Achillemque suasu Heleni sepulturae redditum fuisse. Agamemnon ex consilii sententia Heleno et Cassandrae libertatem reddit. Helenus pro Hecuba et Andromacha Agamemnonem deprecatur commemoratque semper ab his esse dilectum. Etiam his ex consilii sententia libertas concessa est. Interea praedam omnem exercitui ut decuit divisit, diis gratias egit, hostias immolavit. Quinta die domum reverti constituunt.

D. 42.   With the coming of day, Agamemnon called all his leaders to a meeting on the citadel. After giving thanks to the gods, he praised the army and ordered that all the booty be gathered together and fairly divided. At the same time he asked them what they wanted to do with Antenor and Aeneas and those who had helped betray Troy. All of them answered, with a loud shout, that they wanted to honour their promise to these.

Thus Agamemnon, having summoned all of the traitors, confirmed them in all of their rights. Antenor, when Agamemnon had granted him leave to speak, began by thanking the Greeks. Then he bade them to remember how Helenus and Cassandra had always pled with Priam for peace, and how Helenus had successfully urged the return of Achilles' body for burial. Accordingly, Agamemnon, following the advice of the council, gave Helenus and Cassandra their freedom.

Then Helenus, remembering how Hecuba and Andromache had always loved him, interceded with Agamemnon in their behalf.

And again Agamemnon, by advice of the council, gave these their freedom.

Then he made an equitable division of the booty and rendered thanks to the gods with the sacrifice of a victim.

The council voted that they should return to their homeland on the fifth day.

D. XLIII. Ut dies profectionis advenit, tempestates magnae exortae sunt et per aliquot dies remanserunt. Calchas respondit inferis satis factum non esse. Neoptolemo in mentem venit Polyxenam cuius causa pater eius perierat, in regia non esse inventam. Agamemnonem poscit conqueritur, exercitum accusat, Antenorem accersiri iubet imperatque ei, ut inquirat eam inventamque ad se adducat. Antenor ad Aeneam venit et diligentius quaerit, ut, priusquam Argivi proficiscantur, Polyxena Agamemnoni praesentetur. Polyxenam ab eis absconsam invenit, ad Agamemnonem adducit: Agamemnon Neoptolemo tradit, is eam ad tumulum patris iugulat. Agamemnon iratus Aeneae quod Polyxenam absconderat eum cum suis protinus de patria excedere iubet. Aeneas cum suis omnibus proficiscitur. Agamemnon postquam profectus est, Helena post aliquot dies maesta magis quam quando venerat domum reportatur cum suo Menelao. Helenus cum Cassandra sorore et Andromacha Hectoris fratris uxore et Hecuba matre Cherronensum petit.

D. XLIV. Hactenus Dares Phrygius mandavit litteris, nam is ibidem cum Antenoris factione remansit. Pugnatum est annis decem mensibus sex diebus duodecim ad Troiam. Ruerunt ex Argivis, sicut acta diurna indicant quae Dares descripsit, hominum milia DCCCLXXXVI et ex Troianis ruerunt usque ad oppidum proditum hominum milia DCLXXVI. Aeneas navibus profectus est, in quibus Alexander in Graeciam ierat, numero viginti duabus: quem omnis aetas hominum secuta est in milibus tribus et quadringentis. Antenorem secuti sunt duo milia quingenti, Helenum et Andromacham mille ducenti.

D. 43. When the time for sailing arrived, a great storm arose and raged several days; Calchas informed them that the spirits of the dead were displeased.

Then Neoptolemus, remembering that Polyxena, the cause of his father's death, had not been found in the palace, voiced his complaint; he blamed the army and demanded that Agamemnon produce her.

Agamemnon summoned Antenor and told him to find Polyxena and bring her there.

Accordingly, Antenor went to Aeneas and earnestly begged him to hand over Polyxena, so that the Greeks would set sail and thus, having found where she had been hidden, he took her to Agamemnon.

Agamemnon gave her to Neoptolemus.

Neoptolemus cut her throat at the grave of his father.

Agamemnon was angry with Aeneas for hiding Polyxena and ordered him and his followers to depart from their country immediately. Thus Aeneas and all of his followers departed.

For several days after Agamemnon set sail, Helen, home with Menelaus, her husband, was grieved more deeply than when she had come. Helenus went to the Chersonese, accompanied by Cassandra, his sister, and Andromache, the wife of his brother Hector, and Hecuba, his mother.

D. 44. So much and no more Dares the Phrygian put into writing, for, as a faithful follower of Antenor, he stayed on at Troy.[34]

The war against Troy lasted ten years, six months, and twelve days.

The number of Greeks who fell, according to the *Journal* that Dares wrote, was 866,000; the number of the Trojans 676,000.

Aeneas set sail with the twenty-two ships that Alexander had used when going to Greece.

He had about 3,400 followers, people of all different ages; Antenor had about 2,500; Andromache and Helenus about 1,200.

---

34 According to Schissel von Fleschenberg, this section is probably based on an original Greek Preface. See Introduction, pp. 13-14.

BIBLIOGRAPHY

This bibliography lists the latest editions of Dictys and Dares along with some of the most important scholarly books and articles which deal with them and their influence.

EDITIONS

Daretis Phrygii De Excidio Troiae Historia, ed. Ferdinand Meister. Leipzig, 1873. *Dictyis Cretensis Ephemeridos Belli Troiani Libri*, ed. Werner Eisenhut. Leipzig, 1958.

SCHOLARSHIP

Greif, Wilhelm. *Die Mittelalterlichen Bearbeitungen der Trojanersage.* Marburg, 1886.

Griffin, Nathaniel Edward. *Dares and Dictys, An Introduction to the Study of Medieval Versions of the Story of Troy.* Baltimore, 1907.

"The Greek Dictys", *American Journal of Philology*, XXIX, 3 (1908), 329-335.

"Un-Homeric Elements in the Medieval Story of Troy", *The Journal of English and Germanic Philology*, VII (1907-1908), 32-52.

Schissel von Fleschenberg, Otmar. *Dares-Studien.* Halle an-der-Salle, 1908.

Young, Karl. *The Origin and Development of the Story of Troilus and Criseyde*, Chaucer Soc., 2nd Ser., No. 40. London, 1908 [for 1904].

INDEX OF PROPER NAMES

This index is based on the English translation. Its preparation, however, was facilitated by the use of the indexes of Eisenhut and Meister to their Latin editions. References are to page numbers: 3-289 refer to Dictys, 291-375 to Dares.

Calypso, 271.

Camirus, 191.

Canopus, 269.

Capaneus, 27.

Capys, 225.

Carene, 69.

Caria, 107, 205, 325.

Cassandra, 91, 141, 207, 243, 251, 253, 259, 299, 307, 313, 315, 371, 373, 375.

Castor, 297, 301, 309, 313, 315.

Caucasus, (mountains) 191.

Cebrenians, 261.

Cephalenia, 287.

Ceteian, (forces) 207.

Charybdis, 271.

Chersonese, 77, 375.

Chiron, 27, 275.

Choeradian, (crags) 263.

Chorithan, 197.

Chromius, 107.

Chryses, 71, 77, 79, 97, 99, 127, 215.

Chrysippus, 275, 277.

Ciconia, 325.

Ciconians, 107, 121.

Cilicians, 77.

Cilla, 69.

Cinyras, 277.

Circe, 271, 289.

Cleomestra, 225.

Clonius, 25, 33.

Clymene, daughter of Aethra, 9, 253, 265.

Clymene, mother of Palamedes, 7.

Clytemnestra, 39, 43, 265, 267, 309.

Clytius, 225.

Cnossos, 3, 5, 261.

Cobis, 69.

Colchis, 93, 293, 295, 297.

Colophon, 33, 325.

Concord, the goddess, 29.

Corcyra Melaena, 261.

Corianus, 69.

Corinth, 265.

Cormos, 325.

Corythus, 237.

Cos, 33.

Crapathus, 33.

Cretan, (king) 3.

Cretans, 265, 269.

Crete, 3, 5, 7, 9, 33, 93, 267, 269, 271, 273, 283, 319.

Crissaean, (Schedius) 155.

Cupesus, 325.

Cyclades, 33.

Cyclops, 271.

Cycnus, 67, 69.

Cynossema, 259.

Cyphians, 161.

Cyphos, 319.

Cyprus, 13, 269.

141, 143, 153, 163, 165, 171, 175,
177, 179. 181, 183. 191, 209, 215,
219, 221, 223, 225, 227, 233, 235,
237, 239, 241, 245, 247, 249, 251,
253, 255, 257, 261, 265, 279, 281,
291, 297, 299, 305, 307, 313, 315,
321, 323, 325, 327, 339, 359, 361,
363, 369, 373, 375.

Tyndareus, 19.

Ucalegon, 303, 367, 369.

Ulysses,11, 23, 25, 31, 33, 39, 41,
43, 51, 57, 61, 71, 73, 79, 81, 83,
87, 93, 97, 103, 111, 113, 125, 129,
133, 139, 157, 167, 169, 171, 187,
195, 197, 201, 203, 211, 215, 217,
225, 235, 241, 243, 247, 249, 253,
255, 257, 259, 271, 273, 287, 289,
317, 319, 323, 325, 333, 349, 363,
369.

Venus, 305, 309.

Vulcan, 71.

Xanthus, father of Sarpedon, 65,
107.

Zacynthus, 273.

Zelia, 95, 325.

389

SOPHRON CATALOGUE
2012

Caesar's Commentaries: The Complete Gallic War. Revised. 8vo., xxiv,507 pp.; Introduction, Latin text of all eight Books, Notes, Companion, Grammar, Exercises, Vocabularies, 17 Maps, illus. all based on Francis W. Kelsey   ISBN 978-0-9850811 1 9 . . . .$19.95

Virgil's Aeneid Complete, Books I-XII. With Introduction, Latin text and Notes by W. D. Williams. 8vo., xxviii, 648 pp., 2 maps, Glossary, Index.
    ISBN 978-0-9850811 6 4 . . . . . . $24.95

Praxis Grammatica. **A New Edition.** John Harmer. 12 mo., xviii,116 pp.; Introduction by Mark Riley.
    ISBN 978-0-9850811 2 6. . . . . . . $3.95

The *Other* Trojan War. Dictys & Dares. 12 mo., xxii,397 pp.; Latin/English Parallel Texts, Frazer's Introduction & Notes, Index.   ISBN 978-0-9850811 5 7. . . . . . $14.95

The Stoic's Bible: *a Florilegium for the Good Life.* Giles Laurén. 8vo., xxvi,610 pp., 2 illus., Introduction, Bibliography.   ISBN 97814538162 2 6. . . . .$24.95

Why Don't We Learn from History? B. H. Liddell Hart. 12 mo., 126 pp.   ISBN 978-0-9850811 3 3. . . . .$4.95

Available from: SOPHRON
    73 Dean Road #3
    Sacramento, CA 95815
    liberdux@gmail.com
and Createspace or Amazon worldwide.

Check or PayPal. Media mail: $3.50 first book $1.00 thereafter. Allow 4 weeks.